Toward a New Cuba?

Toward a New Cuba?

Legacies of a Revolution

edited by

Miguel Angel Centeno
Mauricio Font

LYNNE
RIENNER
PUBLISHERS

BOULDER
LONDON

Published in the United States of America in 1997 by
Lynne Rienner Publishers, Inc.
1800 30th Street, Boulder, Colorado 80301

and in the United Kingdom by
Lynne Rienner Publishers, Inc.
3 Henrietta Street, Covent Garden, London WC2E 8LU

Library of Congress Cataloging-in-Publication Data
Toward a new Cuba? : legacies of a revolution / edited by Miguel Angel
Centeno and Mauricio Font.
Includes bibliographical references (p.) and index.
ISBN 1-55587-632-3 (hc : alk. paper)
1. Cuba—Politics and government—1959– 2. Cuba—Economic
conditions—1959– I. Centeno, Miguel Angel, 1957– . II. Font,
Mauricio.
JL1010.T69 1996
320.97291'09'049—dc20 96-32581
CIP

British Cataloguing in Publication Data
A Cataloguing in Publication record for this book
is available from the British Library.

Printed and bound in the United States of America

The paper used in this publication meets the requirements
of the American National Standard for Permanence of
Paper for Printed Library Materials Z39.48-1984.

5 4 3 2 1

Para
Pepe Wangüemert
—M. A. C.

❖

A Cuba:
Tan próxima y tan lejana. Tan desafiante y difícil.
—M. F.

Contents

Part 2: Toward the Market

Part 3: Postscript

Acknowledgments

The authors owe a great deal of appreciation to various parts of Princeton University: the Program in Latin American Studies, the Center for International Studies, the Council for Regional Studies, the Research Program in Development Studies, the Sociology Department, the History Department, the American Studies Program, and Mathey College. Without them this book would not have been possible.

Good individuals make generous institutions, and we especially want to thank Tom Bogenschild for all the effort and laughs. He fully deserves his name on the cover. Rose Rivera's patience knows no bounds, and, as always, Cindy Gibson, Blanche Anderson, and Donna DeFrancisco tried hard not to laugh at our antics. Christopher Britt came through in a bind. David Carrasco and Viviana Zelizer have been friends and supporters for too long not to know how much they are appreciated.

Our thanks to Lynne Rienner for all her support and to the anonymous readers for their input. Thanks also to the staff at Lynne Rienner Publishers for a great job.

Thanks to D. A. for a great poster and to A. G. for liking it so much.

Thanks as always to Elba Barzelatto for more than she is credited with here.

Deborah A. Kaple and Alex Centeno put up with far too much—when you see the Malecón, you will know why I care about the doves.

M. A. C.
M. F.

Introduction

Miguel Angel Centeno & Mauricio Font

Like most books, this one began with a conversation. A casual meeting at the annual conference of the American Sociological Association in 1994 turned into several lunches and innumerable coffees. We kept asking ourselves a single question: What would happen in Cuba? We wondered if the experiences of Eastern Europe and of the rest of Latin America were at all relevant. Or perhaps the key path was China's? We knew of many books on Cuba published in recent years, but none of them seemed to explicitly address the question of the island's future. So we decided to write our own.

Our title implies that Cuba will have to transform itself. We do not mean to suggest that this will be in any particular direction. We do believe, however, that whether socialist or capitalist, democratic or authoritarian, Cuba will undergo dramatic change in the coming years. Two themes guided our efforts. First, for good or ill, the legacy of the Cuban Revolution cannot be ignored and will help determine the process of change. Second, the experiences of other countries undergoing political and economic transitions can help us better understand the changes occurring in Cuba.

As a first step in addressing these issues we organized a conference of leading scholars on Cuba. This was held under the auspices of the Princeton Program of Latin American Studies on April 7–8, 1995. The conference allowed us to familiarize ourselves with the admirable scholarly work being done on various facets of Cuban society, and also to engage in those invaluable informal conversations that so often generate the best ideas. Forty-eight hours of fascinating and intense discussions were capped by a moving address by Manuel Moreno Fraginals.

With nearly twenty papers to chose from, we sought to create a coherent whole that would describe current conditions in Cuba and, more important, would provide a base from which to view coming events. None of the chapters that follow attempt formal predictions. Rather, we sought to define and illuminate those variables that might play the biggest roles in defining Cuba's future. As Cubans, we hope that some of our pessimistic expectations are wrong. The level of consensus regarding the path on which Cuba is traveling, however, would indicate at least a high probability that the island will have to suffer a while longer before it arrives at new and stable social, political, and economic conditions.

How to explain the Cuban transition (or lack thereof)? A variety of methodologies and general models have been offered to explain the global transformation underway since the 1980s. Some suggest that international constraints are critical, while others emphasize domestic politics. Some offer a variety of "new institutionalisms" that analyze the structures of political power and the games that are played within them. Others suggest that political culture may be decisive. While some analyze the negotiations at the commanding heights of power and capital, others focus on the creation of civil-society pressure from below.

Here, we prefer an eclectic historical approach. The path taken by Cuba is being shaped partly by the options available and the perceptions thereof, and these in turn are historical products. We reject, however, purely deterministic arguments. The Cuban transition is constructed by choices made in a variety of locales. The contributors to this volume discuss how the various social, political, and economic sectors respond to a variety of transition scenarios. Based on these structural limitations and on estimations of the choices made by these contemporary agents, the authors then offer their visions of Cuba's future. Finally, they use the large amount of information available on political and economic transitions to place the Cuban experience into a comparative context.

The book is divided into three parts. The first discusses possible political scenarios in Cuba's future and the most significant influences on those outcomes. The second part analyzes past and present Cuban economic policy, the successes and failures of recent reforms, and the likelihood that Cuba can retain its current "dual economy." Part 3 includes an edited version of Professor Manuel Moreno Fraginals's remarks at the conference.

Toward a New Politics

In the opening chapter, Centeno provides an overview of the various paths available to Cuba and discusses the likelihood of each in light of current Cuban studies, including the chapters by the other contributors. According to Centeno, the Fidel-led status quo is not sustainable in the long run, nor can Cuba easily follow the Chinese market-Leninism model. The absence of alternative political institutions may doom post-Fidel Cuba to at least a temporary period of military-authoritarian rule during which economic reforms will be imposed. Pérez-Stable follows on the theme of deinstitutionalization, noting that the regime's famous legitimacy and support may have significantly eroded during the past five years. Nevertheless, she does not believe that a transition is imminent given the control still maintained by the government. She emphasizes that the refusal by the current elite to adopt new ways of governing may make a peaceful transition impossible.

De la Fuente and Glasco and León focus on the often neglected Cuban civil society. León challenges the dominant state paradigm that has ruled Cuban studies for many years. Partly because of political changes, partly because of the economic reforms, new forms of social exchange have developed in Cuba that may represent a new challenge to the government. Important developments include the rise of self-employment and increasing social stratification based on the availability of dollars. De la Fuente and Glasco detail the attitudes of the black population, which is perhaps the single most important group in Cuba today. They find considerable support for the accomplishments of the revolution, and some trepidation regarding the changes a transition would bring. The black population, however, is not monolithic; it reveals the generational splits found throughout the island. Its automatic support for the revolution may also be waning.

Moving across the famous ninety miles, Gunn Clissold analyzes the relationship between Cuba and the United States and questions the basic assumptions that have shaped it during the past three decades. She then discusses the likely consequences of these policies in light of feasible scenarios, concluding that a continuation of the foreign-policy status quo (on both sides) threatens Cuba's chance for a more democratic future. Castro discusses the Cuban diaspora and its possible role in a transition. As in the other chapters, the findings are not optimistic. Despite some setbacks, the traditional hard-line opposition to compromise with Fidel continues to dominate the political voice of the exile community. Because the ideological inflexibility of the island has its counterparts in Florida, it may be difficult to develop the kind of dialogue between the two communities needed to establish a peaceful transition.

All six chapters focusing on political change are pessimistic regarding the likelihood of a smooth transition to a more democratic government. A new civil society may be arising in Cuba, but the regime refuses to change the manner in which it rules. Precisely because it has avoided the kind of dramatic political shifts seen in other communist countries, Cuba may be ill prepared for the disappearance of Fidel Castro. Of equal concern, external actors, such as the diaspora and the U.S. government, are not likely to play constructive roles. If peaceful change comes to Cuba, it must begin on the island and it must begin as soon as possible.

Toward the Market

Font opens Part 2 with an overview of the reforms adopted since 1990 and their relationship to the economic crisis that followed the demise of the

USSR and the socialist bloc. His chapter traces the character, origins, and strength of the distinctive institutional form of Cuban socialism. Font argues that this institutional framework shapes and constrains the process of change, imposing limits to how far the reforms can go in altering the established model. Market-oriented change is here to stay, but the future is less than clear.

The three chapters that follow provide in-depth treatments of critical aspects of the reform process. Eckstein highlights the growing fiscal crisis of Cuban state socialism. Her analysis of the post-1990 state responses reveals a curious mix of socialist, market-based, and even precapitalist policies. But, in the end, socialism "as we know it" is losing out to market forces due to a combination of external and fiscal pressures. Ritter analyzes the bifurcation of the Cuban economy into an internationalized and dollar-based sector and one encompassing the traditional, socialist, peso-based economy. He emphasizes that this duality leads to costly and dangerous pathologies. Differences in real prices between these two structures provide strong incentives for Cubans to engage in rent-seeking behavior. The pathologies also include negative distributional effects. This highly dysfunctional pattern calls for effective policies to heal the split of the Cuban economy and society and create conditions for overall economic recovery. Pérez-López's chapter probes the rise of the second economy in Cuba and its expansion in the context of the post-1990 reforms. The second economy is a prominent feature of all transitional postcommunist societies, with positive and negative components: It is a source both of badly needed entrepreneurship and efficiency and of corruption and crime. Pérez-López points out that the property grab by the nomenklatura, a well-known phenomenon in the transitional societies of Eastern Europe, is also taking place in Cuba.

Carranza Valdés, one of the two young Cuban economists in this volume, makes clear that Cuba has to define a new economic policy with which to attack the basic disequilibrium of the economy. He confirms the role of military officers in the rise of a new entrepreneurial class. He claims that Cuba needs to create a new form of socialism suited to its national characteristics. Carranza argues that the dual-economy model is not sustainable and calls for a more integrationist approach. His recommendations have considerable affinity with those of Ritter and several of the other contributors to this volume. Monreal presents an overview of the relationship between theory and reform in Cuba. He notes the absence of a theoretical paradigm that could serve as a blueprint for Cuban economic reform and suggests that without such a development, Cuban economic policy may face a series of unsolvable contradictions.

Whatever their emphases, the authors of Part 2 agree that Cuban society is changing in major ways. Traditional state socialism has already given way to new structures that give markets a prominent role. New questions and ideas, institutions, actors, and processes are gradually emerging. At the same time there is wide agreement that the current situation is transitional—fraught with tension and ambiguity, shaped by the search for more stable arrangements, and marked by structural heterogeneity and complexity. There is thus a protean character to it. The policies that are adopted now and in the near future are likely to be of enormous importance in defining more precisely a transitional path for Cuban society.

The final contribution by Moreno Fraginals is a moving account of how the prominent historian perceives the Cuban transition. Asking where Cuba is going, Moreno Fraginals sees a largely negative future. He ends his presentation with a call for cooperation and unity for the Cuban community as a whole.

Overall, the book has a sobering message for all those interested in the future of Cuba. It appears that what has worked so well for thirty-six years may be precisely what is preventing Cuba from developing a more democratic and economically viable future. We hope, nevertheless, that much of our pessimism will prove to be unfounded.

PART 1

Toward a New Politics

◆ 1 ◆

Cuba's Search for Alternatives

Miguel Angel Centeno

◆

When Fidel Castro announced the beginning of the Special Period in Time of Peace in the fall of 1990, he changed Cuba's old battle cry to "socialism or death." Immediately, wags in Havana wondered aloud if there were a difference between these two alternatives. Others wanted to know if these were the only two options available. This book tries to answer the latter question. What paths are open to Cuba thirty-seven years after the triumph of the revolution and seven years after the collapse of the Berlin Wall? What will Cuba look like in the twenty-first century?

To consider the alternatives a preliminary series of questions is required. How much popular support does the regime enjoy? How organized are the various internal opposition forces? How strong are the glasnost and perestroika wings in the ruling elite? How much institutional control does Fidel really have? What will the United States do? What about the exiles? How much sacrifice (pre- and post-transition) will the population put up with?

Under the best conditions one hopes to find a democratically elected regime that has been able to make significant changes in economic policy while maintaining public order. Unfortunately, there are few examples of this model. The Czech Republic and Poland are the best examples from 1989; Spain in the late 1970s and early 1980s may be another. A second transition type sacrifices democracy for order and economic change. This is the classic variant of Pinochet Chile, PRI Mexico, and Deng China. Contemporary Russia may be an example of a third type: significant accomplishments in democratic reform at the cost of levels of public order and the ability to transform the economy. A fourth version is order maintained by stagnation. One example is post-1989 Romania; another may be present-day Cuba. A final variant is chaos and failure on all counts, which is best exemplified by Yugoslavia and Haiti.

This chapter uses these models to explore and define the special challenges facing any Cuban transition. In the final section I focus on the obstacles on Cuba's road to a market democracy. One clear pattern emerges: the absence of institutional mechanisms through which Cuba can proceed to a political and economic redefinition. The three requirements for a successful transition (which I call contracts, domination, and trust) demand the development of strong political institutions. Unfortunately, the factor that may best account for the longevity of the regime—Fidel's nationalist charisma—may be hampering the very developments that would make the transition smoother. Because of his central role, the discussion is divided into two parts: scenarios including Fidel Castro and those requiring his exit.[1]

Con Fidel

Most observers of Cuba agree that the status quo does not represent a viable long-term option.[2] The economic collapse following the Soviet pullout does seem to have stopped in 1994. Early estimates that the economy declined by 50 percent from 1989 to 1993 now appear too pessimistic; the rate was closer to one-third (Pérez-López 1992b and 1994; Mesa-Lago 1993; Svejnar and Pérez-López 1993; Zimbalist 1994; ASCE 1993; Carranza Váldez 1992; the *Economist,* April 6, 1996). Despite this correction, however, few perceive a significant improvement in the Cuban economy in the near future; in any case, stability with relative enmiseration does not make for a secure political base.

With a good price for sugar and an increase in production, optimistic forecasts call for 5 percent growth in 1996. Even if this could be maintained it would still take ten years to return to 1989 levels. The economy may be stabilized, but it may not have extra resources to purchase a population's loyalty. Tourism has improved, but its potential is limited by the buyers' market in tropical paradises and the special pressures on Cuba. Moreover, with greater publicity about the difficulties facing the population, a visit to Cuba may no longer enjoy the political cachet of the past. The frantic growth of the resort of Varadero is also running into the classic production problems of any socialist economy. It is not clear how much more capacity Cuba can create even if demand continues to increase (Espino 1994). The investments made by foreign businesses in other sectors (e.g., nickel) will take some time to develop, and even then it is unlikely that they will replace the collapsed Council for Mutual Economic Assistance (CMEA) trade and investment (Pérez-López 1994). Although European and Latin American investors do not appear to take the Helms-Burton law very seriously, the threat of potential legal action in the United States will no doubt cool some of their ardor. Most important, as several of the chapters make clear, the institutional constraints on the Cuban economy (e.g., state dominance in the distribution of agricultural goods; refusal to allow private employment) remain.

Measures of social well-being follow a similar pattern. In the summer of 1994 the nutritional and health standards of the population had reached crisis levels. The monthly rationed food basket only provided about twenty days of sustenance, and hospitals no longer had basic medicines (Rodriguez Calderón 1995). The desperation of the *balseros* (rafters) was obvious, as was the almost skeletal appearance of many bidding them goodbye. By 1996 the outlook had improved or at least stabilized; travelers' anecdotal evidence describes a less desperate food situation. It is unlikely, however, that Cuba can maintain its well-deserved reputation for protecting basic health and welfare.

The strategies that the government is using to provide some relief also present possible dangers. Farmers' markets and the legality of dollars have made conditions bearable for those who are lucky enough to have generous relatives in exile or a plot of land on which to plant vegetables. This money also allows Cuba to import those goods necessary to maintain the minimal economic infrastructure and tourist services. But it also serves to reinforce the "dollar apartheid," which is increasingly resented by the unlucky half (see Chapters 9 and 10). The fact that such a division is highly correlated with skin color (the result of the racial makeup of the exile population sending remittances, and the apparent discrimination in hiring for tourist services) makes for a particularly explosive situation. As in many of the formerly socialist societies, the entry of the market has also produced a reversal of class positions in which professionals and managers have less access to key resources than do some blue-collar workers and farmers (Reed 1995; McFadyen 1995). This has generated noticeable social and political tensions. Moreover, the markets and the greenbacks serve as daily reminders of the failure of a regime and the collapse of its bravado.

Although Fidel and the regime still enjoy considerable support, especially in the countryside, discontent is growing. For example, in the National Assembly elections following the fourth Cuban Communist Party (PCC) Congress, 31 percent of the ballots were invalidated or left blank (Baloyra 1994, p. 31; Domínguez 1994). The local elections of 1995 also revealed significant discontent, especially in La Habana. The riots of August 1994 and the balseros phenomenon would suggest that at least a sizable minority of the population is dissatisfied with the current system and surveys indicate considerable dissatisfaction with living conditions.

In short, the current system contains the seeds of its own destruction. It is not flexible enough to allow new dynamics to generate growth (with which to buy political peace), yet it has also created new divisions and sources of discontent. It is therefore relatively safe to assume that whether socialist or capitalist, democratic or authoritarian, the country will have to undergo dramatic change in the coming years. Cuba has rather successfully used aspects of the market to rescue its economy while rejecting those parts that threaten the system, but as various chapters in this volume make clear, it cannot expect to continue doing so indefinitely. The Special

Period, by definition, cannot be politically or economically maintained for much longer.

The Cuban leadership may be aware of the impossibility of maintaining the status quo, and may also be wary of the chaos often associated with transitions. In that case, and in combination with some healthy self-interest, the Chinese model may appear quite attractive. Such a strategy would involve not only encouraging foreign investment outside the entrepôt economies of mining and tourism, but also allowing Cuban nationals to develop private enterprises. The state's economic role would be limited to regulatory oversight and guardianship over some strategic sectors. The preferred model may be described as "socialist openings to the capitalist world" or "islands of capitalism in a sea of socialism," much like the Chinese policies (Roca 1993). Certainly the ability of the Chinese communists to remain in power and the willingness of the global community to accept Tiananmen Square would appeal to those who want to keep at least some aspects of the regime, if not only their jobs.

It is important, however, to emphasize that the Chinese model is not simply a policy of perestroika without glasnost;[3] the key to its success is the selective application of economic reform. China has managed to create extremely dynamic private entrepreneurship while maintaining much of the public sector. This has allowed it to grow at a fantastic pace while minimizing economic and social losses for large parts of the urban population. The model is based on an overpopulated countryside whose excess workers are willing to migrate and work for low wages and no benefits at the private firms. The government's share of these profits goes to maintaining the inefficient public sector, which employs large parts of the population in the most strategic cities. The system is also fueled by the import of billions of dollars in international capital and from the overseas Chinese community, and ensured by the political stability of the PRC.

What are Cuba's chances of replicating such a model? Some of the conditions exist: a rural sector able to pump food into the cities in response to economic liberalization, potential interest from foreign investors, and an exile community that for a variety of reasons is willing to send large amounts of cash. One possible obstacle is that although the global market is willing to ignore China's politics in return for China's economics, Cuba would not enjoy the same largesse; especially not from the United States or even from a Latin America ever more sensitive to the desires of Washington. Cuba is not a large enough plum to justify the political backlash that such a permissive attitude would create; Florida's electoral votes weigh more than the potential returns from the Cuban market.

More important, Cuba cannot afford the massive budget deficits with which China has maintained its "iron ricebowl" (see Chapter 8) and thus secured political stability. Nor can Cuba sell its population at quite the same rate as the Chinese proletariat, nor maintain its huge and often idle workforce. In early 1995 there were discussions among Cuban policymakers regarding the effect of laying off close to a quarter of the working population.[4] Even if it possessed the political will to do so, it is not clear that Cuba could afford to maintain a minimum social-welfare net for such a large part of its population. Equally important, unlike China, Cuba is already an extremely urban country. The government cannot count on a reserve army of peasants willing to work for minuscule wages in miserable conditions in exchange for access to better urban services. The expectations of the Cuban working class may make exploitation-wage development improbable.

Finally, the political dynamics of post-1978 China were also quite different from the Cuban case. The "repression card" was played before and after Tiananmen, but may be of questionable use in Cuba. The purges of the PCC (del Aguila 1994b) may have strengthened the capacity of the central authorities to withstand the economic crisis, but they also weakened its capacity to control without explicit violence. The regime's continued dependence on Fidel's charisma makes it difficult to imagine how it could survive such a blow to the already frayed image of *el comandante* (the commander) as televised shootings in the Plaza de la Revolución. It will also be difficult for the regime to continue basing its claim to power on the defense of *la patria* (the homeland). Transforming the PCC into a Party of the Cuban Nation (Dilla Alfonso 1994, p. 58) would certainly be consistent with the recent rhetorical turn of the leadership (e.g., once again celebrating dates from the Independence Wars and the resanctification of José Martí). But can such a strategy survive the closing of Varadero to Cubans, the exclusion of islanders from most businesses, the easy terms offered multinationals, and the profits accruing in the nomenklatura businesses? At some point, it will occur to a few that la patria and Fidel are not the same thing.

In any case, the Cuban authorities, much like the Chinese in the 1980s and the Vietnamese of late, resent the cultural mess that comes with the market: public greed, conspicuous consumption, foreign influence. Recent events indicate that the purists (or that side of Fidel's personality) have won out. As described in later chapters, it is unlikely that the current regime will be willing to permit the type of social and economic developments seen in China over the past two decades. Regardless of the government's public discourse, China's is not an acceptable path.

The Autumn of the Patriarch

Despite the limitations of the Special Period and the fact that the Chinese option may not be viable, it would be a mistake to underestimate the political genius of Fidel and his apparently inexhaustible number of lives. Since early 1995, Fidel and the regime in general have made a considerable comeback. As of early 1996, authorities felt strong enough (or threatened enough?) to clamp down on domestic dissidents, roll back some market measures, and defy the United States. The shooting down of the Brothers to the Rescue planes and the defiant response to Helms-Burton would indicate a regime with a great deal of faith in its survival. Yet such apparent stability is ephemeral. The resource and legitimacy constraints under which the current regime operates require a change sooner rather than later. Fidel might survive tactical crises, but the regime will not survive the strategic dilemmas it faces.

It is safe to say that Fidel will not go gently into that good night. It would go against everything known of his character and personality for him to retire to Galicia or accept a gradual diminution of his power and an ideological shift away from his values. Although he could have played such a role even in the late 1980s, it does not seem likely that Fidel will be a Gorbachev, a Nyerere, or a Juan Carlos. The elite's readings of the collapse of communism emphasize the weakening through democratic opening and political softening. From this point of view, compromise leads to disaster (Smith 1992, p. 98). Yet as long as Fidel exists he will draw the wrath of enough political factions in the United States to make a negotiated transition practically impossible. That is, Fidel remains too much of a lightning rod for both opposition to the regime and support for its continuation. Whereas Deng could make China less Maoist, a Cuba under Fidel will always be *Fidelista*. Cuba's transformation will require that he be pushed from the leadership by the frailty of his own body or that of his bodyguard.[5]

Despite the growing discontent and the Malecón riots of August 1994 it is unlikely that Fidel will be removed by a popular revolt. One of the few things on which sociologists of revolution and social movements agree is the importance of organization and resources: Revolutionaries must have them, and the representatives of the status quo must not. The situation is quite the opposite in Cuba. Even if the situation has changed since 1989, the state is still strong and civil society is weak. Although the political events of the last few years should make one wary of predicting anything, it is improbable that the transition will begin from below. The wild cards in this scenario are the increasing importance of the informal sector (see Chapters 3 and 10) and foreign investment. As control over the economy (or at least parts thereof) passes from public to private hands, new organizational dynamics may emerge to create a political challenge, such as small-business and labor associations.

In the absence of privileged information the intraregime security situation in Cuba is unclear. The Abrantes and Ochoa case (and the less dramatic purges that began with the rectification campaign in 1986) demonstrated that Fidel still had the influence and control to define the composition of the elite. Years later it still appears that Fidel has strong control over the PCC, the Revolutionary Armed Forces (FAR) and the Interim Ministry (MININT)—the only political institutions that count. The fact that the military as an institution is closely involved with the new economic order and has access to a large part of food production may also lower the probability of armed discontent. Fidel's relationship with the next in command (his brother Raúl) lowers the probability of a coup. The move to the market since 1993 appears to have produced the same kind of intra-elite debate and conflict that accompanied the institution and then prohibition of the free peasant markets (Rosenberg 1992). In the spring of 1996, however, Fidel again demonstrated his mastery of palace politics *a la cubana,* successfully purging those he deemed to be exceeding their limits and reestablishing his personal mark on economic policy.

Yet, as the various apparatchiks and middle-level military officers consider their lives, those of their children, and the fate of many of their Eastern European counterparts, they must at least wonder whether the patriarch might be better off dead. Alternatively, they might see Fidel as the only guarantor of their privileges (Schulz 1993). An important factor will be the expectations among the cadres of the likelihood of maintaining their relative position in a new economic order (Nee 1995). On less self-interested grounds, if the military sees itself as the only guarantor of political stability or independence (e.g., in view of a threatened U.S. invasion), it might act against the regime.

Will the regime collapse in some Wagnerian finale featuring either a hasty mock trial of Fidel and Raúl or street fighting between various successors of Fidel? Or will forces inside the regime be able to negotiate a transition from Fidel? Let us for the moment assume that Fidel is gone. What then?

Sin Fidel

The only certainty at this juncture is that Fidel's departure will signal the end of the regime. It is difficult to imagine that large parts of the population would not use this occasion to demonstrate their discontent. Although the government was able to put down the summer 1994 riots, it probably could not deal with much larger manifestations. A Cuba without Fidel will produce a political vacuum, at least in the short term. The sudden departure of el comandante would make a moderate "Brazilian-style" transition very unlikely. It will be sudden and at least initially will involve the threat of violence.

The two most likely candidates for leadership would be Raúl Castro and some junta including Carlos Lage, Ricardo Alarcón, and Roberto Robaina. The first could count on the immediate support of the armed-forces high command, but would have to carry significant political baggage. The second might be more acceptable to the United States and other foreign actors as well as to the domestic opposition, but could not necessarily count on the support of any armed forces. Neither would be able to maintain the balance between forces that has sustained *Fidelismo* for almost forty years. The potential outcomes of the resulting conflicts are as follows.

Chaos

Studies of transition periods indicate that very strong hands are needed to manage such dramatic social changes; political chaos is not a route to democracy or the market. But maintaining public order and political legitimacy in the midst of radical transformation is a challenge. Perhaps the most surprising aspect of post-1989 Eastern Europe is that the institutional transfer of power went relatively smoothly. In no country (with the exception of Romania) was the period following Communist Party rule marked by prolonged confusion regarding who would take over. Again with the exception of Romania and the special cases of Russia and China, there was surprisingly little violence involved.

The worst possible scenario is the breakdown of all institutional and social order accompanied by little substantial change. Fortunately for Cuba, the most dramatic cases of political chaos in the past decade (Yugoslavia, the ex-Soviet Caucasus, Rwanda) have been largely driven by forces alien to the island: regional differences and ethnic conflicts. Although there remain critical gulfs between the famous plains and mountains and between the east and west of the island, the solidity of Cuba as a nation-state is as assured as any political institution can be. Racial politics represent a large question mark. De la Fuente and Glasco's analysis in Chapter 4 is one of the few that take into account race in Cuba, and it does not suggest the kind of cleavage that makes for civil war. Then again, similar studies in Bosnia in the mid-1980s might have been equally optimistic. Precisely because we know solÿittle, it may be important to keep race as a critical unknown variable in all of our Cuba equations.

The capacity for order will rest on the ability of the FAR or the Interior Ministry to maintain some institutional coherence. Whether this will take the form of an explicitly military government or tacit military support for a civilian regime is impossible to predict. Both MININT and the FAR seem to be organizationally dependable, and the long-standing quarrel between the two appears to have been resolved after 1989, so a Romanian scenario seems less likely. There is considerable tension within the FAR, however, between military professionals and party apparatchiks, between generations, and between Angola veterans and those who did not participate in their "international duty" (Greene Walker, p. 61). Despite these tensions, at this point it appears that the FAR could provide the basis for a post-Fidel regime and thus avert a total disintegration.

It would seem, then, that the best way to preserve order would be to offer those institutions with access to the means of violence some role in the new Cuba. This would require one of two general strategies. In the first, the level of repression and authoritarian measures would be such that questions regarding the legitimacy of the new powers or their role in the previous regime would be forbidden. The second path would involve forgiving some sins and forgetting slights. The cooperation of the FAR and/or the Interior Ministry may be so essential as to justify a loss of memory. This in turn would require a considerable degree of cooperation with the Miami community.

The diaspora could represent a significant challenge. If the post-Fidel government fails to resolve the succession quickly enough, if demonstrations go on over an extended period, if forces such as the Cuban American National Foundation (CANF) perceive a weakening, or if enough individuals decide that this is the moment to intervene, a process of political violence could begin in Cuba that would be difficult to stop or control. The violence of the transitions in 1933 and 1959 should serve as a warning. The emotional baggage of almost four decades is considerable, especially when combined with those aspects of Cuban political culture that so venerate the violent and futile gesture. The cooperation so emphasized by León (Chapter 3), Castro (Chapter 6), and Moreno Fraginals (Part 3) in this volume may be of greater immediate importance to the transition than even they realize.

In the most spectacular confrontation scenario, enough chaos and political anarchy would result in political pressure for the United States to intervene. Despite the new Republican isolationism, it would be difficult for even Pat Buchanan to resist calls to "save Cuba from a return to communism," especially given the many debts to the Cuban exile right. Such an intervention would be a disaster. Whatever the weakness of the regime, an intervention by the United States would touch so many historical memories as to unite much of the island to resist. The FAR may not be up to the levels of efficiency it demonstrated in southern Africa, but it would provide much greater resistance than have the Haitian police or the Somali clans.[6]

The Russian Nightmare

Chaos scenarios do not have to be as dramatic as those in Yugoslavia and Rwanda. A somewhat less sensational alternative is a Russian scenario in which the central government maintains command over military and major political functions, but loses control over much of the country to local powers and control over the streets to a variety of criminals. In this case, the trains would still run on time, but you could be mugged while riding them.

It may be important that Cuba has not developed the type of underground economy seen in the last ten years of the Soviet Union (see Chapter 10). That is, the black market that exists involves sales of consumer goods and prostitution, but not million-dollar deals with mineral exports to international buyers. There is no evidence of organized crime in Cuba equivalent to the *mafiya,* for example, that runs a good part of Moscow. This is not to deny the increases in juvenile delinquency and petty crime that have been observed since 1990. But the next Cuban government will not necessarily have to fear an already organized, trained, and armed criminal force ready to pounce on the market. The one possible danger here is that the drug cartels may see a political weakening in Cuba as an opportunity to establish a haven only ninety miles from Florida. Certainly the experiences of Panama and Colombia make this a potentially critical issue.

Nor does Cuba have to deal with the geographical distances and linguistic and cultural barriers that have made federalism something of a euphemism in Russia. Although it is not impossible to imagine some guerrilla activity in the Escambray or the Sierra (from a variety of political viewpoints), whoever controls Havana will also control Oriente.

A more applicable lesson from the Russian experience is the political vacuum left by the disappearance of the one institution on which the organizational infrastructure of the state depends: the Communist Party. Even if the FAR can provide some basic order, it is not the kind of political machine on which a new democratic regime could be based. The problem is that Cuba has not developed intermediary organizations capable of managing the transition (Baloyra 1994, p. 26). If Cuba is to avoid the fate of the former Soviet Union, the continuity of some of the political organizations may be essential. There has been a continuing debate regarding the degree of bureaucratization of the regime (Domínguez 1978; Fitzgerald 1990; Roman 1994). The critical issue is not the extent to which Fidel rules, but the survival of some level of institutional rule following regime change.

Even discredited political institutions are better than none, as Ernesto Zedillo has found out. The technocratic revolution in Mexico, for example, owed a great deal to the institutional continuity of the so-called dinosaurs. It was the thousands (if not millions) of party hacks and associated hangers-on without Ivy League degrees that provided the political stability with which to impose economic draconianism. Again, Cuba does not posses such institutional resources. The Committees for the Defense of the Revolution (CDRs) are remarkably efficient repressive mechanisms and the local governments have served to provide some response to daily problems and complaints, but neither one can deliver the population. Precisely because of overreliance on Fidel's charismatic authority, which has increased following the purge of the elite in the late 1980s, the regime does not have the symbolic or institutional slack needed to manage the delicate balance of imposing new economic policies while maintaining legitimacy and control.

Authoritarian Capitalism

Given such constraints, there is a distinct possibility that a post-Fidel regime would have to abandon all trappings of the communist past following a military coup or at least a Romania-style imitation of one. The major difference from the Chinese scenario would be the much more forceful imposition of a new economic order accompanied by more explicit and systemic violence. This might even be accompanied by the participation of elements of the exile right wing, whose commitment to democratic values often seems limited by expediency. Such a regime would resemble Pinochet Chile or pre-1992 Korea more than PRI Mexico or Kuomintang (KMT) Taiwan.

What is the logic behind this path? It is often argued that it is impossible to deliver both economic benefits and democracy (cf. *Journal of Democracy*, October 1994). Let us follow the rationale of this assertion with one simple example: the Cuban health system. No politician is going to win a democratic contest in Cuba running on the abolition of a system that has accomplished so much (Feinsilver 1993). Yet it is likely that the economic regeneration of Cuba will require either spending fewer government resources or shifting attention toward medical tourism and away from basic public health. How can the political rationale of one and the economic logic of the other be reconciled? Another example is the battle over work discipline, an old issue in the Cuban economy (Pérez-Stable 1990, p. 27). Various studies have documented the extremely lax work discipline in Cuban enterprises; anecdotal tourist accounts tell of terribly rude and inefficient service. If Cuba is to reconstruct its tourism industry it will need a workforce ready and able to perform at the snap of the visitor's fingers. A population not accustomed to this may respond with organized-labor action, with the expected counter-response of foreign investors. On which side will the government fall?

An answer to this question may be detected in recent proclamations from the Cuban government. In a speech to foreign investors at the Havana International Fair in 1994, Carlos Lage emphasized the appeal of Cuba as an "orderly country [with] a hard working, devoted, highly educated and trained people; a society without terrorism or drugs" (*Cuba Update,* February/March 1995, p. 18). Already the regime has followed the pattern of the newly industrialized countries (NICs) in creating a cadre of technical and professional personnel who have (in Fidel Castro's words) "mastered the science of organization and management" (Fitzgerald 1990, p. 199). An alliance of technocrats, military personnel, and foreign interests looks very much like the recipe for the authoritarianism of 1970s Latin America.

Even if many of these experts appear to have suffered during the purges of the spring of 1996, enough remain to provide a technocratic core to some future regime.

It is unclear how the United States would respond to an authoritarian-capitalist Cuba. Over seven years of chaos in Russia and the more recent shocks from Mexico have done a great deal to reduce U.S. observers' threshold of political respectability. One can imagine editorials in the *Wall Street Journal* castigating radicalized Cubans for demanding more than their now fiscally responsible government can provide, and offering sympathetic support and understanding to the post-Fidel Cuban National Front of Salvation.

The longer current conditions continue, the longer the Cuban economy degenerates, and the longer organized and institutionalized politics becomes a thing of the past, the more likely is a military alternative. Before accepting this fate, however, let us analyze the likelihood of a more democratic transition.

Markets and Votes

Although it may be an empirically null set, the possibility of a democratically elected government maintaining control over the economy is worth analyzing. It is not impossible that the Cuban population would at least attempt to express its political and economic views while also choosing to maintain the economic equality and social services under which it has grown. Whatever other problems are involved, such a transition would face two overwhelming obstacles. First, it is unlikely that the United States and the exile community would accept that democracy had produced a still-socialist Cuba, yet without their blessing a transition would be doomed. Second, the Cuban welfare system may have been partly a product of the regime's policy of collectivizing social goods, but it also depended on considerable Soviet largess. In an ironic twist, the only chance Cuba has of preserving its remarkable accomplishments in health and education may be to follow Mexico's strategy—to serve as a model of U.S.-inspired policies and make its survival politically vital to the United States.

The other desirable scenario would be a democratically elected government overseeing a conversion to the market and regenerating the economy. This is the pattern followed most successfully by the Czech Republic and Poland in the 1990s. Cuban appears to lack the capacity to use mechanisms that seem essential to a peaceful and successful transformation. In a previous article I called these mechanisms contracts, domination, and trust (Centeno 1994).

Contracts include elite agreements, transition bargains, and social pacts that seek to prevent violence by providing assurances to the various players that even worst-case scenarios within agreements are preferable to likely outcomes of breaking the rules. Contracts require police enforcement—domination—to guarantee compliance. Without such assurances the transition process will be so pervaded by fear that all parties will be tempted to behave opportunistically. Trust is necessary to allow flexibility and ambiguity in contracts and to prevent temporary domination from becoming permanent hegemony.

The Spanish case illustrates perhaps the ideal combination of these three mechanisms. Political parties made contracts negotiable. Suárez's Unión del Centro Democrático (UCD) avoided some of the most difficult choices in dismantling the Franquist corporatist state, but did provide an interim during which democratic politics and legitimacy could mature. Gonzalez's Partido Socialista Obrero Español (PSOE) used this foundation and its political control over and support from key social actors to impose more drastic reforms. Meanwhile, external actors served to guarantee the rules of the game. The position of the potentially destabilizing armed forces was defended and even improved through entry into the North Atlantic Treaty Organization (NATO) while the plum of European Community (EC) membership helped constrain challenges to democracy and economic reforms. Finally, the memory of the Civil War and the figure of the king were able to provide a symbolic center around which to consolidate social trust (Bermeo 1995).

Contractual problems in the Cuban case might include the institutional viability of the FAR, continued employment within the PCC and government apparatus, and, perhaps most important, the status of property claims. This issue will be especially difficult given many exiles' expectations of financial revenge. It is unlikely, for example, that the large numbers of islanders living in formerly middle-class neighborhoods such as Miramar will accept being thrown out of their homes in the name of democracy and the sanctity of pre-1959 property. The establishment of "registrars" of prerevolutionary property in Miami may have extended the regime's life by several months, if not years (Reznick 1993; Oppenheimer 1992). On the other hand, no post-Fidel government can ignore the issue of privatization and the many claims that will be made.

The absence of organized forces that can legitimately represent large sectors of the population and assure compliance with agreements once they are made represents a major obstacle. Contracts require negotiators, and it is still unclear who these would be in the Cuban case. Political institutions provide channels for articulating demands, distributing political favors, and imposing a level of discipline on political actors. Finally, through representation and control, institutions limit the number of relevant parties to any negotiation and thus facilitate the bargaining that must take place before, during, and after the transition.

The absence of government institutions has a parallel in the lack of organized dissident groups in Cuba. The combination of nationalist legitimacy, efficient repression, and the opportunity for exile have contributed to Cuba's relatively feeble dissident movement. The church certainly does not provide the kind of institutional base that was so important in both the Polish and East German cases. So far there is no Václav Havel around whom various forces can unite, at least for the short term. Arnaldo Ochoa might have served as a Yeltsin, but no one inside the government seems willing to challenge Fidel's power.

In order to ensure a successful transition, independent institutions must begin to develop in Cuba. Whether these be explicitly political or more representative of what Robert Putnam has called "civic communities" does not matter. What is important is that the atomization produced by three decades of authoritarianism and the political vacuum following its collapse be curtailed through collective memberships. Only though such combinations can Cuba's future be protected and negotiated.

In any discussions of contracts it is also important to keep in mind the potential benefits available to the population from various outcomes. Cuba may have a much more difficult time in a transition precisely due to the extent of state penetration into the society. The level of socialization of economic activity was more extensive in Cuba than in Eastern Europe, and the provision of social services was more advanced (Svejnar and Pérez-López 1993). Thus, for large segments of the population, transition to the market may mean a loss of benefits without any obvious gain—not the best circumstances under which to strike a bargain!

Whatever the promise of freedom, all parties involved in the Cuban transition must accept new limits on their actions. The exile community, for example, can no longer engage in the kind of fruitless confrontational politics at which it has become so expert. The post-transition forces will have to place some limits on the popular demands they are willing to meet. The new state must be strong enough to ensure respect for private property, but it must also be able to impose fiscal controls so as to continue delivering public goods and preserve the incredible social and economic equality of the revolution. Unfortunately, the democratic states that are produced by transitions tend to have all the problems of newborns: They are weak and require a great deal of loving care. They certainly do not have the capacity to guarantee fragile agreements.

In other transitions, external actors such as the United States or the European Community have guaranteed the rights of all relevant players, thereby enabling contracts to be negotiated and kept. Unfortunately for Cuba, the most likely candidate for this position, the United States, is so closely associated with one side as to make its role problematic, to say the least. The only hope in this regard is a strong commitment on the part of Latin American countries and/or Spain to serve as guarantors of any post-transition bargain. Without such guarantees it is difficult to imagine how the various interests and factions can ever agree on a political solution, much less how to apportion the inevitable economic sacrifice.

Guarantees are particularly relevant in a situation of such mutual social distrust as in Cuba. The first obvious divide is between the population on the island and the exile community. One need only spend five minutes with representatives of either to realize that there is not much faith in the trustworthiness of the other. The exiles see the islanders as failures requiring their guidance; the islanders see the exiles as potential oppressors. The escalating duels between the government and Brothers to the Rescue, and the resulting tragedy, indicate that the political passions continue to hinder any notions of long-term interests.

Great divisions also pervade the respective communities. Despite its claims to be a monolithic force, the CANF only represents a part of the community, arguably a small minority. Other exiles see it as a threat to democracy, but have yet to produce an equally viable or public alternative. On the island divisions are even more complex. To begin with, Cuba avoided the civil-rights movement of the 1960s by proclaiming racism dead on the island. Few would agree that this is true or that the Afro-Cuban population has truly been integrated. Afro-Cubans will be quite understandably nervous about their status in any transition. Those who have benefited from the social programs of the revolution will also distrust those who might benefit from its revocation. The divisions stemming from access to dollars or to nomenklatura privileges may also represent a significant obstacle.

Unity cannot be preserved forever, nor is it desirable in a country with as many real cleavages as Cuba. But during the transition it may be essential for all participants to agree that they are part of a community that all have a share in maintaining and defending. Who or what will provide that cohesion is impossible to tell.

Given Cuba's past experience with demagogic leaders, it might appear foolhardy to suggest that the island needs yet another to assure a successful transition. But if not a *caudillo,* Cuban society requires a symbolic center on whose legitimacy and trustworthiness all can rely. Ten years ago, even Fidel could have metamorphosed into such a transition figure, but no one has appeared on the horizon to assume this role. Combined with the organizational vacuum likely to follow a change in regimes this might make a democratically managed transition impossible. Much like in the periods after 1898, 1933, and 1944, the Cubans may once again regret the loss of José Martí.

Conclusion

During the Special Period it appears that Cuba's problem is what Gramsci once called "a disastrous equilibrium." The regime may not collapse soon, but it is also not a viable choice. It needs the formulation of an alternative, yet has closed internal dissent and delegitimized external pressure. The transition will require some institutional assistance, but only the patriarch can provide this and he prefers to live in his isolated autumn.

As I have emphasized, the most difficult obstacle facing the transition is the absence of political organizations to negotiate and enforce the new social and economic contracts. Fidelismo may be the most significant legacy of the revolution. As was the case during the rebellion against Batista, few institutions have survived in the wake of Fidel. His leadership brought victory in 1959 and may even bring survival nearly forty years later, but it is worth estimating the political costs associated with it.

Perhaps the best model for the beginning of the Cuban transition is 1933. As in those years, one is likely to see (or is already seeing) the slow collapse of an institutional order whose legitimacy is increasingly suspect and whose ability to produce and distribute goods is ever more strained. The fall will be accompanied by random violence, the appearance of new political groups, and social conflict. In 1933 Cubans were unable to create a viable institutional order. It can only be hoped that this time a Batista does not appear. Whatever body establishes authority—a reconstituted army, some civic alliance of technocrats and popular groups, or a Miami-led exile vanguard backed by U.S. Marines—will have to deal with the dilemma of how, after many years of sacrifice and hope, to satisfy the population's political and economic aspirations.

Notes

1. For a similar exercise (with different conclusions) see Mesa-Lago and Fabian 1993 and Suchlicki 1992. The personalization of power of the regime even after thirty-six years has been noted often (cf. Baloyra 1993), yet no systematic work has been done to explain it.

2. For a dissenting view see Donald E. Schulz 1994.

3. For the application of the Chinese model in general see Berliner 1994. This section owes a great deal to my conversations with Xiaonong Cheng, Princeton Sociology Department.

4. From a confidential interview in the summer of 1995. The fact that those associated with the government could speak publicly of laying off 300,000 to 400,000 workers (10 percent of the workforce) indicates the extent of the crisis.

5. The power of the latter is considerable. For example, the 2,000-person special troops of the MININT are under Fidel's direct command (Greene Walker, p. 56).

6. In combination with the militia and the CDRs, the Cuban armed forces present over 1.5 million potential fighters.

◆ 2 ◆

The Invisible Crisis: The Exhaustion of Politics in 1990s Cuba

Marifeli Pérez-Stable

◆

Cuba is in the midst of an invisible political crisis. By drawing heavily on reserves of goodwill and popular fears of the unknown, the government, which has long been led on the basis of charismatic rather than institutional authority, has maintained an appearance of normalcy. Just below the surface, however, the foundations of the regime have been largely depleted by thirty-seven years of revolutionary appeals, and corroded by widespread cynicism.

Since 1959 Cuban leaders have relied on Fidel Castro, single-party politics, and mass mobilizations to govern the country. Although they are reluctantly and belatedly carrying out economic reforms, they still resist changes in the political realm. In the aftermath of the Cold War, the Cuban leadership continues to act in almost the same way as in the past, claiming to be the sole standard-bearer of national sovereignty and social justice. Out of conviction, fear, or helplessness, the Cuban people have acquiesced to the leadership's self-reaffirmation. The fact that, in the early 1990s, under markedly inauspicious international circumstances and an unprecedented economic collapse, the government avoided the fate of its former allies in the Soviet Union and Eastern Europe is an indication of its political resilience. That it relies so heavily on the presence of Castro, the monopoly of the Cuban Communist Party (PCC), and the rituals of mass mobilization is, however, symptomatic of the latent political crisis. This pattern does not provide the means for long-term governance.

Cuban leaders refuse to recognize that politics lies at the heart of their predicament. To acknowledge the political nature of the current crisis would edge them toward pluralist democracy. But truly free elections would entail the possibility of turning over the reins of government to a different constellation of elites, an option that Castro in particular is unwilling to entertain. Instead, Cuban leaders have stayed the political course, hoping that economic changes will suffice to deter a popular explosion and that they can remain in power without incurring the unbearable cost of deploying massive force. The strategy has so far succeeded. Authoritarian regimes in Latin America and Eastern Europe collapsed because they could not answer two critical questions: Can those who govern persist in governing in the same way as in the past? Do the governed continue to consent to those ways? Cuban leaders have managed to craft positive, if by no means permanent, responses to these crucial questions.

In order to understand the how and why of Cuba's continued exceptionalism this chapter first discusses the nature of the current crisis, and then turns to four critical elements in the Cuban strategy. First, it examines the ideological response by the regime. Second, it turns to the elite dynamics helping to shape that response. Third, it looks at how these have played out in mass politics. Finally, it analyzes the management of economic reform.

Political Trends of Late Rectification and the Special Period (1989–1995)

The 1990s have reaffirmed the long-standing political pattern in Cuba but have not permitted politics as usual. In 1989 domestic and international events forced the leadership to take the measure of its political foundation. Domestically, the trials of General Arnaldo Ochoa, Colonel Antonio de la Guardia, and their associates bared the central predicament of Castro's leadership and the weakness of Cuban institutions. Although loyalty to *el comandante* (Fidel Castro) was the integument of elite unity, such fealty fell short of assuring elite accountability. The rectification process, which Castro had launched in 1986 by proscribing peasant markets, taking measures to revitalize the Communist Party, and appealing to the revolutionary "spirit," failed to prevent the exceptional domestic crisis of 1989.

Internationally, mounting crisis in the Soviet Union and the fall of Eastern European communism signaled the end of the "socialist camp" and belied the premise of the irreversibility of socialism. Single-party politics and centrally planned economies had run their course without attaining socialist democracy or sustained economic progress. The people, in whose name the Communist Parties had purported to govern, decidedly repudiated state socialism. These changes sent shock waves through the Cuban leadership, which for three decades had steadfastly subscribed to communism as a superior form of society and had followed the tenets of Marxism-Leninism (albeit *a la cubana*) as an ideological linchpin of its rule. Thus, domestic and international factors imposed on the government the challenge of renewing the political system without compromising its well-established bounds.

In the mid-1980s, when Mikhail Gorbachev was taking the first steps in his ultimately failed program of glasnost and perestroika, Fidel Castro turned to the fount of the Cuban Revolution in addressing the crisis of socialism, the manifestations of which were also palpable in Cuba. Just when liberal communists in the Soviet Union were attempting to refurbish socialism by sanctioning political diversity and implementing market reforms, Cuban leaders were reaffirming the principles of unity and equality. The trends since 1989 underscore their steely determination to remain in power; politically, Cuban leaders have left little room for compromise.

The National Origins of Cuban Socialism

The struggle for national sovereignty, defined against the United States, lies at the heart of the Cuban Revolution. While the thirty-year dependence on the Soviet Union undoubtedly constrained the island's autonomy, it allowed Cuba to be independent of the United States. But the Soviets were also ideological allies. Although with reservations, Cuban leaders embraced the Soviet Union as an alternative to capitalism and representative democracy. Thus, when its patron disintegrated, the Cuban government lost more than trade, credit, and aid; it lost its ideological progenitor. The symbols and history of *la patria* (the homeland) are now the sole remaining source of ideological legitimization.

At the party congress in 1991, Cuban leaders regained their ideological bearings. The PCC issued a document invoking the legacy of Baraguá, where Antonio Maceo protested against the peace treaty with Spain that ended the Ten Years' War (1868–1878) without achieving Cuban independence. The congress itself met on the 123d anniversary of the start of that war, frequently invoking parallels between today's revolutionaries and those who had then taken up arms for Cuba's liberation. With the Sierra Maestra and the Moncada Barracks looming in the background, the delegates declared the PCC "the sole party of the Cuban nation" (*Granma,* October 13, 1991, p. 7). In his address Castro unequivocally established the inviolable boundaries of Cuban politics in the 1990s: "We are the only ones and there is no alternative" (*FBIS,* October 15, 1991, p. 25).

The identification of the nation with the current leadership has precluded the possibility of launching a process of liberalization through which an opposition, or even dissidents within the governing coalition, could begin to gain some public space. In 1992 the government had an opportunity to signal a political opening with the modification of the electoral law to allow for the direct election of deputies to provincial and national assemblies of Popular Power. Instead, the revised law made it virtually impossible for anyone except an officially sanctioned candidate to run. Although campaigning was officially prohibited, Castro fought hard to cast the February 1993 elections as a matter of national survival. He called on the electorate to vote "for Cuba," implicitly responding to Radio Martí's appeal to abstain from or annul the ballot (Pérez-Stable, 1993b).

Officials issued a similar call in the July 1995 elections for municipal-assembly delegates (*El Nuevo Herald*, July 4, 1995, p. 3). As the nation marks the one-hundredth anniversary of the War of Independence (1895–1898), the government is stepping up its exclusive claim to the mantle of la patria.[1] Ideologically, the boundaries drawn by the Cuban leadership do not augur well for meaningful political reforms.

The Character of Cuban Elites

For over thirty-seven years the Cuban leadership has proven particularly adept at keeping a united front and promoting mobility within its ranks. In the 1990s it succeeded in reconfiguring itself without changing the long-standing pattern of governance. Inordinately inhospitable circumstances might have provoked a schism in the leadership over which course to follow; that they did not and, moreover, that the government effectively promoted significant elite rotation are important measures of political adaptability and endurance.

Since 1989 the leadership has successfully met the challenge of rotation and unity in at least five instances. First, in 1989 the Ochoa–de la Guardia trials shook the armed forces and, particularly, the Interior Ministry, the two institutions at the medulla of the regime. After the military effectively took over the Interior Ministry, extensive turnover of high- and middle-level state-security officers followed (*Granma,* June 16, p. 1; June 29, p. 1; July 14, p. 1; July 31, 1989, p. 11; *Granma Weekly Review,* August 20, 1989, p. 3). The armed forces also experienced turnover, though not as widely. Second, the most important outcome of the 1991 PCC Congress was the renovation of the Central Committee (CC). More than two-thirds of its members were newly elected or promoted to full membership; the 1991 CC was also more representative of ordinary citizens (as opposed to cadres), the under-fifty generations, and the provinces than previous central committees (Pérez-Stable, 1993a, p. 172). Third, the profile of National Assembly deputies elected in 1993 showed a similar trend.[2] Fourth, in 1994 the party replaced seven of the fourteen provincial secretaries with younger cadres; in 1995 three additional provinces received new PCC secretaries (*Cuba en el mes*, July 1994, pp. 44–47 and July 1995, p. 47). Finally, in January 1995 the Council of State announced a major cabinet reshuffle, in which seven younger, presumably more reform-oriented individuals assumed the economic ministries (*El Nuevo Herald,* January 25, 1995, pp. 1 and 4).

Rotation has also taken place at lower levels of the PCC, the ministries, the mass organizations, and Popular Power (*Cuba en el mes,* August 1994, pp. 20–25 and September 1994, p. 42). The government has emphasized the routine nature of these changes at all levels. Normalization of staffing alterations has reached the point, in fact, that following the early-1995 cabinet reshuffle, the ministries introduced "transition ceremonies" in which the old team passed the torch to the new. In reporting these ceremonies the press noted the valuable experience of the armed forces in the promotion, evaluation, and rotation of cadres, underlining the crucial role Armed Forces Minister Raúl Castro and his chiefs of staff are playing in this process (*Cuba en el mes,* March 1995, p. 51). Earlier, Minister Castro had observed that cadres should generally not remain in office more than five years (*Cuba en el mes,* September 1994, p. 32). The army's role in these matters calls into question that of the Communist Party. Who supervises whom? On paper, the party is the vanguard; in practice, decision-making seems tilted in the military's favor.

Although these changes fall well short of promoting the decisive form of elite rotation—that of elections giving an opposition the opportunity to become the government—their impact has been far from inconsequential. That Cuban elites have weathered what seemed to be insurmountable difficulties underscores their mettle and bolsters their self-confidence. Nonetheless, Cuban leaders also know that someday they will have to face the death or retirement of Fidel Castro; without him, they may not prevail. The current resistance to political reform is not preparing them well for that inescapable day of reckoning.

The Dynamics of Popular Support, Quiescence, and Opposition

In 1959 the Cuban Revolution elicited extraordinary popular support around a program of national sovereignty and social justice. Although the revolution left no options to its opponents but jail, death, exile, or silence, this seemed less compelling then to most Cubans than its promise of a *Cuba para los cubanos* (Cuba for Cubans). Even when, at the height of the Cold War, the revolutionary government turned to the Soviet Union and embraced communism, its nationalist and egalitarian appeals proved stronger for most Cubans than the anticommunism to which they had long subscribed. Rejecting representative democracy, the Cuban leadership established an alternative basis upon which to govern by turning to the model of a single party and combining it with the authority of Castro and the widespread support of the Cuban people for the revolution. The leadership's challenge lay in translating the remarkable effervescence of the revolution into institutions capable of addressing the mundane endeavors of daily life. Thirty-seven years later, the Cuban government is farther from meeting that challenge than it was when the revolution was vigorous.

During the preparations for the 1991 PCC Congress, Cuban leaders succinctly recognized a crucial failing of the political system. Although they claimed that precongress assemblies yielded unanimous support for "the Party, the Revolution, and . . . comrade Fidel," they simultaneously underscored the imperative of overcoming the pernicious pitfalls of *la doble moral* (duplicity) and *el afán de unanimidad* (eagerness to achieve unanimity).[3] The political system, however, is bereft of institutions and guarantees to overcome these pitfalls. Cuban politics is absolutist—that is, it allows no quarter for compromise on the vision of patria consecrated by the revolution.[4] Ironclad unity is the sine qua non of national sovereignty; the expression of individual or sectoral interests is regarded as contrary to the national interest; acceptance of el comandante's incontestable primacy is an inviolable imperative.

Thus, only masses, not citizens, are compatible with absolutist politics. To overcome duplicity and conformism, the political system would need to promote an integrative politics, supportive of the diversity in Cuban society and respectful of the expression of individualism. These values are clearly in conflict with charismatic authority, a vanguard party, and mass mobilizations. Yet the Cuban leadership has no other way of rallying the support, or at least the acquiescence, of the masses.

Cuban politics has long deferred coming to terms with its central contradiction. From the outset the leadership faced the daunting chasm between revolutionary ebullience and quotidian exigencies. Though manifested in different ways since 1959, the tension between institutionalization and mobilization was a constant; at its core lay the question of channeling the spirit of the revolution into the flesh of life. At no time has the political system created the institutions to renovate elites and forge a standard of citizenship requiring something less than full mobilization.

Indeed, this is the crux of the political crisis. In its origins the Cuban government drew support and legitimacy from the fount of nationalism and the ideal of egalitarianism. Subsequently it failed to create the institutional foundations for the Cuban people to renew their commitment to the ideals of 1959. In fact, Cuban politics left no room for the natural cycles of support and disaffection. The absolutist politics of la patria penalized or ostracized citizens known to harbor even the most trivial reservations. Cubans still have no options but to support the government unconditionally or to face jail, death, exile, or silence; the political system provides no space for partial or halfhearted support, let alone peaceful opposition. Even if with diminishing returns, the masses have continued to dominate the political purview of Cuban leaders. Two recent experiences exemplify the strengths and weaknesses of their governance.

The Popular Power elections of 1992–1993 reconfirmed the leadership's dependence on the masses. The elections took place in two stages. First came the elections for the municipal assemblies of December 1992, a routine process since 1976. Second, in February 1993 Cubans voted for the first time for provincial and national assemblies. The December outcome was a jolt: Up to a third of the electorate abstained or cast invalid ballots, options tantamount to an antigovernment vote, which pierced the myth of a united *pueblo* supporting la patria and the leadership. Consequently, the February election acquired an immoderate significance: More than merely a vote, it became a test of the government's ability to rule in the same way, or almost the same way, as in the past. The wayward third of the electorate had to be persuaded to vote "for Cuba."

For nearly two months Castro campaigned in favor of voting for the entire slate, and the government resorted to extraordinary measures (such as reviewing voter registration rolls and visiting people in their homes to instruct them on electoral procedures) to shore up his call. The results formally assuaged the December embarrassment: 88.5 percent voted the straight ticket (Pérez-Stable, 1993b, pp. 52–57). Although in February the government displayed a certain strength in gaining the population's compliance to its demands for a show of unity, the outcome confirmed a glaring weakness: The Cuban political system lacks the wherewithal to gauge and abide by the popular will. When the electorate sent the government a strong message in December, Cuban leaders resorted to the self-fulfilling formula of mass mobilization, which succeeded in preventing citizens from voting No but failed to infuse their Yes vote with meaning.[5]

Although massive demonstrations have been trademarks of Cuban politics, the government has infrequently resorted to them in the 1990s. During the summer of 1994, when 32,000 people left on rafts, there was only one such expression of "popular support," organized to mourn a young black policeman who died in an attempt to stop a boat hijacking. After the government stopped patrolling Cuban coasts, the would-be rafters openly paraded to the points of departure, carrying their boats or the materials to build them, without interference or denunciation. In contrast to the Mariel exodus of 1980, the government never resorted to el pueblo to repudiate those who were abandoning the island. On August 5, 1995, the first anniversary of the antigovernment riots on the Malecón (Havana's waterfront), the leadership convened a mass demonstration of "revolutionary affirmation"; tens of thousands responded and the government mobilized a large security contingent for their protection (Reuters, August 5, 1995). Only with such careful controls could the government use the once-genuine expression of popular support.

If Cuban leaders at one time mustered overwhelming active support and, later, a combination of such support and a more passive disposition to listen to their directives, they are now mired in a conundrum. They continue to have a core of adherents, which allows them to resort to their long-standing pattern of governance; at the same time, they have lost the acquiescence they once had from a majority of the population, and the long-standing pattern does not afford them the means to renew popular confidence. Indeed, la doble moral and el afán de unanimidad are unbridgeable pitfalls within the jagged terrain of Cuban politics. Even without the goodwill, let alone the endorsement, of the majority, the government can survive if the population remains indifferent, fearful, or paralyzed by a sense of helplessness. What, from their vantage point, Cuban leaders must thwart is the coalescing of this discontent into an opposition movement that can jeopardize their rule, or into mass disturbances that would result in the decision of whether to shoot. Battered legitimacy is not a lethal threat; the organization of alternatives is.

The Politics of Economic Reform

Although the Cuban government has been cautiously moving in the direction of economic liberalization since mid-1993, it seems to lack the conviction to formulate and carry out a coherent program of reform. Making the U.S. dollar legal tender, authorizing many forms of self-employment, and expanding agricultural cooperatives had been long overdue. Once decreed, these measures pointed to more comprehensive reforms aimed at broadening the role of the market in resource allocation and promoting the private sector (foreign and national).

The government, however, hesitated. In the December 1993 meeting of the National Assembly of Popular Power Castro railed against capitalism and the "excesses" of the profit motive, and called for workplace assemblies (*parlamentos obreros*) to discuss additional economic reforms. Held in early 1994, the assemblies predictably yielded the support of el pueblo for Castro's position. Economic reforms had to be "politically correct" as well as technically sound, and they could never compromise socialism. These assemblies were a show of strength by the hard-liners against reformers.

Nonetheless, by the end of 1994 the reformers appeared to have gained the upper hand. After the popular "consultations," the government cautiously moved forward on the economic front. It announced price increases on selected goods and services and imposed a charge on others that were previously free. The government also revealed plans to phase in a new tax system, and put state enterprises on notice that it would gradually reduce subsidies. In the fall, individuals, cooperatives, and state enterprises began selling their products in agricultural markets and special consumer-goods stores at freely established prices. These measures have reduced the budget deficit and strengthened the peso against the dollar.[6]

Although the tense summer of 1994 temporarily tilted the balance of power in favor of the reformers, it shifted back again in 1995. The government vacillated on the full liberalization of Cuban entrepreneurship. It authorized additional job categories for self-employment while dampening private initiatives by sporadically confiscating "illicit gains" and harassing "profiteers." In July Castro denounced mounting levels of corruption and reaffirmed that "revolution is our religion. There will be no transition to capitalism." In September the National Assembly of Popular Power passed a widely anticipated new foreign-investment law that embodied the official ambivalence toward economic restructuring. On the one hand, the law allows for wholly foreign-owned ventures, sanctions foreign ownership of real estate, and generally improves the climate for foreign investment. On the other hand, the state retains full control of labor; foreign investors still cannot hire and pay workers directly. Moreover, the assembly declared the law to be "an opening to defend and develop socialism . . . not a transition to capitalism." Castro concluded the debate with a note on economic reforms: "If there has to be more opening, we will do it, though I do not see an immediate need for that" (Associated Press, September 5 and 6, 1995 and the *Washington Post,* September 6, 1995). Cuban leaders have not shown they are ready to relinquish state control over most of the economy, which is ultimately the road they must take if they are serious about long-term economic recovery. The reform process remains mired in the perpetual uncertainties of Cuban politics.

In ways recalling the early 1970s the armed forces have assumed greater responsibility in civilian politics and economic matters (Domínguez 1978, pp. 341–378). They have played a central role in the nascent reforms; Raúl Castro and the chiefs of staff wholeheartedly supported the reopening of the agricultural markets. "Today the main political, military, and ideological problem of this country is to increase the food supply," said Raúl Castro in announcing the markets. Initially, military farms supplied much of the produce for sale.[7] In 1994–1995, military councils discussed economic and political-ideological issues as a matter of course. Generals attended and often presented the concluding remarks at PCC and government forums to assess the state of the provinces and the ministries.[8]

Raúl Castro has acknowledged some discontent within civilian sectors of the government. "No one should worry that we guards, as we are commonly known, are involved in all these matters," he said. "Before we were guards we were communists" *(Cuba en el mes,* September 1994, p. 34). The regime's need to resort to the military, of course, underlines its failure to consolidate a capable civilian institutional order and puts into question the vanguard role supposedly performed by the Communist Party.

Transition, Transformation, and Democracy: Comparative Perspectives

Currently the Cuban government is stable. Its leadership appears too uncompromising and the population far enough from a state of revolt to augur its imminent demise. Nonetheless, a political transition from the long-standing pattern of governance will eventually take place, even if only when Fidel Castro passes from the scene. The outcome of this transition in Cuba will likely parallel recent changes in Latin America and Eastern

Europe resulting in pluralist democracy. Future challenges will pivot on the complexities of consolidating and institutionalizing democracy. Before this can occur, however, Cuba must first depart from authoritarianism, a process that, while setting the stage for democratization, is itself distinctive. The starting point of this "first transition" is the political crisis besetting the Cuban government. Its present stability aside, the regime suffers from a terminal cn‹dition: Cuban leaders will not be able to govern indefinitely within the familiar parameters. Thus, the first step for moving away from authoritarianism is evident, if not yet mature. A quick review of recent transitions in Latin America and Eastern Europe and of the dynamics of stability in China, Vietnam, and North Korea, however, limits possible contours of transformation in Cuba.

Three Settings: Latin America, Eastern Europe, and Asia

Latin America offers attractive scenarios of transition. Culturally and historically it is Cuba's natural context. Although, unlike all the other authoritarian regimes that until recently prevailed in Latin America, Cuba's is rooted in a radical, nationalist revolution that eliminated capitalism on the island, the Latin American experiences valuably highlight three issues. These are the need to calm the fears of capitalists regarding the economy; the imperative of placating the military concerning its institutional integrity, while returning it (more or less) to the barracks; and the importance of moderates reigning in radicals in the opposition. To a democratic Cuba the Latin American transitions recommend offering limited guarantees to those who have benefited from authoritarianism or who have perpetrated crimes and injustices on behalf of the old regime; strengthening civilian elites who can form parties and coalitions capable of bringing about and consolidating democracy; and observing moderation, which means looking mostly forward in a spirit of compromise, rather than primarily backward with a thirst for retribution (Przeworski 1991; Mainwaring et al. 1992; Karl and Schmitter 1991; Centeno 1994).

Although negotiations among contesting elites are a prerequisite for ending authoritarianism, Cubans have not yet shown the disposition to bargain. Under Castro the government adamantly dismisses the need for political reform; the opposition—on the island and in exile—has not, thus far, demonstrated the capacity to constitute an alternative. That the United States is the inveterate antagonist of the Cuban government and the ally of the hard-line exile opposition is not easing these negotiations. The renewed preeminence of the Cuban military, though a certain guarantee of order in a situation potentially fraught with chaos, underscores the imperative of civilian control over national affairs for the eventual consolidation and institutionalization of democracy. The military might prove instrumental in the transition from authoritarianism, but democracy unequivocally demands that, afterward, officers and soldiers respect the boundaries of politics and civil society. National reconciliation is more than an emotional call. It is the indispensable platform from which a new coalition of elites could extricate Cuban society from the present and mobilize the antiauthoritarian sentiments of the citizenry in favor of democracy. The rule of law is the only feasible context for national reconciliation.

Although culturally and historically quite foreign to Cuba, Eastern Europe had state socialism in common with the island (Kornai 1992; Szelenyi and Szelenyi 1994; Walder 1994). In Eastern Europe the transition from Stalinism to "normal" state socialism took place before the definitive crisis of 1989. After the 1960s, elites lost faith in the promise of socialism (particularly given the stark, dispiriting contrast with Western Europe) and their conviction about their right to wield power. This demoralization made all the regimes except Romania's unwilling to give the decisive order to shoot when thousands of citizens took to the streets.

To varying degrees, Poland, Hungary, and Czechoslovakia experienced the emergence of a second society even within the framework of authoritarianism. In the 1970s and 1980s Adam Michnik had called on Polish dissidents to live "as if" they were living in a free society, unmindful to the extent possible of the official reality. In so doing, citizens and their alternative associations exercised, in Václav Havel's words, "the power of the powerless" (Michnik 1985; Havel 1985). Moreover, in Poland and Hungary economic reforms had advanced considerably; in Czechoslovakia the economic crisis never reached the levels it did elsewhere. In Romania, Bulgaria, and Albania, where neither economic reforms nor a second, or civil, society had quite jelled, the ruling Communist Parties called elections amid the regional revolutionary wave of 1989–1990. Although they won the first round, they also established a new basis for the political system—one that did not invest the vanguard party with an inviolable right to rule but paved the way for the alternation of power (Rothschild 1993; Stokes 1993). Under Eastern European communism, civilians generally exercised control of the armed forces and state security.

Eastern European experience suggests important distinctions. State socialism in Cuba never acquired the "normal" dynamics it did elsewhere. Economically, when compared especially to Poland and Hungary, the old model of market socialism barely flourished on the island. Politically, the continued presence of Fidel Castro prevented the institutionalization of one-party politics. A measure of the weak institutional basis of the PCC is its inability to do what the parties in Romania, Bulgaria, and Albania did under comparable circumstances of fledgling civil societies: call and win a first round of elections. A second society has decidedly emerged in Cuba after 1989, even if it is not yet fully manifested in the ways envisioned by Michnik and Havel. But Cuba's second society has yet to articulate a collective "we" that could snowball into a challenge to the "they" in power.

Although the collapse of communism in Europe, the crisis of the domestic economy, and the political erosion of the Cuban leadership have irreparably discredited the regime, the citizenry has opted for private solutions, such as leaving the country or doing whatever is necessary to put food on the table.

China, Vietnam, and North Korea have, like Cuba, so far averted the fate of Soviet and Eastern European communism. Not coincidentally, these regimes all originated in genuine revolutions, largely propelled by their national histories rather than extraneously imposed. Initially their leaderships commanded significant popular support, which has helped them to retain a measure of legitimacy even amid domestic crisis and the collapse of communism. Consequently, with the disintegration of Marxism-Leninism as a viable ideology, their leaders have placed nationalism in the forefront in justifying their rule. State socialism in these three countries, however, reveals varied dynamics of stasis and change: North Korea, a hermetic status quo; China, aggressive economic reform; Vietnam, economic liberalization and, much more timidly, political reform. They have three important points in common: Their governments have survived the death of a charismatic leader; their societies are at relatively low levels of modernization; and their regional context is one in which political authoritarianism and economic progress have successfully coexisted (Scalopino 1992; Turley and Selden 1993; and Tu Wei-ming 1994).

The present stability of Asia's communist regimes also points to important considerations for Cuba. Nationalism remains vigorous in spite of many Cubans' exhaustion with incessant patriotic rhetoric and the willingness of thousands to risk their lives to leave the island. Waving the flag and invoking the past still galvanizes significant numbers of Cubans behind their government. Opponents at home and abroad will not weaken the government until they grapple with the intolerable one-sidedness of the U.S.-Cuban relationship before 1959. A new vision of Cuba is urgently needed to overcome the present without repeating the past.

Cuban leaders look toward China and Vietnam for examples of Communist Parties managing economic reform without conceding their monopoly on power. But does the Cuban government have the disposition to carry out a coherent reform program, and will Cuban society, with its much higher level of modernization than China and Vietnam, tolerate full-fledged economic reform without concomitant political transformations? The evidence points toward negative answers. Finally, the regional context of Cuba is much less propitious. Not only is the United States set on a collision course with the Cuban government, but Latin America fails to present the "pull" that Western Europe did for Eastern Europe and that East Asia does for China and Vietnam. It might eventually be significant, however, that for the first time, the U.S. government appears to be truly supportive of democracy in Latin America, and that the Latin American left is fully committed to pluralist democracy.

Conclusion

The conditions for the transition—the inability of elites to continue governing in the same way and the unwillingness of the citizenry to accept being thus governed—have not yet coalesced in Cuba. In other words, the political crisis has yet to become visible.

Although Cuban leaders insist they will not initiate political reforms, circumstances might convince them to the contrary. A moderation of U.S. policy, for example, could be a catalyst for the transition from authoritarianism; the call for ironclad unity on behalf of la patria might then ring hollow with elites and the citizenry. The leadership would quickly have to establish new political bases if Castro were to die or fall gravely ill. If the population were at or near a state of rebellion, Cuban elites would face the decision of giving the order to shoot, which might indeed strain their unity. Finally, if economic reforms continue and the economy begins to recover, the government might feel more confident about initiating political reforms. Then the armed forces might cautiously support a political opening just as they now promote economic changes.

Social scientists were not particularly prescient regarding the collapse of Eastern European communism; it would be hazardous to predict the timing and nature of change in Cuba. Given the absence of institutions, actors, and interests independent of Fidel Castro, many scenarios are possible. However it begins, the transition from authoritarianism is likely to respond primarily to one of two processes. The first is one of liberalization, by which government and opposition elites negotiate, bargain, and agree to a timetable for open elections and a new constitution. The second is one of collapse and defeat for the government amid a popular explosion and possible U.S. intervention. Naturally, a scenario of liberalization would be much more propitious to the eventual consolidation and institutionalization of pluralist democracy.

Notes

I am grateful to Miguel Angel Centeno, Arcadio Díaz-Quiñones, Mauricio Font, and Jay Kaplan for their thoughtful suggestions on earlier drafts of this chapter. Naturally, I alone bear responsibility for its content.

1. See Ricardo Alarcón's speech to the National Assembly on February 24, 1995, the centennial of the beginning of the War of Independence (Cuba-L Service, March 4, 1995) and Carlos Lage's commemorating the one-hundredth anniversary of José Martí's death on May 19, 1995 (*Granma*, May 20, 1995).

2. Pérez-Stable 1993b, pp. 56–57. In the July 1995 midterm local elections almost 52 percent were first-time delegates. Cuba-L Service, July 14, 1995.

3. For the first quote, see *Granma,* January 28, 1991, p. 3; for the pitfalls of la doble moral and el afán de unanimidad, see *Granma Weekly Review,* March 25, 1990, pp. 2–3 and *Granma,* April 13, 1990, p. 1.

4. I am using the concepts of "absolutist" and "integrative" politics as per Víctor Pérez-Díaz 1993.

5. In July 1995 official results in the midterm elections posted a combined 11.3 percent blank and annulled ballots; unofficial estimates claimed about 20 percent. Cuba-L Service, July 14, 1995, for the official figures; *El Nuevo Herald,* July 11, 1995, for the unofficial estimate.

6. I am grateful to Nelson P. Valdés for his useful correction on the chronology of the 1993–1994 discussions in the National Assembly and the parlamentos obreros.

7. *Cuba en el mes,* September 1994, p. 35, for the quotation. In August 1995 independent farmers were supplying up to 43 percent of the produce; the rest came from state farms, military farms, and cooperatives.

8. See, for example, *Cuba en el mes* (1994), January, pp. 23–27; March, pp. 34–35; June, pp. 47–48; July, pp. 38–39; October, pp. 28–30 and (1995), January, pp. 60–61; February, pp. 37–46; April, pp. 44–47 and 56–57; May, pp. 69–72.

◆ 3 ◆

Socialism and *Sociolismo:* Social Actors and Economic Change in 1990s Cuba

Francisco León

◆

The most common perspective on contemporary Cuba is one in which a powerful state dominates a fragile and weak civil society. This interpretation suggests that the regime has the capacity to survive the current crisis by creating social and political mechanisms of participation and control. These would manage the contradiction between the scarcity of resources and the sophistication and diversity of the population's demands (Suárez 1994, p. 81). How accurate is such a view?

In this chapter I analyze the dynamic of Cuban civil society in the 1990s and its emerging relations with the state. I begin by describing the hypothetical sources of civil society's frailty or its instrumentalization by the state. I then question the validity of this view, given the changes associated with the economic crisis and the measures adopted by the government in order to cope with it. I discuss the rapid expansion of social practices devised to evade the state's control, to extend the private sphere, and to benefit economically from the crisis. The focus is on the persistence of *sociolismo,* or the prevalence of interpersonal relations among "partners," which the government has denounced since the mid-1980s. This social phenomenon includes the creation of a network of client-based relations (Oi 1989, p. 7). I will also argue that civil society has defied government authority, that people of all walks of life have challenged government authority, most typically in nonpolitical ways, and that this has eroded the government's capacity to maintain moral and political order (Eckstein 1994, p. 127).

The perpetuation of the old totalitarian model, both as practiced by the government and as understood by social scientists, has been limited by the effects of the crisis and the measures taken by the government to thwart it.

This chapter was translated by Christopher Britt Arredondo.

Partly as a result of recent changes, diverse interest groups have arisen, frequently counterpoised against each other and against the state's control and management. I do not assume that individuals necessarily behave in an organized fashion, nor that they make use of formal means to their ends. I have in mind, instead, a civil society that is constituted by a wide spectrum of organized and unorganized interests (Oi 1989, p. 3). My aim is to illustrate the relation of this emergent civil society to a double process in which the social power of the state is redistributed among diverse groups of varying degrees of autonomy, and in which these and other preexisting groups oppose the government's efforts to maintain state control (White 1993).

My conclusions underscore not only the need for revising the dominant interpretation grounded in the totalitarian model, but also the similarities and differences of that interpretation with the models typically referred to by the government (China, in particular). My conclusions, furthermore, point to that constellation of forces that are capable of both sustaining the change in relations between the state and the civil society and of motivating a peaceful, humane, and democratic transition to democracy and the development of Cuba.

Assuming a Strong State and a Weak Society

Two factors explain the persistence of a state-centered analysis of the Cuban transition: the state's control over the society and the consensus about the continuing significance of legitimating symbols. Such symbols include charismatic leadership, national identity, and the success of the revolution.

Control

Totalitarian control presupposes the capacity of the socialist state to associate personal success with political integration and ideology. This combines with the state's ability to convert collective events and behavior into instruments of control and domination (Aguirre 1984, p. 563). The crisis of the 1990s weakened both pillars of totalitarianism.

The capacity to reward and punish has been limited by constitutional and legal reforms as well as the economic measures taken to confront the crisis. The effect of these reforms can be seen in the progress made in religious freedom and the new organization of believers. The limitations placed on the state are also evident in the area of education, where the importance of the family has grown to the detriment of the state. Perhaps more important, educational achievement no longer corresponds automatically to certain levels of salary or occupation. The weakness of the state has culminated with the legitimization of foreign currencies (Marquetti

1995) and the decrease in the state's virtual monopoly on labor and the regulation of income attendant to it. The state's repressive power has also been stymied by the growth of international, bilateral, and multilateral pressures, as well as by the vigilance of human rights groups and the Catholic Church.

The crisis also eroded the control over collective behavior through the Committees for the Defense of the Revolution (*Comités de Defensa de la Revolución*) (CDRs) and the Confederation of Cuban Workers (*Confederación de Trabajadores de Cuba*) (CTC). This is particularly true in the case of the CTC given the drastic decline in its influence over workers (for instance, by means of socialist emulation in the workplace), the generalization of a double standard of behavior for the rulers and the ruled, and the imposition of massive layoffs. Finally, the mobilization for mass events, such as the celebrations in the Plaza de la Revolución, and participation in "voluntary" work have diminished as a result of failures in public transport or as a result of popular resistance to forced agricultural labor.

This is not to imply that the Cuban state is dead. The state has demonstrated its capacity to create new mechanisms of control—such as the rapid-action brigades—as well as its ability to transform its traditional modes of influence and control. A case in point is the use of the CTC as a means to gain legitimacy through popular participation. Even when the media's efficiency diminished as a function of its lack of credibility and willingness to inform, the state continued to prohibit social agents from publicly articulating their interests, proposals, and aspirations (Ash 1990). In this respect it is worth noting that the efficiency of the new mechanisms of control can rapidly increase, while the recognition and institutionalization of a right, such as religious liberty, is slower and more subject to regression.

The reduction of the state's spheres of influence in the economy and the society, however, encouraged the development of autonomous activities, practices of mutual help and other forms of cooperation that strengthened family, neighborhood, and occupational relations, and, in general, particularistic relations *entre socios,* or "between partners."[1] These ties existed prior to the crisis, but they expanded along with a growing acceptance among Cubans who found in them a solution to their more immediate problems.[2] This process, beyond its economic importance, has transcendental consequences for the development of a civil society. Of these, perhaps the most important is the reconciliation between family members on the island and in exile. These links have established an interdependence supported by money remittances and conversations (León 1994, p. 105).

Legitimating Symbols

Among the socialist countries, the Cuban regime has always been characterized by its legitimacy. The charismatic leadership of its founding leader, the high value placed on the revolution as the central element in the identity of the Cuban nation, and the recognition by the citizenry of the revolution's conquests constitute the main pillars of popular conformity (Pérez-Stable 1993a). It is the relation among these three components, more than any official ideology, that sustains the regime.

The pivotal point of that trilogy is the leader. In the 1990s Fidel Castro was severely challenged, but he nevertheless seems to have been able to overcome a series of crises. Thanks to Fidel, the Cuban regime survived the crisis and the disappearance of the socialist camp, and remained loyal to the revolution and to socialism. Thanks to him, it has successfully rejected the post–Cold War international order. Despite the United States' disavowal of his legitimacy, Fidel was able to expand and develop direct relations with world leaders and to skillfully maintain a high profile in the international media. In short, he was attacked from all sides and at many levels, including his family relations, but not unlike other contemporary Latin American leaders (Menem, Fujimori) he was able to dodge the blows.

On the other hand, Fidel proved vulnerable in his capacity as ruler and as leader of a transition. Many of the policies with which he is closely associated, such as the livestock program, have recently been subjected to criticism. The defense of such decisions has been left to other members of the leadership. Internationally, the belief that there could be no solution to the crisis *without* Fidel has given way to the suspicion that a successful transition may be impossible *with* him.[3]

Faith and love of *la patria* (the homeland) is the second leg of the legitimizing trilogy. The reconstitution of the nation and Cuban patriotism has been the most important aspect of the crisis and the government's response to it. The government lost the monopoly it had over the definition of the nation. It is from this process that a plural Cuba has emerged whose members recognize themselves and are recognized the world over as Cubans. Similarly, the crisis—understood as a national tragedy—has resulted in Cubans reacting to the problems they face with solidarity, transcending geographic limitations as well as political and ideological differences.[4] The most definitive test of this change has been, without a doubt, the case of the *balseros* (rafters), who, failing to gain their liberty, did nevertheless gain the respect and empathy of their compatriots.[5] The reaction could not have been more dissimilar to that of those same compatriots with regard to the Mariel exodus.

Of the three components of the trilogy it is the revolution that has been affected most profoundly, not only by the economic crisis but also by the constant redefinition of its content and the growing loss of its conquests. It is within that context that the revolution recognizes the need to defend itself. Hence, the repeated emphasis of the official discourse on the level of support (social, electoral) on which the revolution still counts, despite the difficulties suffered by the population. This defense has mostly been left to those who participated directly in the revolution—the official agents whose responsibility it is to assure that the party does not deviate from its traditional goals and that its directors do not become corrupt. They also watch the younger members of the population who did not live the revolution directly, who do not believe and therefore resist the sacrifices required of them.

These changes in the trilogy on the basis of which a consensus has been traditionally forged have obliged the state and civil society to modify their mutual interrelations. Although the regime has tried to protect the leadership of Fidel, he in turn has needed to adopt a seemingly independent or critical position with regard to the economic crisis. He has done so in an attempt to save the conquests and maintain the principles of the revolution, while also reserving the power to define, if not Cuban national identity, then certainly the terms of any dialogue with the opposition.

For the first time since the revolution, Fidel and the Cuban people do not necessarily speak the same language or refer to the same symbols. Combined with the institutional or functional limits on the regime's totalitarian control, this has led to a civil opening of unprecedented importance in the history of revolutionary Cuba.

Sociolismo and Socialist Institutionality

Beginning in 1985 the government's response to the almost continual economic crises has involved attempts to strengthen socialist commitment and rectify errors associated with the emerging capitalist patterns (Mesa-Lago 1991). Along the streets and highways of the island, billboards announced, "Now we are truly going to construct Socialism." Simultaneously, the government campaigned against sociolismo, that supposed enemy that had opened a window to the virulent germs of capitalism, personal interest, and chummy favoritism.

In May 1991, for example, sociolismo was the focus of a meeting held between officials of the government and Cuban youth. The socios were discussed in the terms of a public enemy and characterized as profiteers (*macetas*). They were viewed as such because they benefited from the protection of the socialist institutions (health care, education, food) while also profiting from productive or service activities not permitted by the law. The official statement from the event affirmed that

> Illicit profiteering cannot be viewed as an isolated incident limited to the number of people who have been convicted in recent months. The *profiteers* were born and grew up in a given neighborhood, a block, a certain, concrete environment and we are all, to some extent, responsible for their fruition. . . . Consequently, the disappearance of those elements cannot be

> associated solely with a police operation. The decisive blow to that and other deformations is to come in the form of collective confrontation (*Granma,* May 26, 1991, p. 9).

How successful have these campaigns of rectification been? What has been the response of civil society? Below, I discuss three cases of new civil activity: self-employment, *mensajeros* (messengers), and the rise of collective relations.

Self-Employment

On September 8, 1993, the government decided to authorize self-employment in more than a hundred occupations where the opportunity existed to earn ten, fifteen, or even twenty times more than a university-educated state employee (F. González 1995). Presently there exist more than 200,000 licenses for self-employment and an unknown number of workers who are employed by that sector (Everly and Marquetti 1995). In the face of forecasts that the 130 occupations authorized for self-employment would soon reach the point of saturation, authorities have decided to expand the activities permitted by law and to assimilate up to 350,000 people in the coming years (F. Gonzalez 1995).

Self-employment exemplifies the influence of civil society over the state, in which the microsystems of personal relations begin to affect the implementation of public policies and, given the context of the economic crisis, also compel the state to modify its institutions (Oi 1989; Davis and Vogel 1990). Indeed, the state now allows those who continue to benefit from its protection (health care, education) to obtain exceptionally high incomes—to be officially sanctioned macetas.

Mensajeros

Under the Cuban socialist model, the distribution and subsidy of a wide range of essential and not so essential products of consumption (cigarettes, rum, etc.) has been as important as state control of self-employment. Traditionally this mode of distribution gave way to the exchange or sale of certain products among the beneficiaries; for example, the exchange or sale of cigarettes from nonsmoking to smoking households. Nevertheless, the mechanism of rationing goods with tickets did not permit, or severely limited, the appearance of intermediaries, given that only the members of a family could use the ration coupons.

With the economic crisis the number of products available and the quantities distributed began to decrease. As a consequence, the time required to obtain certain products increased, as did their market value, given the growing difference between the official and black-market prices.

Before the crisis, those in charge of distribution could make exceptions to the rules limiting use of coupons, either for people of high rank or for "friends." In the initial stages of the crisis, the number of these exceptions, in particular for official reasons, grew to encompass households that had entrusted other people, usually retirees, to obtain their products for them in exchange for some sort of remuneration. These are the famous mensajeros. More recently it became not only possible but economically viable for the mensajeros to constitute themselves as intermediaries between households and the official apparatus of distribution, given that they could sell the portion of the products that the households did not consume on the black market. The mensajero appeared as an illicit occupation that nevertheless formed part of the regular function of the official system of distribution.

The mensajero emerged for the convenience of everyone: the state, the households, and the distributors (mensajeros and bureaucrats). With the mensajero the transformation of a basic mechanism of state control over the civil society was consolidated and new links between the official system of distribution and the black market were established. All this allowed households to develop autonomous relations with respect to the state.

Organized Theft

The cases of self-employment and the mensajero illustrate solutions developed by members of the civil society, living under the control of the state, to new situations. These two cases also demonstrate the development of social practices that have transformed socialist institutions while gaining wide acceptance within the civil society. Being a mensajero is not a punishable crime, nor is being self-employed. But one can also see changes in activities that remain prohibited.

Indubitably, the decrease in and basic insufficiency of workers' salaries compared to the prices of the products produced by their labor constitute a formidable motive to steal from companies in Cuba, most of which are state owned and run. Some of this stealing is of a collective nature. The pilfering of beef is a case in point. The sale of beef, as well as of fresh milk, is limited to the black market *(Prensa Latina Informa,* August 26, 1995). In 1994 the theft and slaughter of cattle was estimated at 30,000 head (*Prensa Latina,* January 26, 1995). The theft of a chicken is more likely than not bound to be an individual act, but to steal, slaughter, and market a young bull requires the participation of two or more people. Moreover, a system that has successfully stolen, killed, and sold 30,000 head of cattle annually, despite the government's armed guards, requires a degree of social solidarity superior to or at least equivalent to the state's policing of the cattle. No one doubts that at "household" restaurants, which have been reopening their doors since the beginning of 1995, it is possible to eat meat purchased on the black market.

Beyond a doubt, the government has lost its control over the production and sale of beef to the superior activity of collective groups of anonymous citizens. The most important point is that the society has successfully challenged the state. What form does this new society take?

The Emergence of Interest Groups

In Cuba the changes associated with the crisis, be they through formal economic reforms or ad hoc solutions such as the mensajero, suggest a differentiation of degrees of national consensus, and the development of conflicts and contradictory social interests (Marquez 1994).

The legalization of the use of dollars has perhaps had the most dramatic effect on social divisions. People's reactions to the establishment of agricultural markets in September 1994 often depended on their access to dollars. Those who could pay and thus had access to a variety of products favored the changes. Those opposed included large numbers who had experienced both a relative and absolute decline in consumption. The legitimacy of such stratification was not equally accepted by those who were paid in foreign currencies and those whose salaries were exclusively peso-based. Likewise, the reaction of state-run producers was different from that of the autonomous producers, who were already accustomed to selling and distributing their products on the black market. This obliged the state to develop differential measures of promotion for each category of producer (state, cooperative, and autonomous).

With these economic changes the dynamic of relationships between members of the civil society and the state changed. Interest groups acquired a legitimate social identity as well as access to information regarding their numerical significance and function in the economy. The state had to recognize their importance. Furthermore, the opportunity to view themselves as social agents of change arose as a result of the ability with which these groups transformed the economy.

Education, a basic institution linked to the systematic control and generation of consensus, can illustrate the change in these relations. The state now lacks the necessary economic resources to continue increasing the educational level of the younger generations for whom there exist no adequate jobs. It therefore decided to decrease university admissions and to augment the percentage of youths attending polytechnic high schools. These new policies were resisted by students and families, who used any means available to continue with their professional education (Eckstein 1994, pp. 99–100, 125). This meant shifting control of educational access away from socialism and toward sociolismo.

Another example of the state's eroding influence has to do with agricultural work. Since the 1960s this has been a cornerstone of the Cuban educational system, which has traditionally sought to combine education with labor. By taking the school to the fields, the state insured student participation in harvests. This system broke down with the state's agricultural reforms. With the creation of the Basic Units of Cooperative Production (UBPCs) the tradition of free student labor in agriculture was no longer a given, because it was now up to the UBPCs to decide for themselves whether they would use unpaid student workers. In 1994–1995 a high proportion of the UBPCs decided to contract other workers in place of the students. As a result, the fulfillment of the state's educational objectives was limited.

This was also true outside agriculture. The institution of Popular Power is a cornerstone of Cuban "participatory democracy" and of the public management of localized, day-to-day problems with material shortage. The crises of Popular Power since the end of the 1980s have served to exemplify the efficiency of interest groups in the transformation of Cuba's socialist institutionality. Indeed, the failure of these socialist institutions, not only in terms of management but also in terms of providing a space for discussion and the political resolution of perceived problems, led local groups to question their legitimacy and to form popular councils on a provisional and experimental basis. Such grassroots organizations first had to be approved by the Provincial Assembly in Havana, but later became a general phenomenon throughout the country (Bengelsdorf 1994). This experience has proven the viability of transforming political institutions by means of the creative interaction between the state and the civil society.

Notwithstanding the government's wishes to keep relations between foreign investment and the national economy under its control and vigilance, civil society has also invaded this field. Informally this has happened by means of the corruption of public bureaucrats and the bribes they have accepted from foreign investors (Reuters, July 9, 1995). More formally this has happened through national associations of foreign companies, and their negotiations with the state. The tone of the discussions demonstrates a continued conflict of interest between the government and the relative autonomy of the businesspeople. In the face of the government's opposition to the free hiring and firing of labor, the foreign investors believe that it is necessary to use salary differentials or to seek other more effective mechanisms to reward the workers (*Prensa Latina Informa*, January 26, 1995).

Another break in the monolith of government control is intra-elite disputes that are becoming increasingly public. For example, in 1993 the country was overtaken by an epidemic of optical neuritis. This resulted in a heated discussion concerning the causes and remedies of the epidemic between the medical elite and political leaders. The debate was finally decided in favor of the medical elite and vitamins were distributed on a mass scale, as opposed to attempting to solve the epidemic within the walls of the hospitals alone.

In short, the government's control over civil society has been weakened by several endogenous and exogenous forces. How has it reacted?

State Response

From the beginning of the economic reforms the government has made it clear that it intended to preserve the principles of its political regime intact.[6] There are clear areas in which the state has retained command. The first is the control of critical decisions in the principal spheres of day-to-day life (temporary or permanent leave from the country, employment or occupational licenses, admission to the universities, etc.). The state has abandoned its traditional paternalism and assumed a strategy of selective control of people's access to and permanence in different occupations and job titles. For example, the state has limited the possibility of self-employment to 130 specializations; those who wish to employ themselves in such activities must first obtain a license from the state, which can revoke it whenever it wishes to do so. As a result, the cadre of the party and government continue to act as mediators between the state and citizens (Baez 1994; Oi 1989, p. 226).

The second mechanism is the military. The government has often responded to the development of autonomous civil forces by increasing the presence of the military. For instance, the increased availability of resources and the decentralization of finance since the third trimester of 1994, both of which favor the potential autonomous efficiency of the local groups, were accompanied by an increase in the militarization of popular councils. This has been particularly true in the case of the principal local program concerned with the production of foodstuffs (Baez 1994). Another example is the response to the decline in voluntary labor. As a result of the inadequacy of the voluntary work force, in three municipalities of Havana the military has had to dedicate itself to the maintenance of water pipes and the provision of basic health services (ANCE 1993, pp. 4–5).

The third control mechanism is that interest groups lack the possibility to formally generate and negotiate their proposals. Polls developed by the party have been adjusted to determine the orientation of interest groups, but such information is only available to and used in the interests of the state. The members of these groups are given the opportunity to voice their opinions and generate proposals only on a local level. When these proposals are voiced on a national scale and designed by organizations that enjoy greater autonomy, such as the Catholic Church, the government allows them to circulate but uses all its power, including the party mass organization, to express its opposition.

The greatest difficulty facing the government's project is that the current political and economic crises cannot be resolved without some relationship with at least moderately autonomous interest groups. My hypothesis is that the government's resistance to the autonomous organization of interest groups (e.g., self-employed workers, farmers, state employees) will make its attempts at influencing these groups all the more difficult. The government will have no recourse other than to accept the increasing autonomy of civil society.

The influence of social organizations on some aspects of Cuban society has emerged, as if from a void, in response to the inadequacy of official institutions. For example, the lack of information and the bias of the official mass media have led to an increase in the importance of rumors and the influence of information and analysis from abroad.

The leaders of opposition organizations have survived years of ferocious control and persecution. This fact in itself gives these organizations a certain symbolic power. Such influence is inadequate, however, because these organizations are, more often than not, ill prepared to exercise their potential authority. The inadequacy of these organizations has made the state's involvement and control easier. But increasing discontent may present a problem to a delegitimized government without institutional interlocutors.

The Cuban Path?

As in all cases of transition from socialism, stagnation, crisis, and economic reforms have played a central role in the emergence of the civil society and the change of relations with the state in Cuba. An outline of the similarities and differences between the Cuban case and other experiences is a necessary step in the analysis of the current relations between the state and the civil society in Cuba.

The obvious difference between Cuba and the former Eastern European socialist countries is the Cuban government's refusal to link the economic and political changes with its commitment to maintaining maximum control over the economy and the civil society (Pridham and Vanhanen 1994). From the perspective of the Cuban government, the Eastern European and Soviet experiences are negative points of reference, giving it insights on how to maintain its control and avoid what that government has termed the postcommunist chaos. One consequence was that the Cuban government, in the midst of an economic crisis and confronted by a young generation of highly educated and ambitious people, rejuvenated the ranks of its elite in an attempt to persuade this generation to identify itself with the leadership, and to give a youthful visage to the state's bearing.

China and Vietnam have served as positive examples because they have rejected the model of double transition (Centeno 1994). But even if in the these cases the Leninist state is maintained, there are critical differences between them and the Cuban experience (McCormick 1990). Both

Vietnam and China are primarily rural and peasant societies; Cuba is urban. Cuba does not have the labor reserve of these countries and has to be more cognizant of the particular political challenges of urban populations.

China's success in the production of foodstuffs has permitted vigorous industrialization and the growth of its exports, despite the macroeconomic imbalance that persists to this day (fiscal deficit, inflation). Due in part to the increase in food production, large parts of the population have improved their standard of living. Access to more complete services (education, health care) has become easier and participation in private investments has increased. In contrast, the Cuban government has yet to win the battle over the insufficient production of foodstuffs; it offers only the opportunity to move either to the countryside or from one job to another in a stagnant and deteriorating urban and industrial setting. As far as any direct foreign investment is concerned, the government, hard-pressed for capital, only seems capable of postponing its benefits to the population. Furthermore, the economy is increasingly being "dollarized," which promotes inflation and instability and reinforces dependency on Cubans abroad. This helps explain why, in the face of the relative liberalism of China and Vietnam, Cuba should stand out for its excessive state control.

Conclusion

This chapter has described the link between the Cuban transition and the simultaneous presence of mechanisms of political control, and the transforming dynamic of relations among socios and the emergence of interest groups. The transition involves a change in relations between state and civil society: Limits have been placed on totalitarian means of control; client-based relations have increased in importance; interest groups and social agents have emerged as factors in the transformation of institutions.

The present government, guided by its desire to keep the economy and the society under maximum control, has supported a shallow and timid transformation. The government and its single party do not appear to comprehend that under the present circumstances the state must either encourage the maturation and emancipation of the civil society or devour that same civil society. The latter would make the development of the country and its transition to democracy virtually impossible (Touraine 1994, pp. 227–228). The government has attempted to transform the mechanisms and reestablish the control of a totalitarian regime in order to impede the organization and political action of emerging interest groups. This has led, on the one hand, to the growth of sociolismo and the search for private solutions and, on the other hand, to the state's increasing loss of control over the economic and social crisis.

The Cuban government's recognition of citizens' rights would contribute to the intensification of the civil society, which is a necessary condition for Cuba's development and transition toward democracy. The instigation of a legal context according to which interest groups would be permitted to extend themselves with autonomy also has the advantage that these groups would no longer need to seek out the protection and support of foreign personalities, groups, and governments as has been the case to date. By granting domestic autonomy, the government might obtain greater international independence. The government would then need to stop treating all forms of political opposition, including autonomous social organizations, as if these formed part of an international conspiracy to subvert Cuba's domestic order. (This would, of course, rob the government of one of the last bastions of its legitimacy: resistance to imperialist pressures.)

The emergent civil society can legitimize and sustain the process of transformation of the economic and social institutions necessary to overcome the crisis and achieve growth and equity. Such a transformation, based on cooperation, would be humane; it would be peaceful insofar as it would have reconciliation as one of its primary goals; finally, it would be democratic in that the work involved would be "everyone's and to the benefit of all" (José Martí).

Notes

1. The Cuban expression "my partner" assumes a compromise and complicity between the parties, an agreement to mutual help in the face of adversity or necessity, even at the risk of trespassing legal or administrative rules.

2. Pérez-López, Chapter 10, and Susan Eckstein, Chapter 8, p. 124, who estimate an increase in the black market from 2 billion to 14.5 billion pesos between 1989 and mid-1993.

3. A notorious example of this shift in opinion is to be found among governmental and socialist media circles in Spain.

4. The legitimacy of these changes explains the appearance of testimonies in the official press by certain renowned figures such as the celebrated dramatist Alberto Pedro. In a recent interview Pedro claimed, "My fatherland is the theatre . . . my passport should read: Citizenship: The Theatre . . . It is for that reason alone that I enter and leave the country and none of this is the result of tribalism nor of some superficial pertinence to a place, nor for that matter to my believing that because one is here he is more Cuban or stops being Cuban. One is Cuban because he has no other recourse but to be so, regardless of where he may be, after all, one didn't ask to be born here" (Martínez 1994).

5. To the question "What is your opinion regarding Cubans who attempt to leave Cuba by boat?" Silvo Rodríguez answered: "Theirs has been a particularly bitter destiny. Hundreds have died, I feel sorrow for them. We live a stark reality. I hope that things will go as they would like them to, it is my most intimate wish" (*El Mercurio*, Santiago de Chile, December 14, 1994, p. C21).

6. The Raúl Castro report approved by the PCC (April 1996) aims to return to the days of more extreme political control on social actors capable of intellectual, artistic, economic, and political initiative.

◆ 4 ◆

Are Blacks "Getting Out of Control"? Racial Attitudes, Revolution, and Political Transition in Cuba

Alejandro de la Fuente & Laurence Glasco

◆

On August 5, 1994, a riot took place on the Malecón in Havana, in the heavily black neighborhood of Centro Habana. Incidents of this kind have been very rare in postrevolutionary Cuba, and this was the first to receive ample and accurate press coverage.[1] The rioters destroyed several state-owned dollar stores, and demanded freedom and changes in the Cuban political situation. According to an official report, however, Cuban authorities' main concern was the demographic and social composition of the participants in the riot, many of whom were young blacks[2] and mulattos (Tomás 1994; Alfonso 1994).

The concern and surprise displayed by Cuban authorities is understandable. Blacks have been considered by many as the main beneficiaries of the Cuban postrevolutionary social order, and therefore have been deemed a group from which the current government draws unconditional political support (Medsger 1992; Bardach 1994, p. 131). On the other hand, the Cuban authorities have regarded themselves as "givers," dispensers of government welfare to blacks and other formerly poor social groups. As recipients of such benefits, blacks are in turn expected to show unrestricted loyalty to the established social and political order.

The presence of young blacks and mulattos in Havana streets not only posed a fundamental challenge to these assumptions, but also brought race into the forefront of Cuba's current economic and social crisis. One may disagree with the idea that "race is at the heart of the Cuban crisis" (*Miami Herald,* September 1, 1994, p. 10), but events like the Malecón riot might generate racial tensions in an environment in which competition for scarce resources has been dangerously escalating. Against this backdrop a vision that tends to racialize the Cuban conflict finds fertile ground. A white, middle-class Havana resident referred to the riot with the following words: "The blacks are getting out of control" (*Economist,* September 3, 1994, pp. 43–44).

It might be tempting to draw parallels between the Malecón riot and the experience of other ex-communist countries, where political transitions have been often characterized, among other evils much emphasized by the Cuban press (*Trabajadores,* December 28, 1992; *Trabajadores,* November 8, 1993; Roa 1994), by violent civil strife around issues of race and ethnicity. However, any parallels are more apparent than real. Cuba does not have the ethnic- or national-minority problems that Eastern European countries have. Black Cubans do not constitute a distinct collectivity with a separate history, language, religion, or homeland. Rather, they share all these attributes with the white population of the island.[3]

One can better understand the role that race might play in Cuba's political transition by studying the racial history of Cuba and other Latin American countries with substantial black populations that have recently moved from highly exclusionary, authoritarian regimes toward more inclusionary, democratic political systems. Brazil is a case in point. In Brazil, black mobilization has been often associated with periods of national crisis, governmental change, and political opening. Both the Brazilian Black Front (Frente Negra Brasileira) and the United Black Movement (Movimento Negro Unificado), the two most important black organizations in the country's history, appeared in such periods. The first was formed after the fall of the oligarchic First Republic (1930), and the second during the *abertura* decreed by the military in the late 1970s (Andrews 1992).

In Cuba, too, blacks have frequently gotten "out of control." In fact, most crises modern Cuba has gone through have had a racial dimension or have been racialized by some of the contending parts. The Cuban wars of independence (1868–1878; 1895–1898) were to a substantial degree (or were frequently presented as) race wars. The persistence of racial discrimination under the Republic, aggravated by the U.S. political presence in Cuba (1899–1902; 1906–1909), led to increasing levels of black mobilization and to a racial massacre in 1912, which became misleadingly known in Cuban history as a race war. Racial violence reemerged within the volatile political environment of the 1930s, which witnessed the lynching or near-lynching of black citizens, open racial confrontation, and a sharp polarization of racial politics in several interior towns. Last, but not least, the frontal attack on institutional discriminatory practices by the revolutionary government in 1959 led to what was then described as a racist hysteria among the white population, which claimed that blacks had "mistaken freedom for liberty" and were looting white private resorts. In other words, blacks were again—although this time with government support—"out of control" (Fernández Robaina 1990; Castellanos and Castellanos 1990; Rout 1976, pp. 301–312; de la Fuente 1995).

The Cuban government's concern is therefore well grounded in the country's historical experience. Black presence in violent antigovernment demonstrations has traditionally coincided with periods of deep social and political crisis. The existence of a largely white exile community adds another racial element to Cuba's current crisis, for a political change in the island will almost certainly involve the potentially traumatic reintegration of the white exiles into the economic, social, and political life of a country with a much darker population.

But to say that race will be an issue in the Cuban transition and that blacks will be major actors in that process is to say very little. In contrast with Brazil where, despite its claims of racial democracy, blacks enjoyed few, if any, improvements under the military regime (Andrews 1992), in postrevolutionary Cuba blacks have made impressive gains in several key social indicators (de la Fuente 1995). The real question is, will blacks as a group defend a social order and a government from which they have greatly benefited? Or will they participate in cross-racial efforts to oppose the government, as their participation in the August riot seems to suggest? Together with other traditionally disadvantaged groups of Cuban society, blacks face the dilemma of weighing the social benefits brought by the revolution against the opportunities and challenges that the restoration of capitalism would bring. In both popular imagery and practical terms, such restoration will not come alone: It will imply the reestablishment of some sort of influence of the United States over the country's destiny, and the victorious return of the exile community.

This chapter examines issues of race in Cuba through an exploratory opinion poll conducted on the island in June 1994. The underlying assumption is that the way black Cubans perceive racial issues will profoundly influence their role in a future political crisis. Some argue that blacks support the present government unconditionally, others that they are hostile, rebellious, and disorderly. Both assertions have loaded implications. The charge of blind loyalty implicitly blames blacks for the continued survival of the current regime and the lack of significant political change within the country. The charge of resentment and rebellion, made by some whites on the island, tends to blame them for creating civil disorder. The truth includes elements of both assertions, but is considerably more complex than either implies.

The Survey

Our exploratory poll, conducted without official support, did not cover a representative sample of Cuban society. A total of 200 respondents, not randomly selected, were asked to fill out a questionnaire that contained a number of propositions drawn from thirty-nine interviews previously conducted with Cubans living inside and outside the country. We included a given issue in the questionnaire only when it appeared in more than one of the interviews. Moreover, although our tables present only the percentage of those who agreed with the statements, respondents were always given the opportunity to disagree or to respond "I don't know." One of the remarkable aspects of handing out the questionnaire was to observe the interest in the topic by the recipients, and their lack of fear or nervousness in completing it. In addition, people seemed flattered that someone had asked their opinion about a public matter.

Ninety-three of the respondents were male, and 107 were female. They all lived in urban areas: 93 in Havana, 97 in Santiago de Cuba, and 10 in Santa Clara. Blacks and mulattos are clearly overrepresented in our sample (72 percent), especially in light of the figure provided by the 1981 census (34 percent). This overrepresentation was even more marked in Santiago, where our assistants were asked to go into a heavily black and mulatto neighborhood to distribute the questionnaire; the result is that nonwhites represent 92 percent of the Santiago de Cuba sample. Like any other classification effort concerning race, ours is far from systematic. Because respondents were asked to identify their race, our figures show their self-perception in racial terms, however contradictory that might be. A respondent from Santiago, for instance, classified herself as a "white mestiza," whereas another called himself a mulatto, but referred to his two parents as "blacks." For practical purposes we have dealt with them as a single, "black" group.

Another bias of our sample refers to the education level of the respondents. Santiago respondents display a distribution according to educational achievement superior to the one reported in the 1981 census (although in the last thirteen years changes in that distribution must have occurred), but people with higher education are even more overrepresented in our Havana sample. It is obvious that some of our assistants gave the questionnaire to colleagues and other people within their immediate reach, thereby augmenting the proportional participation of professionals and white-collar workers.

These results should be regarded with caution, as a first approximation to a subject that merits more extensive and systematic research in the future. Although the educational and geographic (urban) biases of the sample limit the validity of our claims and conclusions, they do not invalidate them. By comparing our results with those of other recent efforts, it is possible to know precisely in which direction these biases operate, and how they are likely to affect the responses to our questionnaire. In fact, a recent survey conducted by Gallup on the island, which did cover a representative sample of the Cuban population, found that urban residents and people with higher education levels displayed higher levels of dissatisfaction with their lives, and were more critical of the government, the revolution, and the crisis Cuba has been going through (*El Nuevo Herald,* December 18, 1994).[4] Given that our sample population is concentrated in the two largest cities of the country, and has a disproportionally high education level, it is reasonable to assume that our results would reflect attitudes that are more critical regarding the country's situation than would a representative sample.

The questionnaire attempted to explore Cubans' opinions about five different issues: racial inequality during the prerevolutionary period; the impact of the revolution on race relations and racial inequality; failures of the government to remedy racial issues; the impact of the current crisis on race relations in the country; and how a future political change might affect the black population of the island. Additional anecdotal information was provided by about 10 percent of the respondents.

Results

Prerevolutionary Cuba

Our respondents held a negative view of race relations in prerevolutionary Cuba. Although there are racial as well as generational variations in the responses, there is consensus that pre-1959 Cuba was a racist country in which opportunities for blacks, although far from being nil, were limited in several important areas (Table 4.1).[5]

Fifty percent of total respondents considered that prerevolutionary Cuba was a "very racist" or "racist" country, and only 1 percent thought that it was not racist at all. Curiously enough, blacks have a less negative perception, the majority of them considering that pre-1959 Cuban society was only "moderately racist" (56 percent), whereas the majority of whites (56 percent) regarded it as "racist."

This apparent contradiction is explained by the unequal age composition of each racial group. Whereas "younger" and "older" respondents are evenly distributed among whites (each group having 50 percent), 64 percent of black respondents belong to the older age group. This is an important distinction in that older respondents tend to regard the past in more positive ways, regardless of race. What these responses show is that the perception of the past is more generationally than racially based. Younger Cubans of all colors are more critical of the past, which indicates that the

Table 4.1 Was Prerevolutionary Cuba Racist? (percentage of respondents)

	Whites			Blacks		
	Total	Younger	Older	Total	Younger	Older
Prerevolutionary Cuba was:						
Very racist	15	27	4	10	20	4
Racist	56	69	42	33	43	27
Moderately racist	27	4	50	56	35	69
Not racist	2	—	4	1	2	—

government's campaign to disparage the past has succeeded. Seventy-four percent of younger respondents of all races believe that Cuba was a "very racist" or "racist" country, a proportion double that of the older cohorts'. The only point of cross-generational consensus is that Cuba was not a racism-free country before 1959: Only 1 to 4 percent of respondents of all ages agreed with such a characterization.

This does not mean, however, that blacks' perception of the past is identical to that of whites. As Table 4.1 shows, whites are more critical about the past, with 96 percent of young whites describing pre-1959 Cuba as a "very racist" or "racist" society, compared to only 63 percent of blacks. This might be influenced by the geographic origin of the sample; a large majority of black respondents live in the former province of Oriente, a region where race relations allegedly were always easier. In fact, only 8 percent of black respondents disagreed with the statement that "Oriente was the place where there was less racism."

When confronted with specific issues, however, blacks are as critical of prerevolutionary society as whites. The vast majority of respondents, regardless of race and age group, agree that "there was a lot of racial discrimination before the revolution" and that "it was very difficult for blacks to get good jobs" (Table 4.2). However ideologized this approach to the Cuban past might look, our respondents also recognized that before the revolution Afro-Cubans participated in certain areas of national life, particularly in the educational field. An unnuanced statement such as "before the revolution blacks could not go to school" drew very little support among both blacks and whites (slightly higher among younger respondents in both groups). However, respondents recognized that blacks' access to education was limited to the public school system, and that private schools, which offered higher-quality education, were closed to them. Older black respondents constitute the group with the highest rate of agreement with the last statement (87 percent, compared to about 50 percent of other groups), probably because it directly reflected their personal experience.

A group of questions, also included in Table 4.2, inquired about the nature and agents of racial discrimination in prerevolutionary Cuba. The assertion that "discrimination in Cuba was not racial, but economic" came up in conversations with several white Cuban Americans who had left the island sometime in the 1960s. It refers to the relationship between race and class, reducing the racial question to a problem of maldistribution of resources, and is an ideological construction that clearly belongs to the dominant racial ideology in the country. The majority of our respondents disagreed with that assertion, although the argument was more acceptable to older (33 percent of whites, 41 percent of blacks) than to younger respondents.

Discrimination seems to have been practiced by different social groups, although the majority of respondents, especially older blacks (76

Table 4.2 Racial Discrimination in Prerevolutionary Cuba: Respondents Who Agree with the Following Statements (percentage distribution)

	Whites			Blacks		
	Total	I	II	Total	I	II
There was a lot of racial discrimination before the revolution	66	75	56	60	59	61
It was very difficult for blacks to get good jobs	76	71	82	82	72	88
Blacks and whites had the same opportunities	7	4	11	9	13	6
Before the revolution blacks could not go to school	20	25	15	27	36	22
Blacks could go to public, not private, schools	47	46	48	74	51	87
Discrimination in Cuba was not racial, but economic	20	7	33	35	24	41
Discriminators were not Cubans, but Yankees	9	18	—	2	23	32
Discriminators were the rich, not the poor	49	50	48	65	47	76

Note: Age group I = younger than 35 years; age group II = older than 35 years.

percent), singled out the wealthiest in society as the main agents of racism in the country. This is consistent with recent research results that have shown that indicators of inequality were larger in higher-income sectors of the labor market, and greatly diminished and almost negligible among the poorest (de la Fuente 1995, p. 156).[6] In any case, by identifying discrimination with privilege, our respondents were also implicitly suggesting that the revolution, by displacing the privileged classes, had also dealt a mortal blow to racial discrimination on the island.

Postrevolutionary Period

If this poll shows a widespread negative perception of prerevolutionary Cuba, the opposite is true concerning the impact of the 1959 revolution on the country's racial situation. Policies of the Cuban government since the early 1960s have had a strong favorable effect on the lot of the Cuban population, especially among the poorest, and our sample is not an exception to this trend. At least in two important areas, occupations and education, our results corroborate that blacks have made impressive gains under the socialist regime.

Figures 4.1 and 4.2 and Table 4.3 summarize these results. In occupational terms, the proportion of blacks employed in nonmanual activities has increased steadily in each of the three generations for which information was collected.[7] Only 12 percent of black respondents' parents performed intellectual occupations, but the proportion among their children is more than five times higher, an increase that, by the way, is substantially higher than among whites (Figure 4.1). This should not be surprising. Seizing the opportunities created by the revolutionary government, black Cubans have massively entered white-collar positions, and their representation in managerial, technical and administrative jobs has increased significantly during the last thirty-five years.

Figure 4.1 Percentage in Nonmanual Occupations

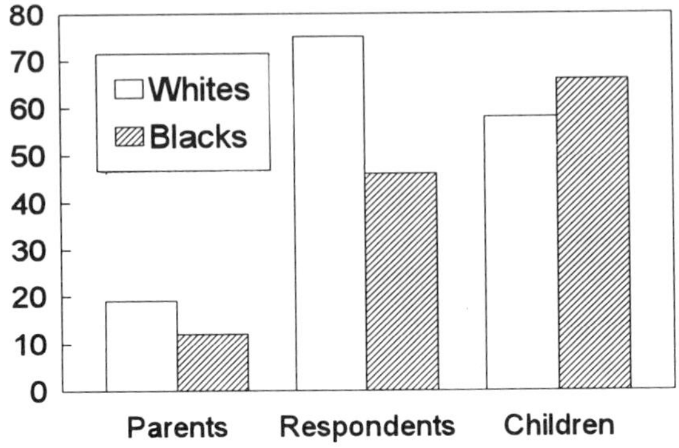

These occupational gains have been facilitated by similar advancements in educational achievement. As Table 4.3 shows, these advancements are by no means exclusive to blacks, but it is they who have taken more advantage of the educational opportunities implemented by the socialist regime in Cuba. This explains why inequality in educational achievement by race declined among respondents (compared to their parents), and has disappeared among their children, who have exactly the same average number of years of schooling as whites (Figure 4.2), and a proportion of college degrees that is virtually identical (41 percent) to that of whites (42 percent). Among blacks, the proportion of individuals with higher education increased tenfold in the three generations for which information is available, from 4 percent among respondents' parents to 41 percent among their children. Whites' proportions also increased, but at a much lower rate; about five times. Illiteracy, which affected 13 percent of black respondents' parents and 6 percent of white respondents' parents, has been wiped out in recent generations. Despite their lack of representativeness, these data corroborate the changes found at a macrostructural level in other studies (de la Fuente 1995).

Given this background, it is not surprising that our respondents have an overwhelmingly positive perception of the revolution, its policies, and its impact on Cuban racial realities. The majority of respondents, especially older respondents (regardless of race), agreed, for instance, that "there is total racial equality in Cuba" and that "without the revolution, blacks would be worse off" (Table 4.4). The Gallup survey asked a similar question, and got an even more optimistic return: 90 percent of their respondents affirmed that skin color does not significantly affect opportunities, nor the way people are treated; 94 percent "believe that persons of color have the same access as whites to a good education," and a similar proportion agreed that they have equal opportunities to get "a good job" (90 percent) or "a position in society" (91 percent) (*El Nuevo Herald,*

Table 4.3 Education by Race and Generation (percentage distribution)

	Parents		Respondents		Children	
	Whites	Blacks	Whites	Blacks	Whites	Blacks
Illiterate	6	13	—	—	—	—
Elementary (incomplete)	7	39	2	6	—	1
Elementary	52	28	2	13	8	6
Secondary	16	8	9	14	8	10
High school	9	8	42	34	42	42
College	9	4	45	33	42	41

December 18, 1994; Levinson 1995). Our respondents, then, share the widespread belief shown by the Gallup survey that the Cuban revolution has eliminated or greatly diminished racial discrimination. In that context, their critical stand simply confirms the expected biases of our exclusively urban, highly educated sample.

How fast was discrimination eradicated, and how important is this in comparison with other areas in which the revolution has been traditionally regarded as highly successful (health care, education)? First, most of our respondents consider that blacks improved their situation under the revolution, but they do not perceive it as a racially differentiated advancement; rather, the prevalent opinion is that they did so "together with the whole population" (Table 4.4). Second, there is no consensus on how fast discrimination was wiped out; whites tend to consider that this happened "immediately" after 1959, and blacks consider that "it took a while."

The fact that institutional discrimination has been greatly diminished or even eliminated does not tell the whole story, however. The predominant

Figure 4.2 Average Years of Schooling

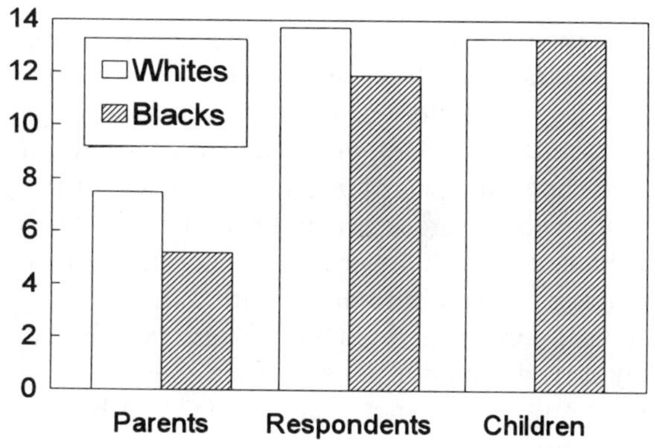

Table 4.4 Racial Discrimination in Postrevolutionary Cuba: Respondents Who Agree with the Following Statements (percentage distribution)

	Whites			Blacks		
	Total	I	II	Total	I	II
Without the revolution, blacks would be worse off	62	64	59	73	64	78
There is total racial equality in Cuba	53	43	63	59	52	62
Blacks' situation improved, more than whites'	13	7	18	13	12	13
Blacks' situation improved together with the whole population	76	79	74	76	76	76
The revolution eliminated discrimination immediately	49	50	48	39	42	38
It took a while to eliminate discrimination	42	39	44	55	48	59
There are racists around, but they are old	25	32	18	63	58	65
The new generations are not racist	47	39	56	66	46	76
Discrimination is over, but there are racial prejudices	71	71	70	79	78	79
The economic crisis affects blacks more than whites	7	—	15	22	20	23
Blacks do not have the same chances in tourism	40	43	37	41	39	42
Blacks are well represented in the leadership	53	61	44	65	50	73
There should be an all-black organization	4	7	—	7	16	2

Note: Age group I = younger than 35 years; age group II = older than 35 years.

belief is that racial prejudice still permeates Cuban society. This is shown by our own figures and is corroborated by other research efforts recently conducted on the island (Alvarado Ramos 1995; Serrano Peralta 1995; Hernández 1995). In our poll, 71 percent of whites and 79 percent of blacks agreed that prejudice is rampant, and the statement drew almost identical support across not only racial but also generational lines. Alvarado Ramos's study, based on 116 interviews conducted in the neighborhoods of Atarés, El Casino Deportivo, and Alamar, shows how blackness is still identified with negative stereotypes such as antisocial behavior and lack of family values and morality. Thus, the majority of whites (69 percent) agreed that blacks and whites do not share the same values and sense of "decency." In addition, most whites (62 percent) have clear preferences in regard to the racial composition of the neighborhood in which they want to live. (In contrast, no blacks and 41 percent of mulattos expressed a racial preference regarding the racial composition of the neighborhood.) Hernández's study of Santa Clara, produced with a stratified sample of 96 respondents, also shows the persistence of prejudice, but the proportion of white respondents who declare that they have racial preferences regarding their area of residence is much lower than in Havana (32 percent).

The coexistence of racial prejudice with a discrimination-free environment in Cuba is explained by some of our respondents themselves, even when they mixed both concepts in their comments. As a white, 35-year-old male respondent with higher education from Havana put it: "I believe that *unfortunately* (because I detest racism) discrimination persists, even though many hide it; *not* at an institutional level, but at the level of social mentality" (his emphasis). His opinion is mirrored by other respondents: "That discrimination is eliminated at a legal or institutional level does not mean that prejudices are eliminated; they disappear more slowly," or, as a black female stated, "currently discrimination exists only in peoples' heads." Most respondents also agree that racial prejudice is a negative legacy of the past, and imply that it should disappear in revolutionary Cuba; a white female engineer summarized this view: "The revolution eliminated racial discrimination, but there are still *remnants* in all the population" (our emphasis).

One area in which prejudice seems to be prevalent, and where racial tensions emerge, is that of interracial love relationships. Although statistical data are scarce, anecdotal evidence suggests that these relationships have increased in postrevolutionary Cuba, but still generate intrahousehold tensions and strong reactions within the family environment, where all the racial demonology persists, and do not always meet with social approval. As a Cuban journalist reported in 1991, there are people who are ardent defenders of equality, but up to a limit—until "his daughter marries one [a black person]" (del Quiaro 1973; Mosak 1991, p. 36). Alvarado Ramos (1995) and Hernández (1995) show that the majority of whites in both Havana (68 percent) and Santa Clara (67 percent) oppose cross-racial relationships and consider them "inconvenient."

If there is racial prejudice in Cuban society, then there are prejudiced people living in socialist Cuba. Older (especially black) respondents believe that younger generations are not racist, so a logical conclusion would be that, as a black teacher we interviewed stated, "there are racists around, but they are old." Perhaps because of its directly accusatory nature, older whites—56 percent of whom agreed that younger Cubans are not racist—strongly disagreed with this statement (only 18 percent agreed with it). Older black respondents, on the other hand, strongly supported the belief that it is the old Cubans who still maintain racist attitudes (65 percent).

According to this vision, the 1960s official hope that generations raised in discrimination-free Cuba would be color-blind has been at least partially fulfilled. A Cuban journalist summarized this view: "The relative absence of prejudice is evident in the generation born after the triumph of the revolution . . . and raised in a society in which discrimination is illegal; where there is a single educational system for all which promotes the value of equality from the earliest grades on; where there are people of all skin colors performing different functions, even though not in the ideal proportions" (Mosak 1991, p. 36; Carneado 1962; Sutherland 1969). It is curious, however, that younger respondents, especially white ones, are not as convinced as older respondents that Cuban youth is racism free. They take a more critical stand on this issue, although a slight majority of black younger respondents agrees that youths are not racist and that the island's racists are mainly old.[8]

Despite agreement that institutional discrimination has been greatly diminished or eliminated, most respondents do not regard this as one of the revolution's major successes, at least not in comparison with other issues such as access to health and educational services. As Table 4.5 shows, higher value is placed on issues like medical care, education, and job opportunities. Again, these results are consistent with those of the Gallup survey, which showed that education and health services are perceived as the revolution's most important achievements (Levinson 1995).

Benefits that blacks and other disadvantaged sectors of Cuban society experienced since 1959 have been threatened by the deep economic crisis the country has faced since the collapse of its former communist allies. The Cuban government has been forced to introduce a number of market-oriented measures, including foreign investment, to foster productivity and restart Cuba's stagnant economy. Measures such as the legalization of dollars, self-employment, foreign investment, and "free" agricultural markets carry with them, as Cuban authorities themselves recognize, a heavy social cost. They unavoidably provoke increasing inequality and resentment in a population that is used to living in a highly egalitarian social setting. As Carlos Lage, vice president of the Cuban Council of State, recently said, "This will create differences among people, greater than what we have now and greater than we are used to having since the revolution . . . the inequality or privilege that can be created are realities we must allow" (Gunn 1994a; Farah 1993; Fedarko 1995; Analco 1993). Although a higher percentage of blacks (22 percent) than whites (7 percent) considered that the crisis has a racially differentiated effect, our respondents' prevalent view is that the current crisis equally affects blacks and whites (Table 4.4). As a black female physician put it, "Here there are not black and white differences. We are all living through the special period" (*Miami Herald,* August 9, 1993, p. 1).

The economic reforms might hit blacks especially hard, however. To start with, the legalization of dollars has exacerbated tensions between those who do and do not have access to hard currency (Lane 1994). Cubans receive dollars from two main sources: the Cuban-American community

Table 4.5 Success of Revolutionary Policies: Percentage of Respondents by Race

	Whites			Blacks		
	Great	Moderate	No success	Great	Moderate	No success
Provided education	88	8	4	93	5	2
Provided health care	92	6	2	94	4	2
Eliminated racial discrimination	24	64	12	15	77	8
Eliminated racial prejudices	14	72	14	6	87	8
Provided job opportunities	80	12	8	77	19	4
Provided adequate housing	6	80	14	17	77	6

and foreigners (through jobs in tourism). Because the exile community is overwhelmingly white, blacks do not get a proportional share of those remittances (Mesa-Lago 1994b). Their opportunities, then, are reduced to the competitive tourist sector where, according to a substantial proportion of our respondents (about 40 percent of both blacks and whites), they do not have the same opportunities as whites to get jobs.[9] "It is difficult to find a black as a manager or as a cashier in a tourist store," a white teacher stated (Serrano 1995). According to a black singer, "Tourist firms look like South African companies in times of Peter Botha. You go there and they are all white. And I wonder: Where am I, in Holland?" (Duharte Jiménez and Santos García 1995).

To be sure, those who work in tourism are a small proportion of Cuba's labor force, and to get a job in such a competitive sector is certainly difficult for everyone, whites included. But some factors, such as the concept of "good presence" so valued in the tourist industry, might work specifically against blacks. In such an environment racial prejudices might play an active role and prevent blacks from gaining access to highly desirable jobs. Prejudices might not be confined to "people's heads" anymore, but may generate positive discrimination. A black female librarian from Santiago told us the story of a friend who had been discriminated against while working in a tourist store:

> I have a friend who finished, with very high grades, a course to work as a cashier in a tourist store. She is the darkest of her group, has a good presence, is a young educated person, and . . . was denied the cashier position. All the cashiers are blond. After having a job designated for her in Havana, she has been transferred three times to different positions, so she is very upset and says that . . . if she denounces what has happened she might get fired.

In addition to Cubans' own prejudices, blacks have to cope with racial prejudices imported by foreign investors and managerial personnel. Blacks will find it difficult to combat such prejudices, however, given that these investors are a key element in Cuban developmental strategy. The government is interested in providing them with as friendly an environment as possible, not the least through the strict control of labor unions and their bargaining capacity. Although investors' access to labor takes place through the mediation of an official body, they have, in Climent Guitart's words, "complete autonomy to select, hire, and, when necessary, fire the hotel's employees." The relationship between investors, the labor movement, and Cuban authorities is a complex one, and blacks might find that it is through the unions—which have been attempting to redefine their role in the new environment—that they can better advance their future claims.[10]

In addition to the current crisis, other factors that might stir blacks' discontent are the lack of black organizations and the alleged underrepresentation of blacks in leadership positions. The latter is one of the most common criticisms directed against the Cuban government regarding racial issues (Moore 1964, 1988; Clytus 1970; Montaner 1976; Domínguez 1978). However, neither of these concerns is considered a problem by our respondents. Most disagree with the idea that there should be an all-black organization on the island, and believe that blacks are well represented in the leadership of the country (53 percent of whites, 65 percent of blacks), although the idea draws less support from younger blacks (50 percent, compared to 73 percent of older blacks). Younger blacks are again more critical of the revolution's performance, and a few respondents bitterly complained about the lack of opportunities for advancement experienced by blacks.

The issue of blacks' participation in government decisionmaking has to be carefully considered, however. So far, the discussion has centered on the proportion of blacks in the highest bodies of the Communist Party (especially the Politburo and the Central Committee), the Council of Ministries, and, occasionally, the National Assembly of Popular Power. It is true that these bodies concentrate most power in Cuba, but to assume that similar organs at other levels of decisionmaking are powerless is a gross exaggeration. Bodies such as the Provincial Assemblies and Provincial Executive Committees of the Communist Party carry a lot of weight in their territories. Although we know very little about the racial composition of these organs, access to them has been greater than to the higher echelons of the party and the government, where the (overwhelmingly white) generation of the revolution still remains firmly in control (Casal 1979; Booth 1976). Moreover, black presence is still strong in the leadership of workers' unions at all levels, as it was in the Communist-dominated prerevolutionary labor movement. Out of 295,798 union leaders elected in 65,356 locals in mid-1990, for instance, blacks and mulattos represent 38 percent. Several national syndicates, such as those of agricultural and cattle workers, education, science, and sports workers, and light-industry workers, are headed by blacks (*Trabajadores,* March 1 and 8, May 24, September 13, and November 15, 1993; *Latin American Labor News* 2 and 3, 1990). Black participation in decisionmaking structures in Cuba needs further research within a wider framework.

The Future

"The future is dark," one of our respondents wrote. Although all Cubans have good reason to be concerned about what a future (in all probability, noncommunist) Cuba will look like, our sample shows that there are important variations in the way the future is perceived. According to our results, one group can be singled out as the most concerned with the possibility of the collapse of the revolution: older blacks. This is the very group that, in general terms, also has a more positive perception of the revolution and its impact on racism in the country (Table 4.6).

First, although most blacks, regardless of age, agree that the restoration of capitalism would mean "to go back to racism," older blacks' level of agreement with this statement is 16 percent higher than that of younger blacks, who in turn disagree with it twice as much as do older black respondents (32 percent versus 17 percent). Second, younger blacks do not equate the fall of the socialist regime with the end of racial equality as much as older blacks do. Both processes are intimately associated for 47 percent of older blacks but for only 28 percent of younger respondents. For younger blacks it is possible to maintain racial equality even if the revolution falls.

The generational gap among black respondents is also evident in their perceptions of the Cuban American exile community. Although most respondents (both black and white) professed not to know whether "generally speaking, Miami exiles are racist," older blacks showed the highest percentage of agreement and the lowest of disagreement with this statement. Younger blacks' responses came closer to whites' perceptions. Older blacks are also the only group of which a majority agreed with the statement, "Those who left are white, and if they come back they will bring racism back" (51 percent). Younger blacks' response is, again, indistinguishable from that of whites; they either are not especially concerned about the racial attitudes of the white exiles, or have misgivings about how racist they actually are.

Either possibility represents a major failure for the revolution's campaign to discredit the exile community. Although race has not played a prominent role in this campaign, given Cuban authorities' own silence around racial issues, the Cuban American community has been systematically portrayed as inhabiting what has been described as a "racial hell in a capitalist paradise." Miami's countless social problems, such as drug trafficking, homelessness, poverty, crime rates, and racial/ethnic tensions, have all received ample coverage in the Cuban press (León Cotayo 1994b; Roa 1993). The failure of this campaign is even more surprising given the city's terrible racial record, the strong evidence characterizing Cuban-Americans as a deeply racist community, and the tense relationship between them and African Americans.[11] These unexpected results also reflect

Table 4.6 Racial Equality in Postcommunist Cuba: Respondents Who Agree with the Following Statements (percentage distribution)

	Whites			Blacks		
	Total	I	II	Total	I	II
Racial equality would disappear without the revolution	25	29	22	40	28	47
To go back to capitalism is to go back to racism	33	36	30	62	52	68
Generally speaking, Miami exiles are racists	27	32	22	33	26	37
Those who left are white; they'll bring back racism	14	18	11	39	18	51

Note: Age group I = younger than 35 years; age group II = older than 35 years.

those found by the Gallup survey, in which 75 percent of respondents referred to the exiles in affectionate terms (*El Nuevo Herald,* December 18, 1994).

At the same time, however, the low proportion of black Cubans among emigrants seems to suggest that they do not find the United States an attractive migratory destination. According to results drawn from the 1990 U.S. census, nonwhites composed only 15 percent of Cubans arriving in the United States between 1985 and 1990. Cuban sources estimate that for the years 1986–1991 the proportion of blacks and mulattos among total emigrants was only 8 percent. With regard to the last wave of *balseros* (rafters), although racial statistics are not available, the widespread perception is that blacks are again heavily underrepresented (Pedraza 1995; Rodríguez Chavez 1992; González 1994b).[12]

As with any potential migratory group, black Cubans react to a number of factors, among which U.S. racism seems to be a major deterrent. Although our questionnaire did not ask about the way racism in the United States is perceived on the island, most black Cubans seem to agree that it is better for them to stay in Cuba. "In the minds of many black Cubans Rosa Parks is still riding around in the back of the bus" (*Miami Herald,* October 10, 1994, p. 2). Popular humor, probably the most accurate expression of beliefs in postrevolutionary Cuba, has reflected the tension between the harsh realities of the domestic crisis and the skepticism with which the United States is regarded as a migratory destination. A popular joke goes as follows: A black guy asked a friend who was going to the United States: "Would you please let me know whether it is as racist there as they say it is? I myself want to go the States." A few days later, the friend sent a telegram: "Desist: I saw a dog eating a black yesterday." The black guy in Cuba replied: "I insist: I saw a black eating a dog yesterday." Judging by such testimonies and the low proportion of blacks among emigrants, most black Cubans have opted to "eat the dog" on the island rather than to face the United States' racist dog. The Cuban government's campaign depicting the United States as a racist, unfriendly environment for blacks to emigrate to—not a terribly difficult task, to be sure—has been largely successful (*Juventud Rebelde,* May 10, 1992; Pérez Martín 1992; *Granma,* January 28, 1993; Montero Acuña 1993).

Conclusion

Black Cubans have benefited from the Cuban revolution and its policies; therefore their positive perception of the socialist experiment on the island is not surprising. Nor is it surprising that blacks' view of the past is negative. The benefits of the revolution are meaningful only when tested against blacks' situation in the prerevolutionary past, which then becomes an unavoidable point of reference not only in academic analysis but also in real life. Congruent with these views is the fact that blacks are more concerned than are whites about the future associated with the possible end of the revolution, the restoration of capitalism, and the return of the former elite—the white exiles and U.S. entrepreneurs.

All these beliefs add strength to the opinion—which is at least partially accurate—that blacks form a solid base of political support for the current government in Cuba. But such an opinion is also an ideological construction that, by exaggerating blacks' attachment to the current regime, tends to blame them for the lack of political change in the country. In other words, blacks' alleged fidelity to the government can be used effectively in the future to prevent them from fully participating in a post-Castro Cuba. Similar constructions have emerged in Cuban history before, when blacks have been linked to fallen authoritarian regimes such as those of Gerardo Machado (1925–1933) and Fulgencio Batista (1952–1958). Curiously enough, blacks are blamed not only for the survival of the regime but also for participating in any form of civil disobedience, in which case they are labeled as "out of control."

Black participation in cross-racial events such as the August 1994 riot is not surprising. Those who rioted at Malecón were referred to as young blacks and mulattos, and our survey shows that, in fact, younger blacks share a more critical view of the revolution and its impact on racism than do older blacks, and are also less concerned about the future. In many important issues younger blacks' responses can barely be differentiated from those of whites.

What is at stake here is a generational rather than a racial issue. As the Gallup survey shows, younger Cubans are those who are the least satisfied with their personal lives (*El Nuevo Herald,* December 18, 1994), and this is true for both blacks and whites. The current crisis has eroded some of the emblematic achievements of the Cuban revolution to such a degree that young blacks no longer perceive the restoration of capitalism as a major reverse. The future might be dark, as one of our respondents stated, but the present is dark enough already. The incapacity of the Cuban government to maintain its previous levels of social assistance, the deterioration of those that still exist, and the introduction of limited market reforms with their legacy of increasing inequality and social polarization are all factors that may contribute to undermining the legitimacy of the political order.

Moreover, the collapse of the structural conditions that used to guarantee blacks' access to education and jobs after the revolution, coupled with the persistence of a widespread racist ideology, may be having a negative effect on the country's levels of racial equality. The thin line that separates subjective prejudice from objective discrimination has become more fragile under the crisis and, it seems accurate to say, in some highly regarded occupational sectors has been openly broken.

It is paradoxical that those who, according to our results, most benefited from the revolution may now prove to be weak defenders. These young, more educated, and upwardly mobile blacks were born and raised in racism-free Cuba; the prerevolutionary, discriminatory social order has not affected their lives or shaped their memories the way it has for older respondents. The latter's fears have been transformed by the success of the integrationist program promoted by the revolution into the former's confidence. Cuban authorities' surprise is largely a function of their incapacity to regard these young black citizens not only as beneficiaries of revolutionary gains, but also as active protagonists of their own well-being and future.

Notes

The authors wish to thank Tomás Fernández Robaina from the Biblioteca Nacional "José Martí" and our colleagues from the University of Oriente, Miguel Matute and Ofelia Pérez, for their help in distributing the questionnaire. We appreciate the critical comments provided by George Reid Andrews, Harold D. Sims, and Rosalie Schwartz to previous versions of this paper. Financial support was provided to de la Fuente by the United States Institute of Peace (a Peace Scholar Award) and the Institute for the Study of World Politics, and to Glasco by the Center for Latin American Studies, University of Pittsburgh.

1. A similar event took place in October 1993 in the town of Regla, near Havana, during the funeral of a young man who had been killed when trying to leave the country. See Santiago (1993) and *El Nuevo Herald,* October 19, 1993, p. 1.

2. "The issue of labels is obviously relevant here. Afro-Cuban has become an extremely polemic and emotionally charged term in Cuba since, at least, the 1960s. The point is that it is a redundant concept: Cuban is already Afro. This is, of course, a cultural construction which tends to obscure the singularity of blackness within a national paradigm, but until I am ready to deal with this issue with all its implications, I prefer to avoid its use" (Alejandro de la Fuente).

3. For a discussion of the role of ethnicity in the transitions of Eastern European countries, see Bugajski (1994); Rupesinghe, King, and Vorkunova (1992); and Sugar (1980).

4. This survey was commissioned by the *Miami Herald* and conducted by CID-Gallup, a Costa Rican firm associated with The Gallup Organization. It covered 1,002 respondents in the western two-thirds of the island (75 percent of the national territory). The team designated to cover eastern provinces was not allowed to conduct its work.

5. We have used two age groups in our results: those younger than thirty-five years old as of June 1, 1994 (born and raised after the revolution), and those older than thirty-five.

6. A similar conclusion was reached by Andrews (1991, pp. 163–165) in his study of São Paulo.

7. We collected information on occupations and education for the respondents, their parents, and their children. The latter were only included, however, if they were twenty-five years of age or older, an age at which, in normal circumstances, they would have finished their education and entered the labor market.

8. The 46 percent of black younger respondents who agreed that "the new generations are not racist" represent the majority; 10 percent answered "don't know" and 44 percent disagreed.

9. The percentages of those who think that blacks do have the same opportunities vary according to race, however, and are higher among whites (44 percent) than among blacks (30 percent). The rest (16 percent of whites, 29 percent of blacks) answered "I do not know." Among those who have an opinion, most whites think that blacks enjoy similar opportunities to work in tourism, whereas most blacks believe that the opposite is true.

10. Climent Guitart is the head of the Guitart Group, which manages several hotels in Havana, Varadero, and Cayo Coco (*Cubanews*, January 1994, p. 11). On the labor conflicts faced by Guitart in Havana and the reaction of the official union, see Gunn (1994a).

11. The most recent episode of tensions between the African- and Cuban-American communities in Miami took place when the Metro-Dade Commission selected a Cuban-American supported by the Cuban American National Foundation for county manager over a female African-American candidate. See Román (1994) and the *Miami Times,* December 29, 1994.

12. We thank Silvia Pedraza for sharing her research results with us.

◆ 5 ◆

Cuban-U.S. Relations and the Process of Transition: Possible Consequences of Covert Agendas

Gillian Gunn Clissold

◆

The relationship between the United States and Cuba will have an obvious and enormous effect on the Cuban transition. This chapter analyzes this relationship and how the relevant pathologies may doom a better future for the island. Cuba and the United States are both pursuing policies that inadequately defend the interests both say they wish to protect: the well-being of their respective populations. The strategies adopted by Washington and Havana to date have not been totally counterproductive, but in the future they could possibly lead to catastrophic consequences. Furthermore, there are other policies available that would further the two nations' declared goals far more effectively. These alternative policies have been considered and, to date, rejected.

Are these policies actually designed to serve quite different, undeclared interests? Are the two governments simply inept, operating on false information and therefore unaware that their policies are inappropriate? Is each confronted with a domestic political context in which adoption of a policy better suited to defending the overtly declared interests is perceived as threatening to the current power structure? Are the transition processes underway in both countries—from Soviet-subsidized communism in Cuba and from Cold War superpower status in the United States—contributing to governmental schizophrenia?

A review of the two nations' recent interactions leads to the conclusion that all four dynamics are at work on both sides of the Florida Straits, albeit with different weights at various moments. Although this is bad news for both the U.S. and Cuban populations—who stand to lose far more than do their leaders if bilateral relations continue to be distorted—it has particularly serious consequences for residents of the island.

The U.S. Strategy

Virtually all United States–based Cuba watchers, from the right and the left, agree about defining U.S. interests in Cuba. They all say that Washington will be best served by a peaceful transition to democracy on the island with a related increase in the space available for civil society, Cuban adoption of market mechanisms, compensation for nationalized U.S. properties, rapprochement between Cubans on the island and Cubans resident abroad, improvement of Cuba's human-rights record, prevention of uncontrolled Cuban out-migration, and avoidance of U.S. intervention on the island. Furthermore, U.S. policymakers agree that expansion of U.S. trade opportunities abroad is wise, though there is considerable variation in the priority given to this concern (Gunn 1993).

Some U.S. policies adopted to date do serve these interests. Despite its explicit opposition to the Castro government, the 1992 Cuban Democracy Act (CDA) permitted U.S. companies to engage in communications-related trade with Cuba, authorized U.S. nongovernmental organizations (NGOs) to make humanitarian donations to Cuban NGOs, and slightly broadened the U.S. travel-ban exemption to include individuals engaged in educational and religious activities. Shortly after the bill's passage, U.S. companies entered into negotiations with Cuba to expand telephone service between the two countries. The discussions were delayed because the U.S. Department of the Treasury objected to the share of revenue the Cuban government firm would receive in the proposed deals (interview with State Department officials, 1994). A compromise was finally worked out, however, and in November 1994 direct dialing between the two countries finally became possible. Although NGO donations technically had been permitted before it was passed, the CDA gave the practice the stamp of congressional approval. After the law's passage the number of NGOs that solicited and received licenses increased considerably. The enlarged travel categories also led U.S. universities and Christian churches to significantly expand their contacts among the Cuban population.

These CDA provisions served U.S. interests in several ways. Scholars who have studied the political evolution of the Soviet Union, Eastern Europe, and China believe facilitating unfettered communication with the outside world is one of the most effective ways to undermine undemocratic political systems. The CDA measures increased the Cuban people's exposure to outside ideas through phone contacts and personal interaction. The phone provision in particular strengthened communication between Cuban Americans and their relatives on the island, building an environment conducive to eventual rapprochement between the two population groups.

The political endorsement of humanitarian donations to NGOs also helped erode the Cuban government's accusation that Washington wishes to "starve the Cuban people into submission." For years the Cuban government brandished the image of a threatening Washington that would exploit any division in Cuban society to foment disagreement and undermine Cuban sovereignty. This rhetoric was used to persuade Cuban reformists to accept domestic repression they would otherwise find unacceptable. The humanitarian impulse reflected in the CDA helped, in a small way, to discredit this claim. The donations stimulated by the bill simultaneously enhanced the prestige and resources of Cuban NGOs capable of expanding civil society, such as churches (Gunn 1995; Fernández 1993).

The 1994 and 1995 migration agreements between the United States and Cuba also served the U.S. interest in avoiding uncontrolled refugee influxes and subsequent domestic problems in the United States. The 1966 Cuban Adjustment Act had previously permitted any Cuban who made it to the shores of the United States, or was picked up by a U.S. craft in international waters, to be given virtually automatic one-year humanitarian parole into the country. At the end of the year the individual would have the right to resident alien status.

The Cuban government's requirement that departing citizens acquire an exit visa, and Havana's willingness to patrol its own shores for violators seeking to reach Florida by raft, generally kept Cuban migration down to a steady trickle. However, Havana constantly complained that the U.S. "open arms" policy unfairly incited "illegal departures" because the same individuals who were turned down for visas at the U.S. Interests Section knew they would be admitted if they arrived by raft. During the 1980 Mariel boatlift Fidel Castro temporarily encouraged out-migration, permitting Cuban Americans to pick up relatives by boat. Over 100,000 migrants arrived before Washington and Havana reached an accord that ended the crisis (Larzelere 1988).

A subsequent 1984 agreement then stipulated that the United States would accept up to 20,000 migrants per year. However, in reality the U.S. Interests Section in Havana had given only a few thousand visas each year. When questioned about this discrepancy, U.S. officials said it was due to the fact that relatively few Cubans take out U.S. citizenship, and therefore only a small portion of Cuban Americans were entitled to bring in their full families. Some U.S. and Cuban scholars doubted that this would fully account for the limited visa issuance, and asserted that Washington purposefully interpreted immigration rules in a strict manner to limit Cuban legal immigration.

Whatever the truth of the matter, the 1966 Adjustment Act remained in force. A slow, steady flow of rafters continued to arrive and be "paroled" into the United States. In August 1994 the Cuban government responded to internal unrest and perceived U.S. provocation by again opening its borders (*Washington Post,* August 17, 1994). This time Washington better protected its interests by discouraging Cuban Americans from going to Cuba to collect their relatives, but admitting the arriving migrants. The seas were awash with Cubans clinging to unseaworthy crafts, and the state of Florida began to complain about the burden the new arrivals would place on taxpayers. Cognizant of rising anti-immigration sentiment, and concerned about protecting the electoral chances of Florida governor Lawton Chiles in the November 1994 gubernatorial race, President Clinton grew increasingly worried as the number of rafters topped 30,000 in late August. The administration took firm steps to stop the outflow.

First it reinterpreted the 1966 Adjustment Act. Previously the simple rescue of a rafter by the U.S. Coast Guard, or a rafter's presentation to the Immigration and Naturalization Service (INS) following arrival on a Florida beach, was considered "inspection into" the United States, required for the act's provisions to be applied to an individual migrant's case. In August 1994 the Clinton administration declared that these procedures no longer constituted inspection. Therefore, Cubans intercepted at sea or washed up on a beach were not eligible for the act's provisions, and could be detained at an INS facility in the United States or sent to the U.S. naval base at Guantánamo in Cuba. This measure "demagnetized" the United States for would-be Cuban migrants, making it clear they would not be welcomed with open arms. The decision also responded to the long-standing Cuban government complaint that the previous policy was encouraging immigration by raft (*Washington Post,* August 19, 1994).

In the September 1994 migration negotiations that followed the reinterpretation of the Adjustment Act, Washington asked Havana to discourage illegal migration as it had prior to the August emergency. Havana agreed, with the caveat that it would use only "persuasion" and not force. In return, Havana asked Washington to increase the number of visas provided. Washington agreed, and promised that at least 20,000 visas would be issued per year. The INS began to interpret rules for visa eligibility in a more flexible manner, and established a lottery for Cubans who could not fit even the more relaxed requirements (*Washington Post,* September 10, 1994).

This solution only partially protected U.S. interests, however; there remained the problem of the approximately 30,000 Cubans interned in poor conditions in Guantánamo. Washington was reluctant to admit them en masse for fear of sending a signal that the immigration gate was open again and thereby triggering another outflow. There were also well-grounded fears that Havana would consider such a move to violate the 1994 accord, and would retaliate by itself relaxing out-migration controls.

Tensions steadily grew in the camps, despite the incremental admission to the United States of children, women, and the elderly. In the spring of 1995 the U.S. Marine Corps general in charge of Guantánamo asserted that riots were "extremely possible" and said that he was "very, very concerned" (Viglucci 1995).

Secret negotiations were conducted with Cuba, and on May 2, 1995, a new accord was achieved. This permitted admission to the United States of Guantánamo refugees on an incremental basis, but also provided for new rafters to be returned to Cuba. Only those who met the standard test for political asylum would be admitted.

The May 1995 accord was a major breakthrough in relations between the two nations. Washington implied that although it still disapproved of Cuba's political system, its abuse of human rights was not so bad as to prevent the repatriation of most rafters. Like the 1994 accord, the 1995 agreement caused a major political backlash by the Cuban American population, and again the domestic reaction prevented the administration from moving forward forthrightly to protect other U.S. interests. But the migration agreements of 1994 and 1995 nonetheless established an entirely new context for Cuban-U.S. relations (*Washington Post,* May 3, 1995).

A final policy that has served U.S. interests is the attempt to build an international consensus on human rights in Cuba. Washington is aware that it is poorly placed to convince Havana to release political prisoners and cease harassment of dissidents. Past U.S. covert action in Cuba makes any individual supported by Washington vulnerable to the domestically discrediting accusation that he or she is an agent of imperialism. Also, the Cuban government believes that Washington will not reward it for incremental improvement in human rights; therefore the incentive to accommodate Washington is modest. The European Union, Canada, and Latin American nations have far more influence. Many of these countries have important investment and trade activities in Cuba that the Castro government would be loath to lose. Many have criticized the U.S. embargo and voted against it in the United Nations, thereby making it harder to accuse them of imperialist collaboration. Washington is aware that these other countries are better placed to pressure for an improvement in Cuba's human-rights record, and has wisely sought to coordinate its activities with them. Unfortunately, the number of U.S. policies that undermine U.S. interests in Cuba is far greater than the number that protect U.S. interests.

One difficulty concerns the overall tone of U.S. policy. Hostile rhetoric that implies that the U.S. government has a greater right than the Cuban people's to determine Cuba's future plays to Fidel Castro's strength. It helps him present himself as the nationalistic figure defending tiny Cuba against the imperialistic, interventionist tendencies of the monster to the north. The Cuban people's deeply rooted nationalism makes them predisposed to seriously consider such an argument. Washington's willingness to let conservative elements in the Cuban American community in Miami influence policy bolsters Castro's claim that if he is overthrown Washington will impose a puppet government of wealthy exiles who will try to return the country to the social and economic structure of the 1950s—a prospect most Cubans fear. The confrontational context also makes it easy for the Cuban government to convince wavering supporters in the military and security forces to stick with the status quo because the successor government would wreak revenge on the henchmen of an overthrown Castro (interviews with diplomats, officials, and dissidents in Cuba, 1990–1996).

These trends have established an atmosphere not conducive to the protection of overall U.S. interests, and several recent policy decisions have undermined specific interests.

First, policy changes that immediately preceded the September 1994 migration agreement have restricted contacts between the Cuban and U.S. populations, limiting the ideology-eroding exposure to the outside world. These measures were imposed on August 20, 1994, at the suggestion of conservative elements of the Cuban American community who were angry about the decision to detain Cuban rafters at Guantánamo. As the price for supporting the detention strategy, they demanded that Clinton cancel the previous policy of permitting Cuban Americans to send limited remittances to their families in Cuba; prohibit travel by Cuban Americans to visit relatives except in circumstances of humanitarian emergency; and impose an additional bureaucratic requirement on U.S. scholars going to Cuba for academic research that they obtain a specific license from the Treasury Department in advance rather than simply signing a form at the airport upon departure. Florida's gubernatorial race, which pitted Democratic incumbent Lawton Chiles against Republican candidate Jeb Bush, also contributed to the administration's desire to appease Miami's Cuban American community.

The measure significantly damaged U.S. interests. The remittance cancellation permitted Castro once again to present Washington as determined to starve Cubans into submission, and gave him an extra scapegoat for Cuba's economic deterioration that deflected responsibility from his own misrule. By removing one source of funds for struggling Cuban families, the policy increased out-migration pressure, the very problem Clinton was frantically seeking to solve. Furthermore, the remittances had chipped away at centralized political power by providing an economic resource not controlled by the state apparatus; now that resource was gone. Cutting personal contact between Cuban Americans and their relatives on the island caused unnecessary personal pain and lessened the corrosive effect of exposure to the outside world. The license requirement for academics initially had only the slightly negative effect of making travel preparation more time-consuming.

Washington has also undermined its own interests by refusing to reward Cuba for significant economic reform. The Clinton administration had long maintained that it would reward Cuba in a "carefully calibrated" manner for positive gestures. The July 1993 legalization of the holding of dollars, which essentially created a tolerated if not approved parallel market economy within Cuba, received no U.S. response. In early 1994 administration representatives explicitly stated that reforms that benefited the average Cuban, such as the reestablishment of a direct market link between the farmer and the consumer, would be eligible for reciprocity. However, when just such a market link was established in October 1994,

Washington refused to any make any reciprocal gesture. The 1994 and 1995 incremental broadening of categories of workers eligible for self-employment received the same nonresponse, as did the September 1995 approval of a new, somewhat more flexible foreign-investment code. Because Castro had implemented the various measures in response to the domestic Cuban situation, not as gestures to Washington, administration officials commented, no reciprocity was required. When Cuba responded to international human-rights pressure in the summer of 1995 and released six political prisoners, Washington barely acknowledged the act.

The lack of reciprocity has undermined U.S. interests by strengthening the hard-line, antireform segment within Cuba. The hard line had long argued that it was not worth making any gestures to the United States because Washington would constantly "move the goal posts." Rather than respond in kind to a Cuban concession, hard-liners maintained, Washington would simply take it as a sign Cuba was on the verge of collapse and it was time to apply more pressure. Cuban reformists had argued that in certain circumstances one could negotiate in good faith with Washington and that positive gestures would be rewarded; they particularly tried to use this argument to call for improvements in the human-rights situation. Washington's lack of reciprocity in the 1993–1995 period seriously undermined the reformist segment in the Cuban Communist Party (PCC). If the United States truly wants a peaceful transition in Cuba, it has an interest in facilitating precisely the reverse trend.

The damage to U.S. interests in Cuba caused by decisions made in the first half of the 1990s are insignificant compared with the March 12, 1996, signing of the Helms-Burton law. The Cuban government bears significant responsibility for the law's approval; its passage was triggered by Havana's February 24 decision to shoot down two private U.S. planes it claimed were violating Cuban airspace. However, the Clinton administration also bears responsibility for letting its policy options be defined by the domestic pressures the incident unleashed. Clinton's hypersensitivity to politics in a presidential-election year has severely damaged national interests; the United States now has to deal with a hostile neighbor over whom it has little leverage.

Originally introduced by Republican senator Jesse Helms on February 8, 1995, the Cuban Liberty and Democratic Solidarity Act tightens the embargo by penalizing the Russian Federation for its remaining economic ties with Cuba; punishing foreign companies that "traffic" in Cuban properties previously confiscated from U.S. owners, or Cuban owners who subsequently became U.S. citizens; denying visas to foreign nationals deemed to be involved in such trafficking; and restricting future policy toward a "transition government." A virtually identical bill was subsequently proposed by Congressman Dan Burton in the House of Representatives. The legislation was drawn up in careful consultation with leading figures in the conservative wing of the Cuban American community. Indeed, one such individual has boasted to colleagues that his organization "wrote the bill" and handed it to Helms in virtually finished form.

The bill was passed by the House of Representatives on September 21, 1995, by a vote of 294 to 130. As of early 1996 approval in the Senate appeared more difficult, but not impossible. Although Secretary of State Warren Christopher criticized major portions of the bill, and recommended that President Clinton veto it if passed, the president himself seemed ambivalent on the matter.[1] The February 24 shoot-down then dramatically increased support for the bill. Conservative Cuban Americans mounted an intense lobbying effort on a Congress already predisposed to swiftly punish the Cuban government. At the last moment a new provision was quietly inserted into the legislation that adopted all past Cuba-embargo executive orders as congressionally mandated. The Clinton administration, with its attention focused on the presidential election and the importance of winning Cuban American votes in Florida and New Jersey, refrained from repeating its previous criticism of the bill, or its dismay at the legislative enactment of past executive orders, and signed the Helms-Burton bill into law (House of Representatives 1996). President Clinton's Special Adviser on Cuba resigned his position a few weeks later, remarking that the passage of Helms-Burton meant he was no longer able to balance pressure on the Cuban government with support for the Cuban people.

The Helms-Burton law will damage U.S. interests regarding Cuba whether it contributes to Castro's overthrow or not. If Castro survives in power, the law will lower the standard of living by discouraging foreign investment and will thereby increase out-migration pressure. Castro is alrady using the law to revitalize his scapegoat strategy of blaming Cuba's economic woes on U.S. policy. If Helms-Burton does contribute to the overthrow of Castro, U.S. interests could still be in jeopardy. Overthrow could lead to massive out-migration, pull the United States into an open-ended conflict, and destabilize the region. Governmental change amid intense economic recession and high tensions with a powerful neighbor is more likely to be destabilizing than in a neutral context.

The law is also hurting relations with important allies who object to its extraterritorial aspects, provoking accusations of violating the General Agreement on Tariffs and Trade (GATT) and the North American Free Trade Agreement (NAFTA), and eroding the United States' ability to influence Russia's nuclear policy. The law has isolated the United States at the United Nations; the April 1996 vote on condemning Cuban human-rights violations was weakened by international distaste for Washington's new policy. Unlike the CDA, which tightened the embargo on Cuba in 1992, Helms-Burton has only a symbolic, insubstantial "Track II" provision. It does little to relieve the suffering of the Cuban population or enhance their ability to communicate with U.S. citizens. This makes it easy for the Castro government to present the United States as acting with callous disregard for the welfare of the Cuban people.

The law's language also restricts diplomacy with a transition government. It lays out such precise criteria for an acceptable transition government that it restricts Washington's ability to facilitate peaceful change in Cuba. For example, eligibility for U.S. assistance requires such a government to make a commitment to reinstate the citizenship of Cuban-born nationals returning to Cuba and to make progress in "granting permits to privately owned media and telecommunications companies to operate in Cuba." Both are measures that an otherwise well-intentioned transition government might well be reluctant to adopt, and they could threaten the cohesion of a delicately balanced coalition. It is ironic that even the United States does not meet some of the criteria, such as the requirement that political parties have equal allotments of radio and television air time. By declaring that the transition government must exclude Fidel and Raúl Castro, the law rules out transition models in which the early phase includes a role for the old guard.

The ideal democratic system described in Helms-Burton has seldom emerged directly from dictatorship elsewhere in the world; usually there is a messy period of compromise and coalition building. By setting such high standards Washington may be prevented from consolidating a transition mechanism that, if imperfect, is nonetheless the most democratic option likely to emerge from the political circumstances of the day. Failure to stabilize the imperfect transition government could then permit a less attractive option to emerge victorious from the race for power. The old aphorism, "The perfect is the enemy of the good," certainly applies to this portion of the Helms-Burton law.

New language inserted in late February 1996, just after the shootdown, restricts policy flexibility even more. By accepting the provision converting past executive embargo measures into law, President Clinton surrendered most of his own and future presidents' power to make Cuba policy and transferred constitutionally mandated executive authority to Congress. Not only can no aid be dispensed, but no past embargo measure can be surrendered until Cuba has a transitional government that meets the law's conditions, or until Congress decides to change the rules.

With a stroke of his pen Clinton has signed away much of the executive's right to make foreign policy on one of the thorniest conflicts in the Western hemisphere. This sets a disturbing precedent for other foreign-policy matters. What happens the next time a foreign leader enrages a politically powerful constituency in the United States? Will the executive surrender to Congress policy on another country?

Furthermore, with the legislative freeze on past executive orders Castro will know that no matter what positive act he might contemplate, be it further market reform or the reduction of restrictions on civil society, unless an antiembargo majority takes over Congress he cannot be rewarded with embargo relaxation by either Clinton or a successor. A proengagement president might be able to make small gestures, such as the signing of agreements on drug-trafficker interdiction or civil aviation, but would be deprived of all substantial inducements.

Paradoxically, Castro can also rest assured that if he again angers the United States, Washington will find it difficult to punish him; with the Helms-Burton law Washington is using up virtually all its economic and diplomatic ammunition. The few remaining options, such as cutting off the small amounts of humanitarian resources and the limited travel still permitted, would only hurt the Cuban population rather than the Cuban government. Washington is thereby left with only armed conflict in its policy arsenal.

Although the United States would win any military confrontation with the island, U.S. strategists have long concluded that such a conflict would cost a considerable number of lives, could not be resolved swiftly, and would trigger a massive refugee outflow. Castro knows that the U.S. population's distaste for both intractable conflicts and uncontrolled migration would make such a military operation politically unsustainable. Possessing the most powerful military in the world, and one of the most able diplomatic services, Washington will nevertheless find it extremely difficult to influence its small neighbor.

Even before the Helms-Burton bill became law it created political pressures in Washington that damaged U.S. interests. Pragmatically minded individuals in the administration sought to follow up the goodwill created in the Cuban government by the May 1995 repatriation agreement with an effort to revitalize the CDA's Track II provision for people-to-people contacts. However, the architects of the effort felt compelled to protect themselves domestically by presenting Track II as an alternative to Helms-Burton that would be more effective in undermining the Cuban government. The Cuban authorities responded by declaring they had no obligation to help the United States undermine the revolution. Shortly thereafter, the Cuban government denied exit visas to a number of Cuban scholars scheduled to speak at conferences in the United States, and reinvigorated its efforts to control NGOs. The spring 1995 effort by U.S. officials to widen Track II actually decreased, rather than enhanced, interpersonal contacts.

The Helms-Burton law provided a plausible pretext for further curtailment of such communication between U.S. and Cuban citizens. Shortly after the bill was approved, the Politburo of the PCC met to decide how to respond. In an atmosphere of virtual economic war with Washington, the Cuban hard line argued, civil society had to be more closely controlled. In a March 23 speech informing the Central Committee of the Politburo's conclusions, Raúl Castro announced a campaign against some of the reformist Cuban scholars who had been involved in dialogue with U.S. counterparts. "Various comrades fell into the spider's web woven by foreign cubanologists, in truth (becoming) servants of the U.S. in its policy of fomenting fifth-columnism," Castro remarked (*Granma,* March 27, 1996). Shortly thereafter the Cuban authorities launched an investigation of twenty-seven Cuban think tanks.

The U.S. tightening of its Cuba embargo also had negative repercussions for economic reform and for dissident activities within Cuba. The Cuban authorities had already been increasing pressure on dissidents in the early winter of 1995–1996, and this escalated after the passage of Helms-Burton. The government claimed that in a circumstance of intense confrontation with the United States, dissident activity had to be controlled much more tightly. In the same March 23 meeting, the leadership pointed out the danger of moving ahead too quickly with further economic reform, and announced a period of "consolidation."

In sum, only a few elements of U.S. policy toward Cuba are actually helping to protect Washington's publicly declared interests. The majority of policies adopted to date, and particularly the new legislation, decrease the likelihood of a peaceful transition to democracy, curtail space available for civil society, provide no concrete encouragement of the adoption of market mechanisms, disrupt the effort to build an international consensus concerning human rights in Cuba, and increase the danger of U.S. intervention on the island. Only the interest in preventing uncontrolled out-migration has been significantly furthered, and even that could be undercut if the other policies contribute to one or more of the scenarios to be described later in the chapter.

Does Washington have a covert set of interests that secretly guide its policy, and no intention to protect its overtly declared interests? The answer is, partly, yes. A minority in the Cuban American community is ambivalent about a peaceful transition, because that would largely cut out the Miami community from leadership roles in a post-Castro Cuba. Cuban Americans would only be accepted as future leaders of Cuba if they were installed by intervening U.S. troops, in the style of Panama's President Endara. United States–based Cubans might be welcomed as high-ranking advisers by a post-Castro government that came to power by peaceful means, but they would not be accepted as leaders. Some individuals support initiatives such as the Helms-Burton law not because they fail to understand that it could contribute to chaos in Cuba, but because they consciously desire chaos in Cuba.

The aims of this domestic special-interest group do not mesh with those of the U.S. government. Most government officials know that intervention would be costly and would inhibit the establishment of stable democratic institutions. However, those in government seeking to defend the real U.S. interests are hindered by a domestic political context in which the defense of the overtly declared interests is perceived as threatening to the current power structure.

Lack of factual knowledge also plays a role in structuring U.S. policy. Many backers of the hard line in U.S. policy, both within government and in the public at large, genuinely believe that the Cuban government is on the verge of collapse. It is easy to understand why so many United States–based Cuba watchers fail to understand the tenacity of the Cuban regime. U.S. travel restrictions and inflexible Cuban-government press policies limit the flow of reliable information. In Europe, where travel to Cuba is not limited, the Cuban reality seems to be far better appreciated.

Finally, the psychology associated with post–Cold War transition plays a role. The United States is accustomed to being a superpower to which allies look for security guarantees and economic assistance, and it is comfortable with a world in which international allegiances are determined by an anticommunist litmus test. Now the United States finds itself in a multipower world. The disappearance of the Soviet threat, combined with the ailing U.S. economy and the growth of a more united Europe, means that Washington can no longer command the support from allies that it once did. It is confused by a world in which pro- and anticommunist labels are largely irrelevant. Cuba presents an opportunity to indulge in nostalgia for the superpower era, the discrepancy in size and resources making the island seem an ideal target for metaphorical muscle flexing. And Cuba is one of the few countries remaining in the world in which the Cold War labels still seem applicable.

For all these reasons, Washington is pursuing a policy that frequently undermines its own interests regarding Cuba. Domestic political pressures currently play the dominant role, and seem likely to for some time to come. If Bill Clinton were to win a second term, and thereby be freed from the need to raise reelection funds and support, it would become somewhat easier to tailor policy to protect U.S. interests. If campaign reform were to limit the role of finances in election races, a similar result would be possible. However, even if these conditions were met, the problems of ignorance, transition confusion, and covert agendas would remain.

The Cuban Strategy

Washington is not alone in its penchant for contradictory policies that fail to further publicly declared interests. Covert agendas, ignorance, domestic-power concerns, and the confusion associated with transition psychology all play a role in Havana, just as they do in Washington. A resident of Cuba would be in the best position to analyze these dynamics, but I put forward the following ideas to stimulate debate and to show that the U.S. ailment is far from unique.

The Cuban government repeatedly declares that its interests would be served by the lifting of the U.S. embargo, the establishment of diplomatic relations with Washington, and an improvement of relations with moderate exile groups. Some policies adopted to date have indeed furthered these interests. In mid-1994 Havana began to raise trial balloons concerning possible new, more flexible mechanisms to compensate U.S. firms that had property nationalized in the early days of the revolution. This was a wise strategy, for it would help build a constituency in the United States with a concrete interest in negotiations with Castro. Under the leadership of Foreign Minister Roberto Robaina, Cuba made overtures to moderate Cuban Americans, inviting some to major conferences in Havana in April 1994 and November 1995. In January 1996 the Foreign Ministry announced streamlined visa policies for certain Cuban Americans wishing to visit the island.

Additional measures have been adopted, primarily to respond to other concerns, but with the side effect of creating a context for improving relations with Washington. Recently Havana signed the Tlatelolco Accord on Nuclear Non-Proliferation, primarily motivated by the interest in building alliances in Latin America. It was hoped that the agreement would be unanimously supported by all states in the region. Moreover, because Washington had been pressuring Havana for many years to sign the agreement, the signature was helpful to their relationship. The decision in the early 1990s to more vigorously implement the 1982 law on foreign investment, and the subsequent decision to redraft that law to make it more flexible, had a similar origin and impact. They were taken to attract investment from other parts of the world, but also drew the attention of U.S. businesspeople to the opportunities that would open up in Cuba should the embargo be lifted. The 1993–1994 decisions to adopt a variety of other market-oriented measures were motivated by economic concerns alone, but were also a modest step toward the type of reform Washington had long advocated.

The list of Cuban policies that do not further overtly declared interests is, however, much longer. Human rights is one of the few issues on which Washington is able to justify its hard-line policy in a manner at least partially convincing to Latin American and European governments. Perhaps even more significantly, human rights is a primary concern of the domestic U.S. left, the natural constituency for lifting the embargo. Havana repeatedly undercuts its own argument against the embargo, and discredits itself with potential supporters, by abusing the human rights of its citizens. The regulations covering employment in foreign-owned enterprises would outrage even the most Cuba-friendly labor organizer in the West. Arrests of dissidents on flimsy charges, and their incarceration for long periods of time after brief trials, cause even greater anger.

Furthermore, Cuba sometimes implements policies sensibly designed to further its interests in such an incompetent manner that they either fail to achieve their potential impact, or are actually counterproductive. The decision to make available to Miami television stations a videotape of moderate Cuban Americans sharing a cordial evening with Fidel Castro discredited many participants in the April 1994 conference. As a result, the conference accomplished less than it might have. After trial balloons were launched concerning compensation for nationalized properties, galvanizing U.S. corporate attention, no follow-through emerged. Details were not provided, and the public-relations opportunity was not exploited. Similarly, although NGO contacts with the United States have proven useful in increasing the U.S. public's understanding of Cuban reality, the Cuban government to date has refused to adjust restrictive laws concerning the registration of Cuban NGOs that inhibit their growth in Cuba. (Specifically, the law still requires that each Cuban NGO have a "state reference institution" to which it must open its books for inspection.)

Perhaps the most flamboyant example of Cuban policies sabotaging publicly declared national interests occurred in February and March of 1996. First, in mid-February the Cuban authorities arrested the leadership of the dissident coalition Concilio Cubano, and denied permission for the group's long-planned February 24 gathering. Cuba adopted this measure even though European Union diplomats, with whom the Cuban government was negotiating a cooperation agreement worth millions of dollars in assistance, had forewarned that closer relations required improvements in human rights. These European diplomats had shown particular concern for the fate of Concilio Cubano.

While the Europeans were puzzling over how to respond to the Cuban-government action, Cuban MIGs shot down two small private U.S. planes on the date the meeting would have been held. The United States claimed that the planes were in international airspace at the time of the incident, and the Cuban authorities claimed that they were inside Cuban territory. Although the action cannot be morally defended, the Cuban-government explanation bears consideration. The Miami-based exile organization that sent the planes, Brothers to the Rescue, had violated Cuban airspace on several past occasions, and in July 1995 and January 1996 it actually dropped anti-Castro political propaganda over Havana. In the days just before the shooting it had been sending funds to Concilio Cubano.

Beginning in July 1995, Cuban diplomats energetically pressed Washington to prevent the infringement of Cuban airspace, and the U.S. authorities had agreed that such acts were a violation of international law. Indeed, after the July 1995 incident the State Department issued a public warning that violators of Cuban airspace were putting their lives at risk, and at the time of the shooting the state was seeking to revoke the pilot's license of the leader of Brothers to the Rescue on the grounds that he had repeatedly filed false flight plans. The United States, however, said it could not stop the flights.

Meanwhile, pressure was growing inside the Cuban military and security forces to put a halt to such activities. Otherwise, it was feared, exile organizations would feel that they could escalate their actions with impunity, and the Cuban population would conclude that the government had lost the ability and/or will to defend itself.

The precise decisionmaking process within the Cuban government on February 24 is still a mystery, but whatever the motive for the showdown the timing could not have been worse. The U.S. Congress was about to enter its final debate on the Helms-Burton bill. Europe was digesting the news of the Concilio Cubano arrests. As a result of the shooting, negotiations with Europe virtually ceased, and Helms-Burton was stiffened and swiftly passed. The impact on Cuban interests was clearly negative.

The state of the Cuban debate about policy regarding the United States is somewhat difficult to gauge, given that much of the discussion goes on behind doors closed to foreign academics. But there seem to be three dynamics at work. First, the hard line argues that Washington will consistently move the goal posts, and will not relax the embargo for anything less than Fidel Castro's overthrow. Washington, they claim, will interpret any positive gesture as evidence that Cuba is "running scared" and on the verge of collapse. Rather than respond with a reciprocal gesture of goodwill, Washington will simply push harder for still greater concessions.

Second, a powerful sector of Cuba's leadership seems to have concluded that a significant improvement of human-rights performance could lead to a dangerous erosion of political control. Dissidents need to be "nipped in the bud," this sector argues, or they will begin to destabilize Cuban society at a moment when the economic situation has created a ready constituency for any leader who claims to have the key to Cuba's salvation. Much of the Cuban leadership also appears ignorant of the seriousness with which potential allies view human-rights abuses.

Third, the institution that pushed the hardest for economic reform in 1993–1994, the Cuban military, is uncomfortable with political reform. It is unclear whether the military was cowed by the 1989 execution of the allegedly reformist General Arnaldo Ochoa after his conviction for drug smuggling, or constrained by a military culture that simply does not lend itself to political pluralism. But the net result is that the economic reform pushed by the military makes it easier for the political hard line to argue against liberalization. The decrease in centralized control occasioned by the economic changes, the hard-line argument goes, makes this a particularly inauspicious moment to implement political reform.

The coverage provided here is insufficient to permit comprehensive conclusions on the counterproductive nature of Cuban policy toward the United States, but some preliminary thoughts are worthwhile. As in Washington, it seems plausible that important sectors of the Cuban power structure actually have an alternative, covert agenda. Some do not want the embargo lifted nor relations with Washington improved because they are afraid that the subsequent flood of dollars and Americans would undermine the present power structure far more than does the embargo. The embargo's usefulness as a scapegoat for economic difficulties supports this hidden agenda.

Havana also sometimes operates on false information. Its diplomats are not rewarded for reporting back to Cuba just how debilitating the human-rights issue is in Cuba's public-relations campaign. Therefore, many otherwise reasonable decisionmakers in Havana genuinely do not understand the cultural resonance of the issue with the North American public. They have convinced themselves that the human-rights issue has been invented by Washington to discredit Cuba, and can be circumvented. The decision to release the controversial videotape to the Miami press can also be explained by ignorance. The Cuban officials concerned have dealt with thousands of tapes of Castro meeting foreign delegations. To them this was no different. They failed to understand how the tape's release would discredit moderate Cuban Americans in Miami to such an extent that many would be fearful of participating in subsequent meetings.

The domestic political context also plays a critical role. The Cuban leadership has to maintain a consensus that unites disparate wings of the revolution. If Castro were to follow the advice of reformers, and alienate the hard line, he would erode his own power. If he were to ignore the concerns of the military and security apparatus, he would damage the unity at the top of the Cuban leadership that has long been deemed essential for resisting imperialist aggression. There is also a fear that some of the reforms would unleash political forces that would be difficult to control, threatening power from without as well as from within the Communist Party.

Transition psychology also plays a role. Cuba is used to the idea that it can metaphorically thumb its nose at the rest of the world. It is used to the language and positions available to a small country backed by a superpower. Adjusting rhetoric and strategy to suit a small country now dependent solely on its own resources is taking some time. The Cuban government is gradually refining its reflexive tendency to respond to challenge with confrontational rhetoric, and is learning the art of diplomatic manipulation that is essential to the survival of small powers, but the cultural adjustment has not occurred overnight.

Possible Scenarios

What will happen to the people of the United States and Cuba if the foreign policies of Washington and Havana continue to suffer from competing covert and overt agendas, domestic power concerns, ignorance, and confused transition mentalities?

Even in the worst-case scenario, U.S. citizens would suffer less than their Cuban counterparts. If misguided policy were to draw the United States into a Cuba intervention, some U.S. sons and daughters would die in Cuba, and the taxpayer would be called upon to finance an expensive bill. Diplomatic relations would be damaged with Europe and Latin America, and the politicians responsible for the decision could end up paying a price at the ballot box. Should policy lead to a migration crisis, the citizens of Florida would have their society disrupted, and again the taxpayer would have to pick up the bill for resettling or detaining immigrants. Should foreign countries impose retaliatory trade sanctions on the United States to protest the Helms-Burton law, U.S. consumers would pay slightly higher prices for some goods, and some export industries might suffer to a small degree.

The costs to the Cuban people would be exponentially higher. In the worst-case scenario of civil conflict and U.S. intervention, many lives would be lost, infrastructure destroyed, and the economy disrupted. The bitterness engendered by such a confrontation would militate against the spirit of tolerance and forgiveness required to build a democratic, stable system in the future. If the economic situation deteriorates still further due to the pressure of Helms-Burton, Cuban families will again be divided by migration, lives will be lost at sea, and the standard of living for those remaining in Cuba will become even more austere.

In sum, both Cuba and the United States are pursuing policies that fail to protect their publicly declared interests. In some ways the Cuban failure is easier to understand than that of the United States; as a small country functioning in an atmosphere of external threat Cuba does not have the luxury of quietly contemplating the long-term consequences of its decisions. Like a small dog, it bites first and asks questions later. However, because the cost of policy failure will fall far more heavily on the Cuban than the U.S. public, the Cuban government has a particular responsibility to adopt a more effective strategy. This is perhaps unfair, but it is the post–Cold War reality Havana faces.

Note

1. Letter from Warren Christopher to Speaker of the House of Representatives Newt Gingrich, September 20, 1995. See also "Statement of Administration Policy, Office of Management and Budget, HR 927—Cuban Liberty and Democratic Solidarity Act," September 20, 1995.

◆ 6 ◆

Transition and the Ideology of Exile

Max J. Castro

◆

On Tuesday, March 14, 1995, the following headlines appeared on the front page of the *Miami Herald:* "Castro finds sympathy in France" and "Mitterrand scorns embargo." Under a large photograph of Fidel Castro clad in a dark suit, looking serious and dignified while reviewing the French Republican Guard, the story detailed a red-carpet reception, complete with drumroll and trumpet fanfare, held for Castro before his lunch with President François Mitterrand.

On the same day the following headlines appeared in *El Nuevo Herald*, the Spanish-language supplement developed by the *Miami Herald* mainly to cater to Cuban American readers: "Castro provokes mixed reaction in Paris" and "Cuba's ruler was the target of protests on his arrival in France's capital."[1] Accompanying the story is a large photograph of a screaming young man with a group of protesters bearing placards in the background. The lead reads: "Surrounded by controversy and with a business-like air, Cuba's ruler Fidel Castro . . . raised a wake of protest and criticism, not only from Cuban exiles, but also from the French . . . who are asking for democracy and respect for human rights in Cuba."

The widely divergent readings of Castro's Paris visit by Miami's two Knight-Ridder newspapers is not an isolated event. A few weeks later, the *Miami Herald* printed a front-page story on a Pentagon-commissioned study of Cuba that found that the regime had weathered the worst of the crisis caused by the fall of the Soviet Union and that Castro had apparently won the political battle (March 31, 1995). The article quoted former hardline Reagan administration official Nestor Sanchez, whose firm had coordinated the study, as saying the U.S. embargo is a failed policy. A translation of the story did appear in *El Nuevo Herald* on the same day—on page 11-A. When President and Mrs. Clinton visited Miami in the summer of 1995, the *Miami Herald* reported that the first couple had eluded Cuban American demonstrators angry at the administration for striking an immigration agreement with Cuba; *El Nuevo Herald* said the demonstrators had dogged the Clintons' every step. Finally, in the fall, Richard Nuccio, the Clinton administration's point man on Cuba, wrote a letter to *Miami Herald* publisher David Lawrence complaining that *El Nuevo Herald* had distorted coverage of his activities on a recent visit to Miami and that the paper had become part of the problem of Cuban American political extremism (July 1, 1995).

There exists a distinct Cuban-exile ideology that, in regard to Cuba, differs systematically with the vision of influential mainstream sectors of the U.S. media and government, as illustrated by the examples given above. Like all ideologies, Cuban-exile ideology is not simply an evaluative structure but also a perceptual lens through which reality is seen, organized, and sometimes distorted.[2] This ideology centers around a loathing of Fidel Castro and, more generally, a staunch anticommunism. It has endured in spite of the passage of time and dramatic changes in the world, including the end of the Cold War. Recently it has broken out of the confines of its ethnic enclave and managed to promote its vision of reality within major U.S. institutions, including at least one newspaper and the U.S. Congress. This chapter describes and analyzes patterns and trends in Cuban-exile ideology in the United States in the 1990s, and suggests political implications for an eventual transition on the island.

Traditional Cuban-Exile Political Culture

Remarkably few social scientists have studied Cuban-exile ideology, although exile politics have been and continue to be important for both the United States and Cuba. Cuban exiles have played a role in several major crises in U.S. politics, including the Bay of Pigs invasion, Watergate, and the Iran-Contra affair. For decades Cuban exiles have played a substantial role in legitimizing U.S. policy toward Cuba, and more recently they have helped define the relationship between the two countries.

The major empirical study of Cuban-exile politics is still Fagen et al. (1968), *Cubans in Exile: Disaffection and the Revolution.* That work is dated and deals mostly with such issues as early attitudes toward the revolution and the decision to leave. The politics of Cubans in exile was the subject of a dissertation by Wong (1974), who argued that a substantial proportion of Miami Cubans fit the profile of traditional migrants rather than political exiles. Dissertations by Torres (1986) and García (1990) provide useful descriptions of the evolution of Cuban-exile politics from the 1960s to the 1980s.

In a more analytical vein, in 1992 Lisandro Pérez defined the ideology of Cuban exiles as being composed of four principal and interrelated components: the primacy of issues that deal with the political status of Cuba; an uncompromising struggle against and hostility toward the Castro government; a lack of debate allowed within the community concerning the exile ideology; and overwhelming support for the Republican Party (Pérez 1992).

Some additional elements and nuances should be added to this analysis. First, underlying both the militancy and the intolerance described by Pérez is the fact that traditional exile political culture and ideology tends toward a Manichaean vision, wherein the prerevolutionary past is idealized and the postrevolutionary period is seen as the embodiment of absolute evil. Thus the struggle of the exiles against the regime is seen as a war of irreconcilable foes. Consistent with this mindset, any suggestion that the revolution has made at least some accomplishments is denied or dismissed as propaganda, and any attempt at compromise is denounced as treason. This view has its origins in the polarizing nature of the Cuban revolutionary process itself, and has its counterpart in the Manichaeanism of the official ideology on the island, where opponents of the system at times have been labeled "worms" and "scum" and treated accordingly. Regardless of its source, this binary perspective has implications for the role exiles are playing and might play in the future in relation to any process of transition in Cuba.

Relations with and perceptions of the United States also serve to distinguish Cuban-exile ideology. Whereas Cuban and Latin American nationalists and progressives traditionally have chafed at the U.S. hegemony in the hemisphere and have opposed the frequent U.S. interventions, from the standpoint of Cuban-exile ideology the problem with U.S. policy in Latin America is that it is not sufficiently forceful.

An additional element of Cuban-exile political ideology is resistance to assimilation and a refusal to adopt a traditional immigrant or minority identity. Although in practice a substantial number of Cubans have benefited from minority status to obtain U.S. government contracts, loans, and other advantages, the predominant discourse holds that Cubans are an exile group and not to be confused with other nonwhite groups. The Cubans have also resented being labeled an immigrant community. One of the main reasons many Cubans in the United States were outraged at the Clinton administration's May 1995 decision to repatriate rafters was that they saw the move as having the effect of equating Cuban political refugees with Mexican, Dominican, or Central American undocumented immigrants. This self-perception of entitlement to a special status as exiles and of not being an immigrant or minority has important implications, especially for relations with minority and other groups in the United States.

Finally, although Cuban Americans overwhelmingly support the Republican Party, it is also significant that the Cuban American community has maintained an asymmetrical but real bipartisanship. The relatively recent partnership between the Cuban American National Foundation (CANF) and the Republican Party obscures the fact that Cubans have been faithful to an ideological vision rather than to a single party. Cuban Americans promoting traditional exile views have been predominant within both the Republican and Democratic parties, and Cuban Americans from both parties have been elected to serve in the U.S. Congress.

The foregoing describes traditional Cuban exile ideology, not all varieties of exile political ideology or thought. How dominant is the traditional exile ideology as of the mid-1990s? Will it continue to endure? What alternative political visions have arisen to challenge the dominant ideology, and what are their prospects?

Pérez noted the existence of deviations from exile ideology in Cuban Miami, but he asserted the predominance of the traditional view. Moreover, he predicted that the succession from the first to the second generation would likely bring a reduction of the level of passion surrounding the Cuba issue, but not a fundamental change in perspective. He predicted that exile ideology would hold sway for some time principally because of three factors: the continuing demographic predominance of first-generation adults among Cubans in the United States, for whom the trauma of the revolution and exile is a lived experience; the political and economic dominance of exiles from earlier waves who are less likely to have relatives in Cuba or to have ever gained anything from the revolution; and the role of an economic enclave composed of a network of Cuban-exile economic enterprises in maintaining and reinforcing the exile ideology (Pérez 1992).

The traditional Cuban-exile ideology represents a worldview that continues to be very influential among Cubans in the United States. Nonetheless, with the passing years nuanced differences have arisen even within the confines of traditional exile ideology. For example, in recent years the two leading hard-line radio personalities in Miami have taken different tacks vis-à-vis debating on the air those considered pro-Castro. As far back as the late 1960s there arose, mainly within the younger generation of exiles, a challenge from the left to the central tenets of exile ideology. More recently, centrist alternatives to the traditional ideology also have emerged. Another indicator of diversity is the fact that some of the actions of Cuban exiles are at odds with hard-line principles. Only a small percentage of Cuban Americans belong to or participate in exile political organizations. Meanwhile, tens of thousands have visited relatives in Cuba, and an even larger number have sent money or goods to relatives on the island, ignoring or defying the admonitions of the hard-liners and, in some cases, breaking U.S. laws.

The Cuban-exile community in the United States is not monolithic and is becoming increasingly heterogeneous. But to what extent does the traditional exile ideology still hold sway among Cubans in the United States in the mid-1990s, and what will be its impact on changes on the island? I will answer these questions by sketching out current patterns of Cuban American politics. For the purpose of this analysis I classify those Cubans in the United States that hold to the tenets of the traditional Cuban-exile ideology as constituting the Cuban-exile right. I include in this category those groups, individuals, and organizations that favor the embargo and oppose normalization of United States–Cuba relations. The CANF and Unidad Cubana are two of the main organizations in this camp. The Cuban-exile center includes those groups that are both opposed to the embargo and in favor of a more democratic and pluralist political system in Cuba. Cambio Cubano, the Cuban Committee for Democracy, the Social Democrats, and the Christian Democrats belong to this group. The left includes groups and individuals whose attitude toward the Cuban government is one of support and solidarity, such as the Antonio Maceo Brigade. Because the left has minuscule influence within the exile community most of my discussion concerns the first two categories.

The Continuing Hegemony of the Right in Cuban-Exile Politics

After three decades of domination by the traditional, rightist perspective, developments in the early 1990s indicated that the politics of the Cuban American community might change. Three trends contributed to an expected erosion of the power of the right: the end of the Cold War, the close of the Reagan-Bush era, and the worldwide trend toward negotiated solutions to seemingly intractable international conflicts.

The end of the Cold War meant that Cuba was no longer a national-security concern for the United States. The Reagan and Bush administrations had unusually close ties with Cuban American conservatives and were noted for their staunch anticommunism. The possibility that struggles as bitter as the Palestinian-Israeli conflict and the South African fight to dismantle apartheid could be settled at a negotiating table suggested that the U.S.-Cuba dispute might follow a similar course. Taken together these developments raised the possibility that those sectors of the Cuban-exile community that favored dialogue with the Cuban government and an end to the U.S. embargo might be strengthened and even find a sympathetic ear in Washington.

The Cuban American right, led but not constituted solely by the CANF, did suffer a number of setbacks and challenges. First, the efforts of the CANF and its allies have totally failed to bring about a regime change or substantial moves toward democracy on the island. The chairman of the CANF, Jorge Mas Canosa, predicted a date for the end of the Castro government, and has gone as far as to declare his group ready to guide a transition. These gaffes, however, did not seriously affect Mas Canosa's influence in Washington nor discredit him widely in Miami.

The hard-line right has also failed to persuade the international community to adopt its strategy of isolating the Cuban regime. The 102-to-2 vote at the General Assembly of the United Nations in 1995 in favor of a

Cuban resolution against the U.S. embargo, and the 117-to-3 vote on the same issue in 1996 are eloquent on this point. The government of the United States is the only one in the world whose policies have been consistent with those of the exile hard-liners. After the U.S.-Cuba immigration agreements of 1994 and 1995, some in the exile right felt that even this ally had been lost.

Hard-liners also failed to win over the bulk of U.S. intellectual and editorial opinion. Among major U.S. newspapers only the *Miami Herald* speaks out frequently in favor of maintaining the U.S. embargo. Even this newspaper, which liberals accuse of catering to the Cuban-exile right, frequently irks the CANF and others on the Cuban right for not coming around completely—for instance not backing a hardening of the embargo—and for publishing material that contradicts the right's views. However, this failure has yet to have policy consequences, and criticism of the embargo by such conservative voices as the *Wall Street Journal,* William F. Buckley, and the late Richard Nixon have had little effect.

The Cuban-exile right also lost its special relationship with the White House. The most recent break with the Clinton administration came in May 1995 over the U.S. decision to reach an agreement with the Cuban government to repatriate Cuban rafters. Hard-liners feared this would be a first step toward broader agreements and openly broke their previously cordial relations with the administration. Although the right lost access to the White House in May 1995, this was offset by the much greater influence it now had in Congress.

The right also has suffered from important defections and dissensions. The CANF and the Valladares Foundation, led by former political prisoner Armando Valladeres, have waged several battles. The CANF is also feuding with most of the Cuban-exile right over leadership and strategy. A project to unite the right under the banner of Unidad Cubana disintegrated in 1994 amid charges of misuse of funds. Yet the CANF has managed to retain its leadership position and marginalize other claimants, and has largely succeeded in avoiding being damaged in intramural fights. The right also failed to prevent the emergence of political organizations offering more moderate programs and expressing alternative visions. Moderate groups have succeeded in diversifying exile politics and discourse, but they have not seriously challenged the right's dominance in either Washington or Miami.

Despite the exile right's multiple problems, the real power of the hardliners, as measured by concrete achievements, not only was maintained in the first half of the 1990s, but actually increased. The Cuban American right overcame the challenges of the early 1990s and strengthened its position in the mid-1990s with the coming to power of a Republican Congress in 1995.

By mid-1995 major victories of the Cuban American right included:

- Obtaining the early support of the Clinton campaign for tightening the embargo through the Torricelli bill and securing its subsequent passage into law as the Cuban Democracy Act
- Introduction and passage in both houses of Congress of legislation to further tighten the U.S. embargo, namely the Cuban Liberty and Democratic Solidarity Act, also known as the Helms-Burton law
- Blocking the appointment of moderate Cuban American Mario Baeza to the post of Assistant Secretary of State for Inter-American Affairs
- Fending off congressional threats to cut funding for Radio and TV Martí
- Taking advantage of the 1994 rafter crisis to obtain from President Clinton the long sought-after banning of exile travel and remittances to the island
- The election of three hard-line Cuban American representatives to Congress

One key element in the success of the exile right is that it continues to enjoy strong ideological support in the Cuban-exile community, at least in regard to relations with Cuba. This social base, contrary to many expectations, does not appear to be eroding.

The polling evidence suggests that while the Cuban-exile community is not monolithic, the right arguably represents the majority of Cuban Americans. The National Latino Political Survey (NLPS) conducted in 1989 and 1990 revealed that 47.8 percent of Cuban Americans are strong Republicans, compared to only 15.7 percent among Anglos. Only 14.4 percent of Cuban Americans are strong Democrats, only slightly lower than the 17.8 percent of Anglos who professed the same identification. Moreover, there is no evidence of a softening of attitudes. The NLPS found that about two-thirds of respondents of Cuban origin—66.5 percent of U.S. citizens and 64.5 percent of noncitizens—opposed the establishment of diplomatic relations between the United States and Cuba (de la Garza et al. 1992). Five years later, in the 1995 Florida International University (FIU) Cuba Poll, nearly three-fourths of the sample favored maintaining the current policy of no diplomatic relations or trade with Cuba. In the same survey, 82 percent favored the tightening of the trade embargo and 84 percent supported increasing international economic pressure on Cuba. The survey also found that since the first FIU Cuba Poll in 1991, "negotiated solutions declined in support while the harder lines were emphasized." Nearly three-fourths approved of exile military action against Cuba, and over half of the respondents approved of a U.S. invasion. The survey attributes this trend to frustration with the lack of fundamental political change in Cuba after the heady days following the collapse of the Soviet Union (Grenier et al. 1995).

Support for hard-line policies may even extend to support for hard-line leaders and organizations, at least among older Cubans of the immigrant generation. A poll of 402 Cuban-born exiles in Miami (three-quarters of whom were over fifty) conducted by the Telemundo network affiliate in Miami found that 77 percent had a positive opinion of Jorge Mas Canosa and 83 percent had a favorable view of the CANF. Armando Valladares, another hard-liner, was viewed favorably by 66 percent; Eloy Gutierrez Menoyo, who now favors dialogue after a career as an anti-Castro commando and more than two decades in a Cuban prison, was viewed negatively by 64 percent of respondents (*Miami Herald,* May 5, 1994, p. 8B).

A second key factor in the right's success is that the long Reagan-Bush era and the Republican administration's promotion of the CANF gave the organization and its views a huge advantage, which it has used in establishing a base of resources and developing a bipartisan set of alliances. This has proved crucial in maintaining and even increasing the CANF's influence despite the electoral defeat of its original patrons. The organization used its early advantage to become the main funnel of political donations from the Cuban American community. The CANF's political action committee (PAC) reportedly gave $758,696 to congressional candidates between 1982 and 1995, and its individual members are said to have given even more.

A third key factor is the bipartisan nature of the Cuban-exile right. Hard-liners on the Cuba issue dominate the Cuban American component of both the Democratic and the Republican parties, and in such enterprises as torpedoing the appointment of Mario Baeza, potentially a moderate voice on Cuba policy. They also cooperate in guarding against dissent by Clinton administration officials regarding the maintenance of a hard-line Cuba policy. The alliance also has anomalous effects, such as Democrats forcing Republicans to shift to the right. For example, candidate Bill Clinton backed the Torricelli bill in 1992 in a quest for Cuban American support (at a time when the Bush administration was quietly expressing its opposition). This forced the Republican administration to change its position and support the legislation, thus moving U.S. policy on Cuba toward an even harder line.

A Center Emerges but Does Not Take Off

The continuing and deepening hegemony of the right was not the only significant development in Cuban American politics in the early 1990s; the time appeared to be ripe for the development of a center in Cuban American politics. According to many observers, the political base for a Cuban American center had long existed in the form of a mass of underrepresented Cuban Americans who constituted a substantial minority or even a majority of the population.

Evidence for this claim came from the NLPS, for instance, which found that despite party affiliations, 45.4 percent of Cuban Americans describe themselves as liberal or moderate. Those who see a growing moderation in the exile community also point out that the 1995 FIU Cuba Poll, which found support for hard-line policies, also found support for negotiations for certain specific purposes. For instance, 65 percent favor negotiations to exclude medicines from the embargo, 82 percent favor negotiations to improve the human-rights conditions on the island, 43 percent favor negotiations to allow unrestricted travel by Cuban Americans to the island, and 24 percent favor negotiations to allow unrestricted trade.

The early 1990s did witness the emergence of a fragile center in Cuban American politics. These groups included Eloy Gutierrez Menoyo's Cambio Cubano, led by a former anti-Batista and anti-Castro guerrilla fighter who had served a long prison sentence in Cuba. The Cuban Committee for Democracy (CCD), formed around a nucleus of Cuban American academics, is another centrist organization. Two of the three parties in the Plataforma Democratica Cubano, the Social Democrats and the Christian Democrats, both of which oppose the embargo, might be put in this category.

In the 1990s these groups were able to broaden the debate over some of the core tenets of exile ideology. Through sponsored radio programs (with revealing names such as "Transición" and "Apertura"), and by making use of the increased openness on the part of some hard-line radio commentators to debate with those outside the hard-line fold, they have been able to gain a foothold in the critical radio airwaves and other sectors of the media. They were successful enough to lead one hard-line radio personality to complain about "the Fidelization of Miami radio."

Moderate groups have also benefited from the delegitimation of both extremes of the political spectrum. The crisis of the left has caused many who formerly professed solidarity with the revolution to move to a more critical, centrist position. On the right, the futility of armed struggle in particular and hard-line approaches in general has led some to reexamine their position. This process led to some rapprochement between previously bitter enemies. The CCD, for example, included former members of the 2506 Brigade, composed of Bay of Pigs veterans, as well as former members of the Antonio Maceo Brigade, the leading organization of the Cuban émigré left.

Despite these accomplishments the moderates have yet to make a significant difference in U.S. policy, and most of their efforts have met with limited success. Various attempts to appeal to such exile interests as family reunification and the right to travel have attracted followers at certain junctures but have never been successfully translated into a political agenda. In fact, no massive protests erupted after the ban on exile travel was imposed by President Clinton in August 1994.

The best example of the failure of the center may be found in electoral politics. This had its most salient moment in the 1992 congressional campaign in Miami, which pitted antiembargo Cuban American Democrat Magda Montiel Davis against hard-line incumbent Republican Ileana Ros-Lehtenin. Montiel Davis lost the election by a considerable margin and lost the Cuban American vote resoundingly.

The CCD's attempt to follow, on a modest scale, the model of the CANF by creating a PAC failed to attract more than a small number of well-heeled moderates willing to commit $1,000 a year to the effort. The group was forced to scale back its dues by 75 percent and was unable to provide campaign funds to candidates favorable to its views. The attempt by a number of centrist groups, principally Cambio Cubano, to compete with the right in publicly mobilizing the masses fell far short when about 1,000 of the predicted 5,000 people showed up at a 1994 rally in a downtown hotel.

Attempts to break the right's monopoly of the airwaves have met with some success, but the bulk of programming still reflects hard-line views. Radio Progreso, which consisted of extensive programming with a decidedly different slant on Cuba issues, and was one of the most ambitious attempts to compete with the right on its own turf, was the object of some violent attacks and never found commercial sponsors. The program was abandoned in 1994, though its director returned to the air in 1995 with a reduced programming schedule.

Moderate groups have also failed to take advantage of the generational gap suggested by the 1995 FIU poll, which found a lower level of support for the embargo among younger Cuban Americans. The leaders of the centrist organizations, like those of the hard-line groups, are all veterans of the revolution, the counterrevolution, or both. A baby boomer may be in the White House, and *yucas* (young urban Cuban Americans) may be very visible on at the local, state, and national levels, but the younger generations have yet to take control of Cuban-exile centrist organizations. In fact, the only two groups with leaders younger than fifty—the Directorio Revolucionario and the Movimiento Democracia—take a hard line on the embargo.

The fragile Cuban-exile centrist organizations face the superior financial, organizational, and media resources of the right, as well as a more hostile ideological climate within their own communities than may at first appear to be the case. Although nearly half of Cuban Americans say they are politically moderate, that moderation does not extend to the issue of normalization of U.S.-Cuba relations or the end of the embargo. The survey data reveal a pronounced rightward tilt in the Cuban American sample compared to all other groups, including Anglos. For instance, excluding the middle category of moderate from the analysis, the ratio of conservatives to liberals is 2.4 to 1 among Cuban Americans, compared to 1.5 to 1 among Anglos, 1.6 to 1 among Puerto Ricans, and 1.3 to 1 among Mexicans. The environment for centrists in the Cuban community continues to be tough because liberals are far outnumbered by conservatives, and many self-described moderates hold very conservative views when it comes to Cuba and U.S.-Cuba relations.

The Cuban American conservative and Republican identification found in the NLPS was not merely a reflection of anticommunism. In response to question regarding government spending on problems facing the respondent's own community in the United States, four out of five (80.8 percent) Puerto Rican respondents favored increased government spending on programs to help Puerto Ricans. Over two-thirds of Mexican Americans (69.2 percent) favored increased spending for programs to help their compatriots. But among Cubans, only 38.4 percent approved of increased government spending on programs to help their fellow Cuban Americans! This finding puts into serious doubt the oft-repeated claim that Cuban Americans are conservative on foreign policy and liberal on domestic social policy.

Such conservatism regarding social programs is sharply at odds with what some surveys have found to be the case in Cuba, where the population regards access to health care and education as genuine achievements to be preserved. It explains the CANF's advocacy of a neoconservative program for a post-Castro Cuba, and raises the issue of whether in a post-transition scenario Cuban Americans will push as hard for assistance to the island as do some Jewish American groups on behalf of Israel, or whether they will behave more like fiscally conservative U.S. taxpayers.

Transition and Cuban-Exile Politics

Cuban Americans appear to be better situated to influence any eventual transition or transformation in Cuba than virtually any other exile or émigré community in recent experience. The reasons for this include the size of the community, its location within the political boundaries of the world's sole superpower, its continuing self-definition as an exile group, the geographic proximity to the island of the largest concentration of Cubans in the United States, and the relative economic prosperity of Cuban Americans within and beyond the confines of the Miami enclave.

Most important, Cuban Americans have attained remarkable influence within the U.S. political system through a set of institutional links and channels. Although Cuban-exile reliance on the United States in the fight against Castro is as strong today as it was in the days of the Bay of Pigs, the relationship has changed. Previously the exiles functioned as mere instruments of U.S. policy; now they help shape that policy.

That influence is now being wielded almost exclusively by the right, and in the form of the Cuban Democracy Act and the Helms-Burton law it seeks to preclude the possibility of certain modes or trajectories of transition. Unacceptable transitions include not only the Chinese model, in which economic liberalization and growth are accompanied by political stability under continued Communist Party rule. Hard-liners also reject a Nicaragua-style transition in which leftist forces maintain a substantial degree of power within the context of a new regime. Also rejected is a sequential negotiated transition such as that in Spain, in which economic restructuring preceded political change by many years.

Ironically, pacted transitions such as Spain's have yielded stable democracies more often than other modes of transition. Conversely, violent transition, a route that may be made more likely by a strategy of economic strangulation, has seldom produced stable democracies (Karl and Schnitter 1991). Thus, one consequence of the exile right's influence on U.S. Cuba policy might be not only to make economic reforms more difficult and less rewarding for the Cuban government, but also to stand in the way of some of the more promising paths to democracy. More generally, by militating for a hard-line U.S. policy toward Cuba, the exile right may unwittingly be retarding the pace of change in Cuba by reinforcing the most inflexible sectors in Cuban society, forcing a choice between sovereignty and democracy, and uniting Cuban ruling elites and some sectors of the population around the defense of the homeland against a looming external threat. The exile right's neoconservative social-policy preferences and its adverse relations with U.S. blacks and other minorities may make some Cubans who favor change on the island skeptical of what the future would hold if the current regime were to fall and be replaced by forces allied to the leading exile organizations.

The strength of the traditional ideology and the exile right should not be underestimated, but there is potential for the development of a more progressive Cuban American politics. Such a politics might be built around the 46 percent of exiles who, according to the 1995 FIU Cuba Poll, support the Cuban Catholic Church's call for a broad national dialogue. Hard-line positions, although robust, are not set in stone among all of the exiles. They also reflect the level of intransigence on the part of the exiles' adversary—the current Cuban government—and the seeming absence of realistic alternatives to a hard-line posture, such as negotiations or elections.

Because of the continuing strength of the right, a fundamental change in U.S. policy toward Cuba will find strong exile opposition under any circumstances. But the U.S. government should consider whether such predictable opposition should outweigh other factors, including humanitarian concern for the welfare of the 11 million Cubans on the island, broader U.S. interests in the world, and the effect of a violent transition on the prospects of a stable and equitable democracy in Cuba. Under the right terms, such as in the context of movement toward political liberalization on the island, a change in U.S. policy could even enlist the support of a substantial sector of the Cuban American population. This would begin with the minority that already favors normalization and the many more who have shown their lack of faith in traditional exile politics through their nonparticipation in its organizations and rituals.

Epilogue

The patterns described in this analysis have been put into stark relief and reinforced by the tragic February 24, 1996, shoot-down by the Cuban air force of two airplanes belonging to the anti-Castro organization Brothers to the Rescue, which resulted in the deaths of four exiles.

The immigration agreement of May 2, 1995, which provided for the direct return of rafters to the island, had raised fears of a Cuba-U.S. rapprochement among exile hard-liners. Their concern was that normalization would allow the Castro government to overcome what they viewed as a terminal crisis and to reconsolidate its rule—with the help of renewed U.S. trade, investment, and tourism—under some variant of the Chinese or Vietnamese models.

To prevent this a collection of organizations grouped as the Movimiento Democracia undertook actions they hoped would spark popular protest on the island before any Cuba-U.S. detente could be set in place. By carrying out acts of open defiance of the Cuban government, such as piloting a flotilla of small boats into the island's territorial waters, they hoped to convey to the Cuban people the message that it was possible to defy the Cuban state: "We are doing it and taking the risk. You can do it too. You will not be alone. We will support you."

The Cuban government was determined not to allow such acts of defiance to recur, nor to be lured into a provocation that would strengthen hard-line forces in the United States. Accordingly, it first tried to enlist the United States in reigning in the exiles. The U.S. government responded by trying to dissuade the exiles from entering Cuban territorial waters, but did nothing to prevent them from doing so, possibly because it did not want to appear to be protecting Castro. The Cuban government responded to the exile challenge with controlled force. Cuban gunboats, with weapons sheathed, confronted the lead exile ship of the flotilla, instructed it to turn back as it approached Cuban waters, and finally slammed into it, damaging it and forcing it to turn back.

While this drama was unfolding in the water, Brothers to the Rescue planes accompanying the flotilla broke away and overflew Havana. Bereft of a mission since May 1995 because the immigration agreement made spotting rafters (only for them to be returned to Cuba) a thankless task, this organization too had adopted a strategy of increasingly bold and public defiance of the Castro government. Pilots overflew Havana on at least two occasions, dropping anti-Castro leaflets, and then boasted of the feat on Radio Martí and promised a repetition. These acts put Brothers to the Rescue and the Cuban regime on a collision course.

In early 1996 the Cuban government was increasingly concerned with the pattern of escalating defiance by exile groups, by the development of Concilio Cubano, an umbrella group of myriad small opposition organizations operating inside Cuba itself, and by the seemingly close relations of Concilio Cubano with the exiles and with the U.S. government. From the Cuban government's perspective, U.S. policy toward Cuba amounted to two tracks of a single hard line: the embargo and increased people-to-people contact under the Cuban Democracy Act—which was acknowledged by U.S. officials to be designed to strengthen the opposition.

In mid-January 1996 the Cuban government decided to crack down on Concilio Cubano and to shoot down any exile planes that entered Cuban air space. To avoid the latter, Cuban authorities issued loud warnings and tried once again to persuade the U.S. government to curb the exiles. It would have taken an act of political will at a high level within the United States to prevent further overflights by determined Brothers to the Rescue pilots, but the U.S. reaction to Cuba's protests over the violation of its air space was bureaucratic and ineffective: an investigation by the Federal Aviation Administration.

The predictable—if unjustifiable—downing of the aircraft provided fodder for exile hard-liners. Because they were well positioned to take advantage of Fidel Castro's characteristically implacable response to what he saw as a deadly threat, exile hard-liners were able to parlay the situation into a significant, and probably enduring, toughening of U.S. policy. Faced with the need to "stand up to Castro" in an election year, President Clinton signed a harsh version of the Helms-Burton bill, a piece of legislation that not only tightens the U.S. embargo but inscribes into law all previous sanctions. This virtually precludes the executive from ending or significantly easing the embargo before a large number of strict conditions are met, including but not limited to the replacement of the current leadership. Not surprisingly, Havana's response to Washington's new move was a defiant one, and in its wake Cuban defense minister Raúl Castro delivered a Politburo report that seemed to augur more repressive times in Cuba: a vicious circle suddenly made more vicious.

A hard-line U.S. policy toward Cuba now seems to be in place for the foreseeable future. The influence of hard-line Cuban exiles was a crucial factor in producing that outcome. Without their influence the United States might have ultimately adopted an approach toward Cuba consistent with its policies toward other remaining communist regimes and with the policies of its allies.

The exiles were not the only factor in the process that set the hard-line policy in stone. Throughout the Cold War, Republicans have sought to portray themselves as tougher on communism. Following normalization of relations with China and Vietnam, and agreements with North Korea regarding nuclear power, Cuba is the only remaining stage of the Cold War, the last place onto which U.S. political conflicts can be displaced and in which the partisan game of anticommunist one-upmanship can be played. In the United States' own backyard, the only country ever to transgress simultaneously the Monroe and the Truman doctrines, and with a perennial leader seen as a demonic figure by many in the United States, Cuba was always a difficult candidate for normalization (Bennel 1994).

These factors explain how an exile lobby that represents only a tiny fraction of the U.S. population was able to leverage its limited power and resources to achieve a significant impact on foreign policy, just as major U.S. corporations and the United States' main allies sought to change that policy. It remains to be seen whether the result is an early transition toward democracy in Cuba or another step in a tragic road toward a national calamity.

Notes

1. All translations are by the author.
2. I use the concept of ideology here in the sense suggested by Michele Barrett (1991, p. 167): "discursive and significatory mechanisms that may occlude, legitimate, naturalise or universalise in a variety of different ways but can all be said to mystify."

PART 2

Toward the Market

◆ 7 ◆

Crisis and Reform in Cuba

Mauricio Font

◆

The size of the Cuban economy contracted by nearly half between 1989 and 1993, dealing a major blow to the project of national development of Cuban state socialism, and raising the possibility of imminent change toward a market economy. The collapse of state socialism in Eastern Europe and the Soviet Union was the main proximate factor in this contraction. By losing its bearings in the world economy, Cuba also faced the challenge of articulating a new development model. Piecemeal reforms since 1990 began to reintegrate Cuba in the market-driven global economy and move it toward internal adjustment. Particularly in late 1993, Cuba entered a broader but still cautious phase of liberalization. The slowdown of the pace of reforms in the second half of 1994 and through 1995–1996, as the regime repeated vows to remain loyal to traditional state socialism, raises questions about its sense of direction. This chapter explores the nature of the reform process—particularly whether it implies a strengthened state-socialist model, the transition to a market economy, or something in between—and the institutional factors shaping it.

To put the current reforms in perspective, the first part of the chapter revisits the evolution of the Cuban model of state socialism, focusing on the rise and collapse of the experiment with liberalization from the 1970s to 1986 and the Rectification drive begun in 1986. The second part discusses the post-1989 reform process. The political-process approach to reforms favored here focuses on the interplay between institutional structures and interest groups. But the dearth of data on groups or factions and on internal political dynamics blocks the development of a full analysis. For that reason, this chapter emphasizes the institutional side of the argument, sketching in that regard a characterization of Cuban state socialism.

Institutional Context: Cuban Socialism, 1959 to the 1990s

The first three decades of the Cuban revolution saw the affirmation of a distinctive form of socialism. After embracing socialism between 1961 and

1963, revolutionary Cuba spent the next two years debating the relative merits of the available models of socialist development—the pragmatic Soviet approach and the more political or ideological approach identified with Maoist China. Much of the debate centered on the relative merits of material versus moral incentives. The latter view won and the period 1965–1970 enshrined very high levels of centralization, moral incentives, and collectivization—what the late Sergio Roca called the "moral economy" (Roca 1988). If by 1963 the revolution had nationalized most of the half-million private businesses existing in 1959, the majority of the surviving very small businesses were taken over in the "great revolutionary offensive" of 1967. By the second half of the 1960s virtually the entire nonagricultural sector, most of agriculture, and the market economy as a whole had been liquidated (Mesa-Lago 1994a, p. 20). Only small farmers escaped the collectivization juggernaut, having benefited somewhat from the agrarian reforms of the early 1960s (Mesa-Lago 1994a; Zimbalist and Eckstein 1987).

By 1967–1968, Cuba had one of the most collectivized forms of socialism the world had known (Deere and Meurs 1992a). The institutional model closely resembled that adopted in the USSR in the late 1920s, augmented by ideas adapted from the Chinese Revolution—the emphasis on consciousness (the "New Man") shaped by collectivization, mass mobilization, voluntary work, and moral incentives. The process leading to its adoption had seen the explicit rejection of a less collectivistic and more market-friendly model of socialism—including the "market socialism" recommended to Cuba by Western marxists (Dumont, Bettelheim, Baran, Mendel, and Sweezy) and defended in Cuba by Carlos Rafael Rodríguez. The leadership saw itself as building a communist society. The highly centralized character of Cuban socialism remained after 1970, when economic-policy failures forced the government to announce a "retreat to socialism" and thereby accept the idea that socialism had to be built by stages. Only after 1993 would property forms and the market experience substantively change (Mesa-Lago 1994b).

The three major pre-1990 shifts in the Cuban model—the 1960s thrust toward collectivization and moral incentives, the post-1970 liberalization, and the Rectification of 1986—have been heatedly debated by two main schools of thought. To "cubanologos" the first and the third reflected the preeminence of ideology-driven hard-liners over pragmatic revolutionaries, thus revealing an inclination to irrationality as well as a built-in tension between hard-liners and reformists. In contrast, authors subscribing to a "political-economy" perspective more sympathetic to the Cuban model have seen coherence and rationality in the shifts. In this view, policy shifts in the Cuban trajectory reflect the unfolding of a coherent strategy aiming at the control of resources required for policy performance. For example, Eckstein (1994) sees the drive for communism as rooted in rational exigencies and priorities. In the perspective developed here, these two approaches point to complementary aspects of Cuba's version of state socialism. Arguments about the coherence of policymaking and those emphasizing the centrality of moral appeals pertain to different aspects of a distinctive institutional form of state socialism. The reliance on ideology and the highly centralized command economy are part of an institutional framework not fully intelligible in terms of narrow economic criteria. In this perspective, such institutional forms owe a great deal to complex legacies linking economic, political, social, and cultural variables.

In spite of interpretive differences, there is agreement on a wide range of empirical issues implied by this approach, including a very high degree of collectivization, the particularly small role of the market, the marked proclivity to rely on moral incentives and appeals, centralization around the charismatic figure of Fidel Castro, and the central importance of relationships with the USSR and the Council for Mutual Economic Assistance (CMEA). Cuba institutionalized a highly collectivized and centralized model in the 1960s and early 1970s that reigned supreme until at least 1990.

Collectivization generated large economic units. The nationalization of sugar, manufacturing, mining, commerce, transportation, and all other sectors meant collectivization into large complexes, the biggest of which were in sugar and nickel. Even small-scale or artisanal establishments were consolidated into larger units. National investments between the 1960s and the early 1990s added almost exclusively to the pattern of growth emphasizing large state enterprises. In agriculture, the least collectivized sector, land reforms gave state farms 76 percent of all agricultural lands by 1963—a figure that increased to 83 percent by 1993. The revolutionary regime allowed the survival of small-scale private agriculture, responding to the priority given to political support from the countryside, but there was relentless pressure on private farmers to join cooperatives or merge with state farms. In 1988 this sector claimed only 8 percent of all land against 80 percent for state farms and 12 percent for cooperatives.

From Liberalization to Rectification

The widely discussed debacle of the 1970 sugar harvest posed questions about the dominant model and led to significant changes, even if centralization was not challenged. Predicting that it would surpass 10 million tons, Castro had defined this harvest as a decisive test for the revolution. Because vast amounts of resources were diverted from other sectors to the sugar harvest, when the harvest fell considerably short of goals it also disrupted the rest of the economy. Moral socialism was now on the defensive. Castro regained control over the situation by shouldering the blame and hinting at an offer to resign. But a major change in policy ensued and Cuba entered a period of mild liberalization in 1971. Castro conceptualized this as a "retreat into socialism" (presumably from the more "advanced" earlier pursuit of communism). Whatever the label, for more than fifteen years after 1970 Cuba adopted an institutional profile comparable to that of the USSR (Mesa-Lago 1994b and Eckstein 1994 discuss the 1971–1985 model). In foreign policy both countries acted together in major military campaigns in Africa.

The 1971–1985 period brought relative decentralization and material incentives, even if Cuba remained a rather centralized command economy. The departure from local orthodoxy represented a limited adaptation of Libermanism in the USSR, particularly the adoption of planning and other institutional mechanisms designed to give stability to economic policy and economic growth. In 1975 the Sistema de Dirección y Planificación de la Economía (SDPE) was inaugurated. With the new emphasis on material incentives and wage differentials also came a stronger reliance on the rationalization of management. In agriculture the gradual expansion of parallel markets meant that surpluses could be sold at prices considerably higher than the ration-card; producer cooperatives gained official favor as the state seemed to abandon the goal of total collectivization.

The most significant agrarian innovation was the 1980 adoption of farmers' markets (Alonso 1992; Rosenberg 1992). With Cuban society still highly dependent on agriculture, this move represented an important form of liberalization. The new law allowed independent farmers, cooperatives, and even state farms to sell surpluses in these markets, excluding export commodities and beef. The experiment apparently resulted from the rise of a reformist coalition involving agencies in the state system, farmers, and consumers (Rosenberg 1992). A slowly building coalition of some state agencies (JUCEPLAN, the central planning board of the Ministry of Agriculture), the interests of private farmers in the Asociación Nacional de Agricultores Pequeños (ANAP), Eastern European advisers, and consumer demands was the central protagonist in the formation of the farmers' markets, lobbying in their favor for eight years. The decision was a result of bargaining among differentiated sectors within the highly centralized polity. But the farmers' markets faced criticisms and restraints from the start. Although they may not have accounted for a large share of registered food sales (Zimbalist 1988b, p. 13), their role in the informal economy was considerable. Party cadres worried openly that the market provided disincentives for farmers to join cooperatives or state farms, and that profit orientation by emergent intermediaries and farmers contradicted equality.

The 1986 closing of the free farmers' market was accompanied by raids on prosperous intermediaries and farmers. The official explanation for the closing emphasized high prices, profiteering, and growing inequality (for a list of official reasons, see Alonso 1992). Others add to the list the illegal use of state resources and tax evasion, as well as the reluctance of farmers to sell to the state and the hindrance the markets provided to the cooperative movement (see also Deere and Meurs 1992). The broader context of the termination of the markets was the shift to Rectification, the policy of "rectification of errors and correction of deviant trends" with respect to the presumably correct and coherent socialist strategy or path chosen in the 1960s. The new policy eliminated gains by independent producers and returned control to a highly centralized system. Egalitarianism was invoked against the inequalities brought about by liberalization. Rectification brought back an emphasis on moral incentives and centralization, as the farmers' markets, the decentralized planning system, and mechanisms of liberalization were eliminated or curtailed (see Pérez-López 1990; Mesa-Lago 1994b; Deere, Meurs, and Pérez 1992; Eckstein 1994).

Zimbalist (1988b) and other authors have argued that the Rectification drive of 1986 represented an adjustment of course in line with a coherent and durable strategy—rather than retrenchment or reversal of the reform process started in the 1970s, as argued by Mesa-Lago (1989), Pérez-López (1992b), and others. Rodríguez (1992) and Eckstein (1994) maintain that it was a rational response to mounting fiscal problems and the need to control slack resources to address them. It was no doubt instrumental action with a clear means–ends relationship. But this implies neither that it was the best option nor that there was an absence of other political and moral contexts defining the meaning of rationality and instrumentality. If the rationality of the action is debatable within a market-sensitive economic framework, the measures are nevertheless compatible with the institutional form emphasizing administrative and political centralization. Likewise, the rather significant changes in policy and personnel that accompanied the demise of the farmers' markets are difficult to subsume under a hard version of the thesis of continuity of a coherent development strategy based on intra-elite consensus. Shortly after 1986 the president of ANAP, who strongly supported the markets, was replaced by one who opposed them. JUCEPLAN's president, Humberto Pérez—a supporter of a managerial economy—was fired. SDPE was subsequently deemphasized and JUCEPLAN's mission diminished. Both agencies would soon be eliminated. Still, the market did not disappear altogether; the weakened small-farmer sector survived and the complementary food distribution system represented by the parallel markets—a mechanism deemed more compatible with egalitarianism—was expanded.

Rectification was surely the result of a process more complex than is implied by arguments over economic strategy and ideology. Rosenberg (1992) points to the dynamics of interest groups. The prior creation of a new cooperative movement weakened the role of independent farmers within the ANAP, the smallholders' association, as consumer complaints about prices were also turned against the markets. Alonso (1992) agrees that the farmers' markets had created a conflict within the leadership. The dearth of data on both policymaking and interest-group action in Cuba prevents a full assessment of the roles of interest groups and the extent of intra-elite differences, but the hypothesis linking policy shifts to institutionally embedded coalition formation is entirely plausible. At the same time, the impressive lack of open conflict surrounding this important reform suggests a highly structured polity.

Cuba's Peculiar Socialism and Its Global Context

Whatever the causes of Rectification—coherent strategy, ideology, institutional dynamics, political calculation, coalition shifts, or a combination of these and other factors—with it Cuba reaffirmed a distinctive brand of state socialism that harked back to the late 1960s. Even if Cuba had already gone beyond other socialist countries in the breadth and depth of collectivization, in 1986 the state reaffirmed in no uncertain terms a near monopoly of all major elements of economic and social organization. In the USSR and Eastern Europe, highly institutionalized ministries coordinated by planning boards emerged as the dominant feature of the state. In Cuba, the centrality of Fidel Castro's charismatic authority, the role of moral appeals, and the degree of collectivization and centralization define the institutional profile of state socialism.

This institutional profile had been affirmed in the 1960s and probably had internal roots. However, consolidation took place in the 1970s and 1980s and was deeply embedded in an international context. The unprecedented latitude with which Cuba's leadership institutionalized this distinctive form of state socialism was largely due to a rather unique juncture in which a propitious international context isolated and protected the project of socialist national development from direct exposure to market forces and external pressure. The 1970s and 1980s were critical in this regard. When deteriorating economic conditions in the mid-1970s compelled Soviet and Eastern European socialism to experiment with stronger forms of liberalization (Szelenyi and Szelenyi 1994), Cuba was largely spared from a similar experience. The two decades after 1970 saw Cuba's command economy receive the resources needed to consolidate only a mildly more liberal but still quite distinctive form of state socialism. This adaptive strategy worked in the geopolitical context of the Cold War.

The economic failure of 1970 had posed anew the question of models, but the enhanced relationship to the USSR inaugurated that year preempted the need for the kind of thorough and realistic reassessment that might have led to a different model of socialism. As a favored Third World partner of Soviet socialism, the island received support, the functional equivalent of "rents," of as much as $6 billion annually during the late 1970s and early 1980s—or a total of $65 billion from 1960 to 1990, according to Mesa-Lago (1994a, p. 1; see also Pastor and Zimbalist 1995, p. 8). Cuba's socialist experiment was supported from the outside probably more than most others. If as a late member of CMEA (1972) Cuba received special treatment and sponsorship from the socialist camp, it fatefully pegged crucial aspects of its development strategy to that camp (for USSR-Cuba relations, see Blasier 1993).

Added to collectivization and centralization, the combined effect of high levels of external sponsorship, barter trade, and the institutionally assured position in the socialist international division of labor meant that the Cuban state enjoyed an inordinate degree of autonomy from market realities and lacked feedback mechanisms favoring economic discipline. The system generally had no direct link between consumers and producers. Most external transactions were conducted outside the market proper. Moreover, after the early 1970s Cuba was the socialist country with the lowest level of trade in hard currency and with Western countries, because state-negotiated barter transactions with the USSR and CMEA countries dominated trade. Production was for distant places and was mediated by interbureaucracy transactions carried out not by firms but by state agencies, often following strategic or political criteria. Because the terms of trade that Cuba thus obtained far exceeded those of the world market, the authorities had plenty of incentives (in a narrow, adaptive sense) to feel disdain for the market. In this context, political and other extra-economic considerations could govern major decisions about distribution and the allocation of resources without the costs becoming visible. In its heyday in the 1970s and early 1980s, Cuban state socialism could draw from large discretionary funds and was able to devote vast amounts of resources to public health, education, the military, sports, and selective economic sectors following extra-economic criteria.

Moral and ideological arguments defined the zeitgeist of Cuban socialism. "Internationalist solidarity" was the primary justification for costly military campaigns abroad. In turn, successes in warfare—as well as basic social policies—reinforced the highly centralized pattern of making decisions and defending them on moral and ideological grounds. Scarcity and imperfections were explained away by reference to epic struggles against imperialism and racism (e.g., the Angolan campaign against South African intervention). Hard times and other challenges could be turned around to document the work of external enemies and justify continuing discipline, sacrifice, and combativeness. Precisely because of the strength of moral and charismatic appeals, planners have always had an uneasy time in revolutionary Cuba. The very primacy of charisma as a legitimizing mechanism means that efficiency and related criteria of resource allocation should not displace it from the role of protagonist; it claims responsibility for successes as well as the leading role in hard times. Since 1990 the system has increasingly relied on morality as defined by national folk heroes and figures such as José Martí, rather than Marxist classics. The prolonged and severe economic crisis is interpreted as resistance to outside imposition and rendered meaningful by reference to the historic quest for a homeland and equality begun by Martí. With this epic as a sacred concern, the leaders embody the people's will and are the trustees of sovereignty and the very survival of the nation.

In any case, Cuba's insertion in CMEA fatefully shaped its economy (Mesa-Lago 1993). One of the most important consequences of Cuba's relationship to the Soviet Union and CMEA was to confirm sugar as the mainstay and top priority of the economy in the 1970s and 1980s. With the leadership arguing that the USSR provided a guaranteed long-term market for sugar harvests, sugar continued to account for roughly 80 percent of exports and a third of economic activity (27 percent of arable land and 12 percent of the workforce) while overall diversification and industry received a lower priority. The socialist division of labor in CMEA did "guarantee" a market for Cuban sugar (at high if not subsidized prices), and Cuba also agreed to import a range of consumer and military goods. At the same time, the sugar sector grew highly dependent on inputs from other socialist countries, including tractors, fuel, fertilizers, pesticides, and partnership in the design and manufacturing of agricultural combines from the USSR. The early and middle 1980s created a unique international context favoring the perception of the Cuban model of state socialism as not just sound but exemplary. The 1970s investments in health care, social services, and sports were then paying off in full—as long as the USSR and CMEA continued their support. In sharp contrast with much of Latin America, which was experiencing the debt crisis and "the lost decade" (in terms of development) of the 1980s, Cuba could boast of impressive social policies as well as moderate economic growth (5.1 percent per year, according to Pastor and Zimbalist 1995, p. 8) and military successes (Turits 1987). The leaders proclaimed the superiority of the Cuban model. The startling contrasts in public health and education above all made it easy to gloss over the reality of Soviet sponsorship; these successes seemed to vindicate Cuban state socialism's distrust of the market and its strong reliance on centralization and moral commitment.

Model and Performance in the Late 1980s

The peculiar character of Cuban socialism asserted itself in reaction to the deepening crisis of state socialism in the eight years from 1985 to 1993. The authorities apparently failed to or chose not to read the writing on the wall as perestroika and glasnost moved the Soviet Union and Eastern Europe toward enhanced liberalization after 1985. Cuba remained adamant about the local brand of socialism reaffirmed with Rectification. In fact, the reforms in the USSR and Eastern Europe aroused an even more defensive posture. A series of decisions to stay the course were accompanied by surprisingly little debate over the role of markets. In 1989, as the latitude Cuba had enjoyed due to international sponsorship began to contract, though still not too dramatically, the government dismissed warnings that the insistence on state socialism and resistance to a new development path would lead to catastrophe. The Cuban model would sooner than expected be served with a definitive test of its ability to maintain the course. As the USSR intensified its fateful transition and the two countries drifted apart, the tone of Cuban socialism exuded self-confidence and Promethean defiance about its ability to prevail against all odds. The system managed to preserve intact through 1990 the traditional accomplishments of the regime in the social policy area—public health, education, culture, sports, and the like. The economic picture did not change much that year, because the Soviets did not stop their subsidies until 1991 and the CMEA arrangement remained in place. The Cuban economy of 1989–1990 did not look very different from that of 1986 or even before.

As 1990–1991 approached, the Cuban economy therefore seemed stronger and more dynamic than it really was. At the end of an exhaustive review of the economy, Pérez-López (1991) concluded that the preeminent role of sugar had changed only marginally and that new investments would ensure this role in the near future; sugar was indeed still king and the country remained essentially a monoculture export economy. A foreign-investment law had been passed in 1982, but it was not until 1991–1992 that joint ventures began to grow rapidly to promote tourism as the most dynamic economic sector. Some authors have emphasized the levels of industrialization reached by the late 1980s. Zimbalist and Brundenius (1989) have argued forcefully about the general extent of a capital-goods industry (see also Rodríguez Mesa 1985). Brundenius (1984) characterized industrial growth and diversification as remarkable. To Zimbalist (1988; Zimbalist and Eckstein 1987) there was strong growth since 1970 and a growth spurt in the early 1980s. Feinsilver (1993) pointed to the growth of the biotechnological sector. A definitive test of the strength of the Cuban industrial sector would be whether it would react to a major external shock in a manner comparable to that of those Latin American countries experiencing import-substituting industrialization after the economic crisis of the 1930s. Not enough time has elapsed to pass definite judgment on that question. But the Cuban industrial sector has been too small and vulnerable to lead the economy out of the crisis. In fact, it would contract significantly in the early 1990s. Gross or even net proceeds from tourism or even remittances from Cuban Americans rank higher than industry in obtaining hard currency.

Crisis and Reform After 1989

Because Cuban government agencies ceased publishing systematic economic data in 1989, estimates of growth rates and the size of the economy after that year have often been based on speeches and partial reports by government officials and therefore lack precision. Various estimates indicate a contraction of 35–50 percent between 1989 and 1993—with GDP decreasing by approximately 3.1 percent in 1990, 25 percent in 1991, 14 percent in 1992, and 10 percent in 1993 (EIU Country Report II 1994). Imports and exports in 1993–1995 were roughly a fourth and a third of the 1989 levels, respectively. Meanwhile, the sugar harvests of 1993/94, 1994/95, and 1995/96 have been less than half the average of 7.927 million tons for the period 1987–1990.

Claiming economic growth of .7 percent for 1994, 2.5 percent for 1995, and a projected 5 percent for 1996, the authorities argue that sustained growth resumed after the contraction bottomed out in 1993. However, the small recent sugar harvests point in a different direction, considering that sugar remains the mainstay of the economy. The dramatic mid-1994 surge in rafters fleeing the country, as well as countless other accounts by journalists and visitors, confirm the existence of a deep crisis and the generalized perception that a rapid and sustained turnaround is unlikely in the near future. The apparent near halving of the Cuban economy between 1989 and 1994, and the prospects for a protracted crisis, raise fundamental questions about the robustness of Cuban economic development and the viability of the underlying model.

To put the reforms in perspective it is convenient to first briefly explore the underlying causes of the crisis. The U.S. trade embargo is often mentioned as a key factor. However, although it is a significant long-term constraint, the embargo cannot account for the nosedive of 1990–1992, given that the embargo policy had remained more or less constant from the 1960s through 1992. If the October 1992 Cuban Democracy Act could not have been a major factor in the large GDP declines of 25 percent in 1991 and 14 percent in 1992, the 10 percent contraction of 1993 and subsequent poor performance are easily traced to the same cause as the previous declines. That law did strengthen the U.S. trade embargo after 1992, mainly by sharply curtailing $500–700 million of direct Cuban trade with foreign subsidiaries of U.S. companies. But Cuba enjoyed unrestricted access to other Western and world markets before and after 1992, limited by its own ability to pay. The trade with subsidiaries of U.S. corporations was complementary and easily substitutable (e.g., even in early 1996 tourists were served at least two kinds of Coca-Cola in Cuba, one made in Canada and the other in Mexico). Even if all such trade had disappeared by late 1993, this could hardly account for the sharp negative growth, given that virtually all affected nations rejected the extraterritorial claims in that law. In fact, Cuban trade with such top U.S. trading partners as Canada and Mexico increased so notably in 1993 and 1994 that these countries thereby emerged as Cuba's top trading partners. When Soviet supplies dwindled, several Latin American and other countries offered to sell oil to Cuba at world market prices. Latin American countries, historically among the closest U.S. trading partners, began to account in 1994–1995 for more than 40 percent of Cuban imports, with much of that trade representing post-1992 commercial expansion. Canada and Mexico—the two U.S. partners in NAFTA—have also emerged as key sources of investment. Because Cuba's main economic partners today are capitalist countries with strong links to the United States, the notion that a U.S. blockade explained the 1989–1994 fall of the Cuban economy must be deemed rather doubtful.[1]

The collapse of the Cuban economy after 1989 is traceable to Cuba's loss of trading and economic partners with the coming apart of the Eastern European socialist camp. The economic contraction of the island accelerated immediately after the ending of Soviet subsidies and the CMEA framework in 1990–1991. In fact, the embeddedness of the island's economy in the now-defunct socialist-world economy, and the peculiar character of state socialism consolidated with it, raise doubts about Cuba's ability to maintain its model of command socialism with the disappearance of this global context.[2] This line of reasoning brings the spotlight back on the process of global reinsertion and how the internal characteristics of the Cuban system shape it and the reform process. According to Spain's former finance minister, Carlos Solchaga, an adviser to the Cuban government, Cuba's main problem is the inefficient character of key economic practices. In the sugar sector, for instance, most sugar mills operated routinely in the red in the early 1990s, drawing collectively an operational subsidy of several hundred million dollars per year. Lack of fiscal discipline led to huge deficits and a ballooning excess in the money supply that reached 11 billion pesos in 1993—with this fiscal behavior as the main factor in strong inflationary pressures and currency devaluation. To Solchaga, Cuba's economy needs profound transformations. A durable solution requires painful stabilization and adjustment measures to align macroeconomic indicators and set the stage for sound growth under a restructured economy, even if the precise nature of this transition is unclear.

Response to Crisis: (A Long) Prelude to Reform

Cuba's response to the post-1989 crisis was slow and timid. As Eastern European socialism experienced a transition away from state socialism after 1989, Cuba's international trade generally shifted from barter to market prices (the sugar-for-oil swap with Russia being a noteworthy partial exception) and from the CMEA to Western nations. Cuba suddenly felt the pressure to restructure its economy and engage market mechanisms in international transactions as well as in the internal distribution of food and consumer goods. However, for several years after the 1989 collapse of

Eastern European socialism, Cuba experienced no major reforms, with the exception of the increasing role of foreign capital and joint ventures, largely waiting until 1993 to adopt changes on a significant scale.

That is, for more than three years, as trade and transfers contracted, the government simply upheld its brand of traditional state socialism, maintaining that the model and existing policies were sound and any alternative would threaten the nation. Leaders spoke of "socialism or death" and a near-subsistence "zero option" to resist what it perceived as imposition from the outside. The prolonged defiance owes in part to the traditional response reaffirmed in the years before 1989, including the defensive posture built in the period 1986–1989. The government had gone from Rectification to the even more austere Special Period in Time of Peace in 1990. The initial reaction relied on the Food Program and strategies for increasing self-sufficiency. The Fourth Congress of the Cuban Communist Party (October 1991) rejected pressures for broad market reforms. The regime's response focused on accelerated plans to develop joint ventures with private foreign capital in tourism and the biomedical sector.

The steep declines of 25 percent in 1991 and 14 percent in 1992 went by without major new initiatives. In fact, the response instead was to take the centralized system to new limits. Between 1989 and 1993 the money supply expanded dramatically, the state payroll and state subsidies being maintained essentially by printing more money. The infusion of private foreign capital and management into the tourist sector prevented the sharp contraction from leading to broader collapse. The government was also able to obtain some additional credits and loans from abroad as the foreign debt mounted by 72 percent between 1989 and 1993.

The slow and timid response of the authorities from 1989 through 1993 is compatible with the characterization of the Cuban regime as a peculiar form of state socialism marked by an unusual degree of distance from the market, a high degree of concentration, a voluntaristic and political mindset, and high dependence on external sponsorship. Moral appeals and charisma played even heightened roles. The leadership appealed heavily to ideological commitment and solidarity—with patriotism rather than Marxism now invoked as the central theme. Official discourse equated the regime with the nation, sustaining the theme of continuity of the historical struggle for nationhood begun by José Martí in which the current regime is the culmination of a process of national affirmation against threats posed by the United States. Meanwhile, the leadership continued to define capitalism and the market as anathema to progress.

But by mid-1993 it became clear that the profound economic crisis could deepen even further and that the fiscal and monetary imbalances were rapidly worsening the situation and complicating the process of recovery. It was also becoming clear that foreign capital might not come in a sufficiently large scale under the existing arrangements. The clearest signs of rapidly deepening crisis were the interrelated fiscal and monetary crises. The post-1993 response to the crisis first included such measures as transforming state farms into cooperatives, permitting dollar holdings, restoring farmers' markets, and a variety of fiscal measures. Even then, substantial reforms expected at the meeting of the national assembly in December 1993 were discussed but not approved.

Economic Reforms: Change and Challenge

It became increasingly clear after mid-1993 that Cuba needed fundamental change in several areas. Seven of these areas are discussed below. Since then the government has taken significant steps in most of these and is contemplating further measures (see Rodríguez 1995a; Carranza Valdéz, Chapter 11 of this volume). The process of reform, though uneven and slow, has brought some relief by mid-decade. At the same time, it has also intensified challenges and dilemmas without necessarily defining a coherent development strategy.

Cuba's place in the international economy. The first and perhaps the most urgent dimension of change and challenge—though not necessarily the most important—is that of reinsertion into the world economy. Cuba lost in 1991–1992 almost all key partners providing technology, markets, consumer and capital goods, and overall economic support. A frantic drive to find new trade and investment partners ensued. Trade with Latin America and the Caribbean (particularly Mexico), as well as Canada, has grown substantially. Spain and the European Community have also emerged as central in this offensive. After an initial decline, trade with Britain doubled between 1993 and 1994 and was expected to increase after an early 1995 high-level mission to the island signed an investment promotion and protection agreement. France, which gave Cuba export credits for 700 million francs and a wheat-for-sugar barter agreement worth 120 million francs, aimed at a comparable agreement. Economic relations with Italy are also significant. Cuba hopes for enhanced economic relations with Europe as a whole. Economic relations with China should also intensify after Castro's visit there in late 1995.

Cuba is thus making modest progress in realigning itself with the market-driven global trade system. But it has a long way to go to reach the trade levels of 1990. Trade for 1995 was still a fraction of the previous high. The vitality of the reinsertion process depends on Cuba's own economic capacity. A fundamental problem is how to integrate what is still a highly centralized command economy with a trading system driven by capitalist globalization. No state-socialist economy has been able to compete effectively in the open international economic arena, and there are few grounds to expect Cuba to be different. Globalization is increasing international competition, but Cuban firms do not appear ready for this challenge. Privatization is an obvious alternative to further subsidization of noncompetitive enterprises, and Cuba may have been de facto privatizing important parts of the economy in the tourist, communications, and mining sectors. But such forms of divestiture are partial measures of last resort, adopted under crisis conditions without a clear plan. It will take time for competitive firms to emerge in Cuba.

The centrality of the United States in regional and world trade presents a major challenge and opportunity to Cuban policymakers. Just the lifting of the trade embargo would bring substantial benefits to the island. A settlement between the two countries would give Cuba access to the huge U.S. market—as well as lead to large investment flows and remittances. But several issues stand in the way of healthier economic relations between the two countries and Cuba's integration into the U.S.-centered hemispheric trading circuits. Although some have to do with internal U.S. dynamics, it is far from clear that Cuban authorities do in fact want close economic relations with the United States.

Investment capital. Three main goals make mobilizing external capital an urgent task. The most immediate is to continue the crash program to develop tourism and finance the purchase of inputs to agriculture and industry. The second goal is to attract new investments to generate close to a million jobs for underemployed or unemployed Cubans. The third is to overhaul productive systems made obsolete by the very dramatic changes in the USSR and Eastern Europe—as well as the often inefficient original equipment acquired there.

Cuba's external debt and fiscal crisis leave it few options other than attracting private external investment. The government has been unable to service for several years the mounting debt of $11 billion owed to Western and Japanese financiers. Added to the large debt to Russia (and the $6 billion claimed by U.S. owners expropriated in the 1960s), the total liabilities make Cuba unlikely to receive further substantial loans or credits from Western or Japanese financiers—at least until such time as Cuba can agree to a debt-rescheduling plan. Because the state has exhausted its capacity to mobilize internal funding for restructuring and sustained recovery, it is compelled to implement changes to attract large amounts of foreign investment.

The authorities were only modestly successful in their post-1989 efforts to attract foreign capital on the basis of Law 50, the investment law of 1982 that was the main legislation governing the operation of foreign capital and mixed forms of ownership before 1995. This law offered investors incentives such as tax exemption, partial freedom to hire and fire, full repatriation of profits, and various services. After the formation of the first joint ventures in 1990, foreign investment grew to over 210 joint ventures totaling $2.1 billion in the second half of 1995 (*Wall Street Journal,* August 7, 1995). Partnerships comparable to those first used in tourism have been launched in the biomedical, mining, energy, and sugar sectors (*Wall Street Journal,* March 6, 1995, p. C1), and all but education and health were opened to private foreign investment. Under this framework Mexico and Canada emerged as the largest foreign investors. Still, a *Euromoney* credit report in 1995 placed Cuba as the riskiest investment location in the world (see also Mesa-Lago 1994a, p. 18). Uncertain property rights and commercial laws, red tape and excessive regulation, input and supply shortages and uncertainties, and the restrictions on the hiring process kept many potential investors away.

The new investment law of 1995 gives somewhat stronger guarantees and sketches a rudimentary framework for the development of a private sector and a market sector. Operating rights rather than titles of ownership governed the formation of the first wave of joint ventures, but Law 77[3] expands the forms of investment to include total foreign ownership (rather than joint or mixed ownership) in a more diverse range of sectors, including real estate and "free-trade" or "export-processing" zones. The official rationale for the development of a new framework openly acknowledges that foreign investment is the only possible source of large amounts of capital, modern technology, and trading opportunities. Some success is already evident. Shortly after the investment code was enacted, Canada's Sherritt International announced investment plans of $500 million. However, the government continues to state that the law's purpose is to aid the development of state socialism.[4] It also hints that joint ventures with the government will continue to be the rule, with wholly privately owned establishments to be rare. It remains an open question whether the new framework is sufficient to attract all the venture capital Cuba needs. At the very least, the new investment law is being very slowly implemented with additional legislation governing real estate and private property, banking and finance, labor relations, commerce, and free-trade zones.[5]

The 1995 investment law was partly defended in Cuba as an effort to neutralize the U.S. embargo. Cuba hoped to develop a sympathetic business constituency in the United States oriented to positive economic relations between the two countries. Responding to the changing situation in Cuba, U.S. companies did in fact become increasingly interested in business opportunities on the island.[6] But Cuba's lack of a strong and stable legal framework giving across-the-board incentives and assurances to U.S. businesses, including pending questions related to the nationalizations of the 1960s, presented a massive mobilization in this regard. Cuban Americans and other expatriate Cubans have a potentially significant role in this regard. Remittances estimated at over $400 million a year (Díaz-Briquets

1994) have demonstrated the economic potential of the Cuban American community. There are indications that Cuban Americans will invest substantial amounts once the investment climate improves on the island and the United States lifts the trade embargo. But necessity rather than conviction would make the Cuban government allow expatriate Cubans the opportunities opened by piecemeal market reforms. Pronouncements by the leadership at least until mid-1994 bristled with antipathy toward U.S. capitalism and the Cuban American community. It was clear that the long history of animosity and suspicion would take time to dissipate. The shooting down of two civilian airplanes in February 1996, and the predictable adoption of a tougher U.S. embargo law shortly after, confirmed the less optimistic views in this regard.

Diversification. The traditional mainstay of the economy, and the earliest and most thoroughly collectivized, sugar was confirmed as the top priority of the regime in the context of Cuba's role in the CMEA. The sugar sector has experienced a sharp contraction and its very long-term viability may be in question. Cuban harvests in 1993/94 and 1994/95 were half or less (3.8–4 and 3.3 million tons, respectively) of the average of nearly 8 million tons just prior to 1989. The latter harvest, the smallest since 1959, earned one-seventh of the 1990 earnings. The main factors in the drop are decreasing crops and yields as well as disrupted industrial processes. Only very costly external credits and collaboration to finance the purchase of fertilizers, pesticides, fuel, and spare parts improved the picture in the 1995/96 expected harvest of 4.5 million tons. European trading houses and banks extended more than $200 million in credit to buy fertilizers, pesticides, and other inputs at 12–20 percent interest with full repayment within a year in cash or sugar stocks (Rodríguez 1995). These forms of collaboration may evolve into joint ventures or perhaps foreign ownership. The underlying issue is whether Cuban sugar as currently organized is fully competitive in international markets. It appears doubful that Cuba's lost ground as world producer will be regained rapidly and without major sectoral reorganization.

The disastrous performance and problems of the sugar sector highlight a process of sectoral realignment since the late 1980s. Noteworthy in this regard is the contrasting expansion of the tourist sector. Tourism is now Cuba's leading sector in terms of growth, and generated gross revenues of approximately a billion dollars in 1995 (but in 1994 the island only retained $250 million of the $800 million in gross receipts). This expansion generates a few thousand new jobs every year. Cuba was the top Caribbean tourist attraction before 1959 and has the natural and human resources to regain that status. The tourist sector is likely to increase manifold in a relatively short period. Tourism relies heavily on foreign investment and rents from natural resources (rather than higher yields due to rising productivity and efficiency). The economic growth and the types of jobs generated, though extremely significant, are mostly at the low end in terms of value added, wages, and profitability.

Hence, even with very fast growth tourism will not play the role that sugar has traditionally played, much less serve as basis for the modernization of the economy. Other sectors—mining, agriculture, pharmaceuticals and biotechnology, energy, telecommunications, and information—are being called upon to play enhanced roles with foreign private investment. Canada's Sherritt Inc. entered into a major deal to modernize the nickel facilities in Moa and process ore in its Saskatchewan refinery—nickel production having fallen 25 percent from 1989 to 1992 in response to the closing of Soviet-made plants. Australia's Western Mining Corporation is also increasingly active in Cuban mining. The pharmaceutical and biomedical sectors were affected by supply shortages shortly after 1989, but appear to have improved recently. Current plans to build free-trade and industrial zones are noteworthy, even if such zones are of limited development potential in the context of the low-tariff trade regime born of GATT, NAFTA, and other regional free-trade agreements and Cuba's nonmembership in most of them.

Domestic markets and entrepreneurs. Changes in the first three areas have followed an outward-oriented strategy of liberalization opened in the period 1990–1993. Foreign investment has been the main carrier for an enhanced private economy, but this process takes place in certain segments of the economy and serves to block the impact of linkages on the rest of the economy. By 1994 this response to the crisis had only generated 10–13 percent of the losses since 1989, according to Mesa-Lago (1994a, p. 21). Policymakers did not engage in major forms of internal change until 1993 and after. The fourth set of reforms and challenges pertains to making fuller use of the market and private entrepreneurship. The year 1993 witnessed the decision to transform collectivized state farms into producer cooperatives, the legalization of self-employment in a number of occupational categories, the legalization of dollar holdings and transactions, and a somewhat more liberal approach to the informal economy. In October 1994 farmers' markets were allowed again. In December of that year, markets were also authorized for handicrafts and surplus manufactured consumer goods. Their impact has not equaled that of the farmers' markets, but has been significant. The year 1995 has seen the proliferation of the small private restaurants known as *paladares.* The next logical step would need to be the liberalization of self-employment and private business investment by Cubans.

By the second half of 1995 the still relatively mild internal liberalization demonstrated that different forms of property and a market economy can be more effective in food production and distribution than the highly collectivized and regulated one. The reforms thus showed important advances and potential, as agricultural production increased and prices decreased. However, a great deal of resistance to the idea of enlarging the scope of the market persisted. If much of the rest of the world had redefined development in terms of participation in market-driven globalization, the Cuban leadership clung to a rhetoric of resistance and defiance, maintaining its adherence to the idea of a command economy. The 1995 investment law was not meant to include investments by Cubans on the island. The inequities resulting from the expansion of foreign capital brought pressure for further liberalization. But private entrepreneurship is still largely viewed as an act of deviance in Cuban society, and successful small-scale entrepreneurs are often accused of profiteering, illegal practices, and the like (see Chapter 10 of this volume). If traditional socialism is maintained in the rest of the economy, while outside capitalists account for an increasing share of the economy, the islanders' exclusion from opportunities for legitimate entrepreneurship will create a peculiar structural imbalance. At least a quarter of a million Cubans had applied for or obtained permits to become self-employed as of late 1995, with more than a million Cubans estimated to be employed in the resulting microenterprises. But a major constraint on self-employed and entrepreneurial Cubans through early 1996 has been the legal inability to hire, which puts them at a major disadvantage with respect to other producers. The government may soon feel compelled to guarantee the ability of small private businesses to hire labor, because other reforms are sharply constraining the state's capacity to guarantee full employment. When that happens, the success of at least some of the domestic entrepreneurs will pose more fully the issue of a Cuban entrepreneurial class and whether the regime is ready for the development of a universalistic legal framework for the private economy.

In the current institutional context, deeper market reforms and the growth of a domestic entrepreneurial sector would tend to erode the "totalitarian" pattern of political authority and are probably feared and resisted for that reason. As the scope of operations of the market and private property increase, the regime tends to lose control over the allocation of resources; this would happen at a critical juncture in which problems are increasing. On the other hand, China and Vietnam in particular have managed to use the market and national entrepreneurship more aggressively while retaining stable, centralized rule. The Cuban government will attempt to learn from these experiences, but Cuba is handicapped in this sense by the very limited entrepreneurial sector that Cuban state socialism permitted in the past, as compared to the old Eastern bloc or even China and Vietnam (Perry et al. 1995).

Stabilization and adjustment. The fifth challenge—in many ways perhaps the most pressing—pertains to macroeconomic imbalances, external as well as internal, requiring stabilization and structural adjustment (see Chapter 9 of this volume). Cuba's own fiscal crisis of the state is characterized by massive fiscal deficits, excess liquidity ("monetary overhang"), and external debt (see also Cabarrouy 1995; Hernández-Catá 1995; Chapter 8 of this volume). The fiscal deficit is the heart of the problem. Just before the internal reforms were adopted, the operational deficit of the government's budget had risen to 32 percent and then 40 percent of GDP—largely financed by monetary expansion. With Carlos Lage and José Luis Rodríguez leading the changes, the deficit decreased substantially after 1994 via cuts in subsidies, the closing of insolvent plants, and the imposition of a new system of taxes and fees. The reduction of the monetary overhang lessened pressures on prices as well as on the unofficial exchange rate between the peso and the U.S. dollar.

How deep and orthodox the adjustment process should be in this regard remains a major dilemma. Fiscal adjustment calls next for the laying off of hundreds of thousands of workers, a measure that clashes with the regime's commitment to social programs and full-employment policies. From 500,000 to 750,000 of the island's workforce of 3.5–4 million workers in the state sector are expected to be gradually "rationalized"—dismissed from their jobs with the hope of being reassigned.[7] Even if standards of living deteriorate further and inequality continues to increase, the failure to complete the stabilization program would doom the overall reform effort. With education and health given top priority, other government programs and agencies face the greatest job losses. The external debt to Western nations and to Russia and the ex-socialist bloc presents a related but distinct problem. Solving this problem may mean the transfer of assets, as in the recent telecommunications deal with a large Mexican investor.

Role of the state. The sixth challenge is the redefinition of the role of the state in the context of the liberalization process. If the government did become friendlier to the market in practice, it has yet to formally redefine its mission. Some changes are unexpected and go against the grain of liberalization or privatization. For instance, the Ministry of the Armed Forces (MINFAR) is playing an already large and growing economic role (see Lee 1995). This ministry is deeply involved in the tourist sector—both as owner of the Gaviota complex and as operator of the AeroGaviota tourist airline. The military has also developed a major presence in agriculture, running dozens of large farms, growing crops it consumes, and reportedly generating surpluses for the market. The army has played a key part in the recently created farmers' markets. Industrias Militares Unidas is manufacturing a range of products for the market. This phenomenon raises a number of important questions regarding the extent to which MINFAR may be taking over key functions from the Communist Party, giving rise to a new entrepreneurial class, straying from its traditional mission, and shaping long-term political dynamics.

A series of administrative changes did give important positions to younger and reform-minded figures such as Vice President Carlos Lage, Foreign Minister Roberto Robaina, and parliamentary leader Osvaldo Martínez (former director of the Center for Research on the World Economy). A thorough generational changeover appears highly unlikely in the near future, but the state apparatus is changing and reformers seemed to be gaining on hard-liners as of early 1996. But considering the centrality of the state in shaping reform processes, the Cuban state will need to change in major ways to turn itself into an effective instrument of market-oriented changes.

Culture and ideology. These changes entail a seventh challenge, at the cultural level. The antimaterialist, collectivist, utopian, and hyperegalitarian value system embraced by the revolution clashes with liberalizing reforms entailing the more intense reliance on individual solutions, innovativeness, material incentives, and entrepreneurship (Sanguinetty 1995). The need to articulate a cultural and normative order congruent with the new times and emerging national agenda is very clear with respect to the formation of national entrepreneurs. The ascetic ethic promoted by state socialism defined private entrepreneurship as immoral and criminal (see Chapters 9 and 10). Emerging entrepreneurs operate at the fringe of what is deemed legal and honest, often relying on inputs and resources from the state sector via shady transactions. To the extent that the regime continues to define local entrepreneurship as deviance, it would abdicate a key role in shaping new cultural patterns vital to the reform process. One risk is that this fledgling sector would from birth be particularly corrosive of the polity and the normative order.

Some steps have been taken in this area. The University of Havana recently began a graduate program on standard market economics. The government of Uruguay is training high-level Cuban decisionmakers and bureaucrats in the handling of market-driven processes. The theme of building socialism has given way to that of survival of the homeland and the revolution while retaining past achievements in health care, education, and related social areas. But at the same time the regime escalated through 1995 and early 1996 the rhetoric against market reforms and resists efforts to redefine the balance between state and market. Official discourse remains focused on the sense of an epic struggle for utopian ends rather than the realm of realistic development. It is possible that a long period of crisis and social learning may be necessary for perceptions and behavior to experience fundamental change in this regard.

Assessing the Reforms

The dearth of reliable relevant data on the Cuban economy, society, and policymaking dynamics makes hazardous the full characterization of the current reforms and the trend of which they may be part. Still, the analysis here makes it possible to venture three main arguments. The first is that the reform process deepened through 1995 and may have in fact already reached the point of no return, but—paradoxically—may very well stop short of a structural turning point. The liberalizing reforms have been largely oriented to an external rather than an internal strategy, though independent producers have accounted for much of the enhanced supply of food products, handicrafts, and services. This strategy prevented the structural crisis from worsening after 1994, but will not by itself put the core of the economy on a clear path to sustained recovery and development under a different model. Significant as they are, the internal reforms adopted after 1993 have not altered key features of state socialism thought to hinder growth in the new global context: excessive central planning, large state-controlled enterprises insulated from competition, and highly controlled or regulated markets (Hernández-Catá 1995). Judging by official rhetoric, they are not likely to do so in the immediate future. On the other hand, the reduced ability of the state increases the probability of deeper forms of internal liberalization and the expansion of entrepreneurship—just as advances in this direction will soon be impossible to stop, as Cubans will not easily give up newly gained economic freedoms to return to a hypercentralized system and hard times. Internal liberalization contradicts a resilient form of state socialism and the supporting ideology. A turning point is unlikely without institutional, ideological, and related political changes, but there are few bases on which to predict a clear shift in this regard. The hesitant changes and the growing tension between this trend and official doctrine raise the question of just what model or strategy the country is in fact adopting. Cuban authorities refer to an "irreversible" and unique process of reform comparable to those in China and Vietnam, but the precise nature of this new Cuban model—whether based on centrally planned socialism, market socialism, a mixed economy, or something else—remains unclear and is still much more timid than that of even Vietnam (Quijano 1995). The authorities have ruled out the model of swift transition of the island's former partners in Eastern Europe. Instead, Cuba has been implementing reforms incrementally, with a high degree of ambivalence, and seemingly without a master plan or strategy. It was becoming evident in late 1995 that the elite interpreted the modest growth of that year as firm evidence of recovery and of the feasibility of dispensing with further urgent reforms. A reluctant and minimalist approach to reform may fail to reach beyond the threshold (in depth, breadth, and commitment) required for sustained recovery, and tends to aggravate some problems as it delays the solution of others. The measures adopted thus far have compartmentalized the economy into a dysfunctional pattern. Tourism and the external sector rely on market-driven entrepreneurship, while the internal economy, where by far most Cubans operate, remains largely collectivized and regulated. The articulation of these two economies is highly problematic (see Chapter 9 of this volume). Within the current institutional framework, the linkages between the socialist domestic sector and the capitalist export economy are realized through either the political system or the "second economy" (see Chapter 10 of this volume). The automatic feedbacks and interconnections of market-based systems are absent or deficient. In the framework of this dualism, reforms often create new problems without dissolving constraints on the more efficient utilization of resources and the expansion of entrepreneurship.

Second, if the Cuban case denies the notion of a linear relationship between the depth of a crisis and reform efforts, economistic models are to be rejected and noneconomic factors should be surmised to be conditioning and shaping the latter. The political-institutional context has been and will continue to be of cardinal importance. Ironically, the market reforms themselves lead to the reaffirmation of central authority and moral socialism, including Fidel Castro's preeminent role, as hard-liners react to the new stresses on the structural faults of Cuban society—cleavages or imbalances introduced by foreign capital, stabilization, dollarization, state reform, and the like. The centralized and moral character of Cuban socialism is reaffirmed by reference to the need to steer the difficult process of reform. In this context, political elites heighten the appeal to moral and ideological considerations to attempt to subordinate the market economy to state socialism. The rhetoric of rejection of capitalism and adherence to socialism thus remains a leitmotiv—just as reforms deepen the reliance on foreign private investment and market forces. A market-oriented "reform syndrome," a factor responsible for success in processes of restructuring in much of Latin America and elsewhere, is unlikely under those conditions. Economic policy is hence likely to retain a reactive character, in terms of responding to crises and defending socialism, rather than actively defining a new model or strategy.

Third, a dramatic resolution of the structural tensions and strains in this situation is inevitable, but it is very difficult to predict its form and timing. The dialectical interplay between institutions and reforms shapes the building up and sedimentation of structural tensions in a "path-dependent" scenario (Stark 1992) in which present and future are connected by continuity rather than clear rupture. Will a political earthquake be inevitable? The most likely scenario in the near future is continuity in political parameters, with the leadership dominated directly or indirectly by historical hard-liners. With central authority reaffirmed and a large number of officers playing economic roles in the emergent economy, a military coup seems unlikely in the near future. The regime's mechanisms for social control have performed well under recent threats; a major crisis has seen relatively little protest. Internationally, the system is even able to leverage the potential for crisis and deteriorating conditions by pointing to the probable costs of further worsening. In fact, at least in the short run the very crisis and reform processes tend to enhance the political position of the current leadership, even as market penetration and other aspects of the reform lead to the long-term erosion of the underlying system. More generally, one can safely dismiss the notion of a modal transition to which the Cuban case should correspond. Precisely what kind of path Cuba adopts will remain a puzzle for some time and will eventually be decided by a combination of forces. What is clearer is that factors outside the state proper are becoming increasingly important and that growing structural complexity will help shape this path. The process of transition may take a long time and adopt a range of transitional forms, or even partial reversals.

Conclusion

Cuba faces the challenge of finding a new development model. The unraveling of socialism in Eastern Europe revealed the utter embeddedness of Cuban socialism in a peculiar set of international conditions no longer existing and unlikely to be replicated. But this by itself hardly suffices to explain the actual process of change. The institutional legacy of Cuban revolutionary socialism—including a highly centralized, voluntaristic, and authoritarian political system—is crucial. The version of state socialism Cuba pursued for more than three decades may have run its course, but in important ways the reforms tend to actually reinforce the regime.

Cuba appears to be trying to follow the cautious Chinese approach to reform, "crossing the river by feeling the stones." But China in fact made decisive changes in the 1970s once it decided to adopt market reforms. In 1978 Deng Xiaoping inaugurated a new era of private market prices, stock and commodities exchanges, and considerably more liberalization than embraced earlier in the decade. These changes have led to more than sixteen years of double-digit economic growth. Vietnam has been evolving toward a similar model. In spite of the dramatic growth it has generated, the Chinese model has major shortcomings. It comes at the cost of continued authoritarianism and thus a high potential for instability at some future point. Moreover, faced with the danger of unrest, China's system responds by giving additional resources to state firms plagued by inefficiency and corruption.[8] Cuban state socialism will continue to use its phenomenal autonomy to explore incrementally a way out of the crisis that harnesses in subordinate fashion the powers of the market and private entrepreneurship. But its smaller agricultural and industrial systems make success under such a model much less likely than in China.

Arguably, Cuba's current challenge is not to wade on a shallow river but to set sail on different structural seas. If so, there are few alternatives to deepening an outward-oriented strategy and complementing it with greatly enhanced internal entrepreneurship. The heart of the reform process, the modernization of the productive system, is unlikely without a strong market-oriented entrepreneurial class. Overcommitted and effectively close to bankruptcy, the state is unable to provide jobs for all, find most of the badly needed investment funds, or guarantee economic recovery. The country must rapidly learn to play by the rules of the globalized market economy.

If so, the Cuban reform project is like a ship setting sail on an adventurous journey with a destiny that is not fully known. Fear of losing sight of the originating port and the familiar coastline continues to delay the action. The journey requires a realistic assessment of the current predicament and options. The pressing danger is that the need for change be construed as an unjustified demand to be battled with ideology and the collectivizing impulse. But the peculiar ideological and institutional style of the past will continue to feed voluntarism and distrust of the winds of the market, as the radically altered external environment no longer gives leaders the leeway and autonomy of the past. It is a major contradiction that, just as the country is compelled to find a place in the capitalist world economy, and in fact makes increasing use of private capital and entrepreneurship, those at the helm insist on a highly centralized moral economy and condemn the market. Is Cuba setting sail in two different directions? Are Cuban policymakers and Cubans in general ready for the high seas of the capitalist global economy?

Notes

1. On the other hand, the U.S. trade embargo has constituted a significant long-term constraint, just as its hardening in 1993 entailed extra costs, including a much lower level of remittances from Cuban Americans. (To be sure, laws such as Helms-Burton will, if implemented, turn the embargo into a near blockade.) In fact, the full lifting of the embargo would have a major beneficial impact on the Cuban economy via annual remittances of possibly a billion dollars from Cuban Americans, major infusions of U.S. (including Cuban American) private capital, sharp increases in tourism and visits by Cuban Americans, trade of several billion dollars, and access to modern technology. Meanwhile, the idea of a major impact of the U.S. trade embargo via substantially higher import costs for Cuba is particularly valid to the extent that Cuba would in fact be inclined to develop strong economic relations with the United States. Because the Cuban government seems to believe that the United States also threatens the very survival of the Cuban nation, this premise may not hold.

2. That China's socialist economy is doing well, and state socialism did actually work for several decades in Eastern Europe and the USSR, would however argue against the notion that state socialism is necessarily not viable. Szelenyi and Szelenyi (1994) maintain that the collapse of socialism was due to exogenous factors—a historical contingency owing to a combination of factors—rather than

necessity. Some new version of authoritarian state socialism could be consolidated if private foreign investors provide the resources to stabilize the economy.

3. Travieso-Diaz and Ferraté (1995) discuss the new foreign-investment law and the main problems with Law 50 of 1982. According to these authors (p. 5), there have been three types of business organizations: joint ventures, production agreements (foreign partner acting as exporter or distributor of Cuban products), and joint accounts (foreign operators manufacturing and distributing goods of Cuban design).

4. For example, see the interview of Ernesto Melendez, Cuba's minister of foreign investment, in the *Washington Post,* September 6, 1995. Vice President Lage is on record as saying that it owes to "isolated circumstance" rather than "general policy" (the *Journal of Commerce,* September 13, 1995).

5. Critics of Cuba's investment climate include Castañeda and Montalván 1995, p. 200; the *Economist,* June 25, 1994. Castañeda and Montalván point out that in the rush to attract foreign investment, the terms of concessions over national assets may be considerably less than could be obtained by more transparent procedures.

6. Two noteworthy U.S. business lobbies are the Washington-based American Business Council on Cuba and the United States–Cuba Trade and Economic Council, headquartered in New York.

7. Other components of the workforce are 700,000 in health and education, 2.2 million in goods-producing sectors (including agriculture), and less than 100,000 in tourism (*Los Angeles Times,* February 23, 1995, D6). There were reports in late 1995 that the implementation of the plan to rationalize the labor force was being delayed by the perception that economic collapse had been arrested.

8. In China the state sector is reported as still drawing 80 percent of bank loans (that go unpaid) and more than 70 percent of all investment, as the state sector continues to grow (*New York Times,* December 16, 1994, p. 1).

◆ 8 ◆

The Limits of Socialism in a Capitalist World Economy: Cuba Since the Collapse of the Soviet Bloc

Susan Eckstein

◆

Fidel Castro's government withstood the domino collapse of communism despite the island's heavy dependence for three decades on Soviet aid and trade. It also withstood global political and economic trends despite a crisis of such magnitude that the island's productive capacity and the regime's political legitimacy were challenged as never before. The crisis did not originate with the collapse of the Soviet Union and the Soviet bloc, but was exacerbated by it significantly. This chapter addresses the depth and structural roots of the crisis, and state efforts to mitigate it.

The Crisis: Trade and Fiscal Origins

While the island's financial problems deepened after 1989, their roots can be traced to the pre-1989 period. Indeed, they can be partly traced to the socialist nature of the regime and the historical form the Soviets imposed on Cuba; to production inefficiencies associated with state ownership and regulation, and the Soviet emphasis on large enterprises utilizing internationally uncompetitive technology; to "soft-budgetary" constraints associated with the politicization of fiscal allocations (Kornai 1979, 1980); and to a commitment to universal cradle-to-grave care. By the end of the 1980s life expectancy had become the highest in Latin America (and for men higher even than in the United States) and the government provided the long-living population with free meals, cheap food, guaranteed employment (or generous unemployment compensation), pensions, and universal health care (Eckstein 1994, chap. 5). No other Latin American government provided such extensive benefits.

In years past, the government concealed at the ideological level the extent and nature of its fiscal crisis. For example, when it initiated austerity measures in the mid-1980s to address a mounting hard-currency debt and a domestic budgetary deficit, the national leadership turned to

Guevarist and Marxist-Leninist principles to explain the problem and propose a solution (Eckstein 1994, chap. 3). It mounted a moral campaign to "rectify errors and negative tendencies." Resentment of and resistance to new material deprivations and demands on labor at the time might have been greater had the government not defended new austerity policies in the name of fundamental revolutionary objectives. In the 1980s price hikes in many other Latin American countries had sparked protests and other acts of defiance (Walton 1989), and Gorbachev's perestroika and glasnost had begun to stir turmoil in the Soviet Union.

The Rectification campaign, though possibly politically expedient, left fiscal problems unresolved. Between 1985 and 1989 the government's hard-currency debt more than doubled and its domestic budgetary deficit increased some sixfold (Eckstein 1994, pp. 222–223). Revenue remained relatively constant while expenditures climbed.

Unfortunately for Cuba, the Soviet collapse occurred just when the island's dependence on the CMEA peaked. The Soviet bloc had accounted for some 85 percent of Cuba's foreign trade in 1989, up from 59 percent in 1974. This was particularly significant given that Cuba was a trade-dependent economy: In 1989 trade had accounted for about half the national product. In the next four years imports fell by 70 percent. The government lacked the means to import little other than essentials, and even critical inputs such as oil dropped by half (and more, subsequently). Partly because of the collapse of trade (including imports of pesticides, herbicides, and machinery, as well as petroleum) but also because of such domestic problems as labor productivity, conditions deteriorated to the point that the country came to face a subsistence crisis.

Following the collapse of the Soviet bloc, the economy caved in and the government became for all intents and purposes fiscally insolvent. By 1993 the economy had contracted by some 50 percent, the domestic deficit—already 1,624 million pesos in 1989—had tripled, and the Western debt increased by some 51 percent. Havana owed nearly $11 billion to Western creditors, plus an additional 15 billion rubles to the former Soviet Union (*Latin America Weekly Report,* April 15, 1993, p. 177; *Boston Globe,* December 30, 1993, p. 22).

The adverse effects of the collapse of the Soviet bloc exacerbated problems that the Rectification failed to resolve. As conditions deteriorated, the moral issues raised by the Rectification campaign became a luxury the state could no longer afford; reference to the campaign, and even to Marxism-Leninism, became infrequent. The fiscal deficit continued to rise and production plunged, while the legitimacy of Soviet-style communism was challenged as never before. In place of Rectification the government spoke of a Special Period in Time of Peace. The Special Period combined policies consistent, not surprisingly, with socialist ideological and organizational principles, but also increasingly with capitalist and even precapitalist values. Noted Castro, "This is no time for theorizing but instead for advancing, resisting, and overcoming" (*Granma Weekly Review*, December 30, 1990, p. 9). The term "Special Period" became a catch-all phrase to explain hardship and justify any initiative offered to address the crisis.

The First Response to Crisis: 1989–1994

Socialist-Style Initiatives

Fidel has argued that the strategies of the 1990s were designed to "save the revolution," not to transform it. In response to the emergent crisis the government took a number of initiatives that might be expected of a regime committed to socialist principles. It initiated an ambitious Food Program to make the island as self-sufficient in food as possible. State plans called for greater output and an expansion of the stock of cattle and poultry, and for official allocation of land and labor to the project. Second, the government once again rationed the distribution of almost all consumer goods, both durable and nondurable. In the 1970s and 1980s it had reduced rationing to the point that the regulatory system had come to account for only about one-fourth of family consumption. With rationing, however, there could be "equality of sacrifice," at prices affordable to all. The government recognized that scarcities otherwise would have driven the cost of basic necessities beyond the means of low-income earners, as did neoliberal market reforms elsewhere in Latin America.

Consistent with socialist organizational principles the government also initiated labor mobilizations. Thirty-one agricultural brigades, with 200 cadres each, worked long hours as model workers. In exchange for their hard labor they earned better-than-average wages and they could exercise certain control over the work process. The government also mobilized urban volunteers to help meet new seasonal demands for labor. The demand for labor in agriculture rose with efforts to implement the Food Program, and with a shift from capital- to labor-intensive agriculture owing to import cutbacks of petroleum, machinery, and other farm inputs. As many as 500,000 Havana residents went to the fields for brief seasonal farm stints in 1992 (*Granma International,* May 5, 1991, p. 2 and September 20, 1992, p. 5).

In addition, the government turned to the military to help out in production and distribution. Military involvement in the civilian economy is not an inherent characteristic of socialism, but it reflects a government effort to rely on administrative rather than market mechanisms that is characteristic of socialism in its "statist" form. One-fourth of the defense industry shifted to civilian production (Eckstein 1994, p. 118). The armed forces became particularly active in farming, to the point that Raúl Castro, Fidel's brother and head of the Armed Forces Ministry, proclaimed, "We've defined beans as more important than cannons at this moment."[1] The new soldier-farmers produced for their own subsistence, but increasingly also for city people and export, largely on land owned by the armed forces. Former boarding-school buildings were converted into housing for any soldier-farmer who elected to remain on the land (EIU 1995, p. 14). The government allowed new soldier recruits to choose whether to serve in defense or agricultural units (with the Army of Working Youth, the EJT, set up specifically to work in agriculture). The country's leadership turned to the military because the cadres were seen as dependable; there was no shortage of civilian labor at the time. Soldiers deployed in productive activity were also praised for their discipline and organization *(Granma International,* June 9, 1994, p. 2).

The government turned to socialist-style strategies as means to address official economic objectives. But Castro was also committed to socialist ends, namely cradle-to-grave social welfare. This commitment was political. Castro took pride in not closing a single school, day-care center, or hospital, and in not leaving a single person destitute, despite dire Special Period circumstances. His government did announce an end to guaranteed employment and generous unemployment compensation in 1991, reversing a long-standing commitment to labor. Worker resentment, however, led the government to rescind the proposal soon after making it public. The social programs strained the resources of the bankrupt state.

Market-Oriented Strategies

The government relied on market along with statist strategies to address economic concerns. Indeed, market features became ever more important, while collectivist and statist strategies, except those involving the military, were quietly phased out. The shift occurred at the same time that the national leadership and the Communist Party remained publicly committed to socialism and party membership purportedly rose.[2]

Market features took on special importance in the external sector. Courting foreign investment, Castro defended the "creeping privatization" and economic "denationalization" involved: "We're not violating any principles of socialism" *(Granma International,* May 5, 1991, p. 15). The government accordingly reversed not only its decades-old stance toward foreign investment but its sectoral priorities as well. Tourism had been reined in after the revolution to put an end to the decadence of the old order, but it became a priority in the 1990s. Nonrenewable resource deals included production and risk-sharing contracts for oil and mineral exploration, and nickel refining and marketing. Although Cuba has the fourth-largest known nickel reserves in the world, the sector was in disarray. Forty percent of existing capacity was idle, facilities built by Americans before 1959 were considered superior to those built with Soviet technology since then, and in 1992 Cuba spent about half of each nickel dollar earned on imported inputs.

By 1994 Cuba had attracted about $1.5 billion in foreign investment (EIU 1995, p. 12). Most of the money was linked to some 150 joint ventures with the state, although foreign investment was not confined there. Castro recognized the opening to foreign capital to be "pretty large," but he claimed no intention to restore capitalism *(Granma International,* September 7, 1994, p. 7). In his quest to attract business he offered "stability and continuity" and an "orderly and stable country" *(Granma International,* February 8, 1995, p. 3).

To entice foreign capital the Cuban government offered investors concessions that squeezed labor and undermined its own institutional control over the economy. It allowed investors to hire and fire workers; employees thereby lost the economic security they had enjoyed since Castro's first years in power. The government also allowed investors rights to unlimited profit repatriation, typically for ten years, and agreed to bear the construction and infrastructure costs required *(Granma International,* December 27, 1992, p. 11). It even ceded control over firm-level policies to foreign capital. Joint ventures could operate autonomously from the state and independent of centralized planning (EIU 1992, p. 20). In some instances overseas investors acquired majority ownership, even though the investment code placed the foreign equity ceiling at 49 percent. The government turned ownership rights and management over to foreign companies, including administration of wholly owned national enterprises. This was especially true in the tourist sector, where some thirty-five comanagement contracts were signed as of 1994 *(Granma International,* February 8, 1995, p. 3).

In the process, the government gave up control over investment priorities. Production for the domestic economy came to a near halt owing to foreign disinterest in any but the hard-currency sector. Yet, as of 1993, hard-currency exports stood at only one-third the value of overseas sales in 1989, even with the infusion of foreign investment *(Granma International,* December 14, 1994, p. 7). Since the collapse of the Soviet bloc all trade was in hard currency; thus Cuba failed to attract sufficient investment to its hard-currency or domestic peso economy.

Within the external sector tourism expanded while sugar contracted. Tourism grossed an estimated $700 million in 1993 and $850 million the following year, up from $200 million in 1989 (*Cuba Business*, September 1994, p. 2; EIU 1995, p. 13).[3] Foreigners were known to recoup their investments within four to five years (Eckstein 1994, pp. 102–104). In its drive to attract tourists the government played on the image of prerevolutionary Cuba, an image it initially had rejected as decadent. It allowed

Playboy magazine to feature an article on the "girls of Cuba," and the Ministry of Tourism ran travel advertisements abroad featuring string bikini–clad Cuban women.

Meanwhile, sugar production and sugar earnings, the mainstay of the island's export economy for centuries, declined. By 1993 sugar yields had dropped to half their 1989 level, to a two-decade low. Production suffered from cutbacks in imported inputs and labor flight from the cane fields. Cuba's earnings plunged because of market as well as production problems. The price the commodity commanded in the world market was about one-third of what the Soviets had paid. In the pre-Castro era the United States had paid above world-market prices for Cuban sugar, and it guaranteed Cuba its largest import quota. Following the collapse of the Soviet Union, Cuba became entirely dependent on the nonsubsidized free market, in which only about 10 percent of all sugar is traded.

Hard-currency-oriented joint ventures included overseas service work as well as exports and tourism. Since 1977 Cuba charged for some of the construction, health care, education, and technical assistance its internationalists provided other Third World countries, but in the 1990s it established joint ventures for foreign contracts. UNECA, a Cuban construction company that initially did overseas construction work and then domestic tourist-sector building when external contracts dried up, formed mixed enterprises with foreign collaborators during the Special Period. Cuba offered, above all, inexpensive skilled labor (Eckstein 1994, pp. 190, 192).

Market reforms within the state sector extended beyond the opening to foreign capital, and they affected the domestically as well as the externally oriented portion of the economy. The government, for example, simultaneously encouraged enterprise self-financing, especially in hard currency.[4] It also ceded to firms the right to freely negotiate trade deals. Indeed, without fanfare, the government gradually began to transform state enterprises and agencies into semi-autonomous units.

Other reforms allowed for a privatization of domestic economic activity. The government relegalized self-employment, to the point that by 1994 some 162,000 islanders had authorization to offer repair work, carpentry, plumbing, gardening, and other services. The government had allowed such independent activity in the mid-1970s, but reined it in the 1980s because it undermined the public sector (Eckstein 1994, chaps. 2 and 3). In 1993 the government also instituted a new agrarian reform that transformed 58 percent of state lands into cooperatives (*Latin American Weekly Review,* February 1993, p. 75; *Boston Globe,* December 30, 1993, p. 52).

The government, meanwhile, introduced new material incentives in priority sectors. It raised some farm salaries to the top of the wage scale (average wages in the sector once having been at the bottom); it raised prices paid to farmers for deliveries to the official collection agency; it offered bonus payments to exceptionally productive farmers; and it initiated yield-related wages (*Granma Weekly Review,* January 13, 1991, p. 3). In addition, the government allowed tourist-sector workers to retain their hard-currency tips; until 1993 they were to turn all such earnings over to the state.

The market opening even came to include, in 1993, legalization of the dollar as a domestic currency. Since 1989 the dollar had come to be islanders' de facto currency of choice. According to government estimates, over one-fifth of the population and over one-fourth of Havana residents had access to dollars *(Granma International,* January 4, 1995, p. 4).

Precapitalist Survival Strategies

The government tolerated and even promoted precapitalist survival strategies that further reversed much of what the revolution had stood and strived for until 1989.

In farming, the government encouraged precapitalist techniques and subsistence agriculture, along with statist/collectivist and market features. In place of the petroleum-dependent, capital-intensive technology that the government had proudly and effectively touted for three decades, farmers were called upon to rely on their own labor and draft animals. Castro here turned to au courant international environmental discourse, not Marxism-Leninism, to justify the shift. He pointed out how much better the "new" methods were for the environment (*Granma International,* June 28, 1992, p. 8, supplement). The revolution and socialism were to be saved, said he, with "a machete in hand, with lathes to make spare parts, and with hoes for weeding" (*Granma International,* March 28, 1993, p. 7). At the same time, the government exhorted city dwellers to set up "victory gardens" in backyards, empty lots, and open spaces. There were an estimated million such gardens nationwide in mid-1992.

The economy, meanwhile, deindustrialized. Nearly half of all factories either were shut down or run on a much reduced scale, to the point that the manufacturing sector operated at 15 percent of capacity in 1993 (EIU 1995, p. 6). Industrial facilities, such as the Soviet-assisted nuclear-power plant, stood like abandoned pyramids, in Raúl Castro's words *(Granma International,* May 5, 1993, p. 4). As manufacturing ground to a near halt, the government and the state-linked women's mass organization, the Federation of Cuban Women, exhorted women to make candles for illumination during the many hours of electrical blackouts. Officials also encouraged women to make their own soap and sew their own clothing and shoes. A revolution that had pressed for women's liberation from housework now urged the contrary.

Bicycles became one of the main means of transport, as broken-down buses had to be taken out of service and bus runs were slashed for consuming too much scarce petroleum. The government purchased a million bicycles from China, and planned to replace half the truck fleet used for transporting goods with 60,000 Chinese cargo tricycles *(Granma International,* January 10, 1993, p. 5). In this context as well Castro spoke of an ecotopia, in place of a communist utopia (*Granma Weekly Review,* February 10, 1991, p. 1): Pollution would be much less with the so-called transportation revolution.

Finally, the very government that had striven to become a world medical power came to promote "grandmother remedies" and the natural cures used by "our forefathers in their wars of independence" (*Granma International,* July 13, 1994, p. 5). It even called on doctors to grow their own herbal medicinal supplies. Islanders were left without such basic medicines as aspirins. While emphasizing a "greening" of medical care, Castro remained publicly committed to his ambitious Family Doctor program designed to provide a "doctor on every block." The program should continue, said he, even if we have to go back to using neighbor's rooms [and] . . . garages" *(Granma International,* July 13, 1994, p. 5).

The Reforms of 1994: Whither Socialism?

Production and fiscal problems reached such proportions that the government in 1994 announced a series of additional reforms that further stretched the meaning of socialism in Cuba. The reforms, like preceding Special Period measures, were not justified in the name of Marxist-Leninist and Guevarist principles or the continued construction of socialism. Instead, they were justified on the basis of leadership wisdom and concern for the common good. Castro exhorted his fellow Cubans to have "confidence in what the leadership of the Party and government do" and asked for the "highest level of understanding of the people" *(Granma International,* May 11, 1994, pp. 12–13).

A major problem the government faced was that money, at least the official currency, had lost nearly all meaning, and not, in the main, for the positive reasons Marx argued would lead to its irrelevance in communist society. Marx argued that money would lose meaning as society guaranteed the meeting of all human needs, but the peso had become nearly meaningless because there was little to buy with the money in circulation. By early 1994 excess liquidity amounted to roughly the equivalent of the value of the national product *(Granma International,* May 1, 1994, p. 3).

Castro claimed that the humane focus of the Special Period, which ensured everyone's well-being and left none abandoned, was the source of the liquidity problem *(Granma International,* May 11, 1994, pp. 12–13). True, islanders enjoyed a range of free social benefits that other Latin Americans and prerevolutionary Cubans either had to pay for or go without. The fact that Cubans received them free of charge contributed to but did not alone explain the liquidity problem. The liquidity problem also derived from the decline in the purchasing power of the peso with the dollarization of the economy and growing scarcities. Rationing failed to cover more than half of minimal family monthly needs, and scarcities drove prices up in the growing black market. A vicious cycle set in. As islanders could not cover their basic needs with the money they earned, they became ever more disinclined to work *(Granma International,* January 4, 1995, p. 4). Production thereby suffered, contributing to the paucity of goods and high black-market prices for the goods that were available.

To tackle the liquidity and fiscal problems the government announced price increases, charges for services previously provided for free, and new and increased taxes. These measures were designed to both reduce expenditures and increase state income. The Cuban government's fiscal problems had been rooted since 1989 in expenditures increasing at a faster rate than revenue. The spiraling of expenditures was partially traced to the politicization of allocations, along with the government's commitment to its "social project." To reduce its expenditures and increase its income the government introduced charges for vitamin tablets previously provided free of charge (since the 1992 optic neuritis epidemic). The government also raised prices of nonessentials, namely alcohol and tobacco; it hoped to recover 2.2 billion pesos annually from sales of cigars and cigarettes alone.[5] When announcing the alcohol and tobacco price hikes, a government functionary noted that low-income earners would not be hurt in that access to some supplies would remain on the ration system *(Granma International,* June 1, 1994, p. 4).

The government concomitantly raised charges for services and social programs—for example, electricity rates. Rates began to be pegged to usage; officials argued that this was a progressive tax measure, because the poor consumed the least electricity *(Granma International,* June 15, 1994, p. 3). Second, the government introduced entry charges for museums and sports events; Castro argued that people would thereby get used to the habit of paying for things *(Granma International,* May 11, 1994, p. 13). Third, the government began to charge for all meals at work centers and schools. There is no more free lunch in Cuba. Fourth, as of the 1994–1995 academic year, the government terminated student stipends and started charging all students for their uniforms.[6] Students needing financial assistance were to rely on loans, to be repaid, interestingly, not on a needs but a meritocratic basis. The higher a student's grades, the lower the loan-repayment rate (with top-grade scorers rewarded by a debt cancellation). Meanwhile, the government cut back university admissions: For example, only 2,500 students were admitted to study medicine in 1994, compared to 6,000 at one point *(Granma International,* July 13, 1994, p. 5). Castro continued to define the right to education, along with health care, as sacred achievements to be preserved at all costs, but he felt the state could no longer shoulder the costs of massively upgrading the educational levels of the children of the revolution. It was financially costly to invest in schooling, especially schooling for which there were no jobs, and it was politically risky to "overeducate" youth, to raise professional expectations that could not be met. Viewed from a comparative vantage point, Cuba could afford an educational retrenchment. The island's pupil/teacher and enrollment ratios were exceptionally high by Latin American standards (Eckstein 1994, p. 224).

The government's problems in absorbing schooling costs were exacerbated by declining educational productivity. Teachers (as well as nurses) increasingly absented themselves from work as their peso earnings became worthless. They abandoned their jobs for hard-currency-earning work in tourism, and they took early retirement to set up businesses. Desertion rates were so high that teacher shortages arose in key subjects.[7] Accordingly, the government faced difficulties delivering the educational services intended.

The government, meanwhile, talked of changing its employment policy. It had tried to end all but short-term unemployment compensation in 1991, both to reduce its fiscal expenditures when job opportunities first dramatically contracted and to direct unemployed workers to agriculture, one of the few sectors where the demand for labor picked up in the Special Period. The government understood that workers with a guaranteed income would be disinclined to take up manual work in the fields. It did not, however, enforce the announced unemployment policy, for political reasons. The political risks of firing unnecessary labor and insisting that they do detested farm work came to be seen as too great, as the potential numbers involved came to be massive. Under the circumstances the government chose to subsidize urban employment by keeping "excess labor" on the payroll, and to honor generous long-term compensation for people without work. Cuban economists estimated that one-third of the labor force was underemployed in 1993, and unemployment compensation the preceding year cost the state some 867.4 million pesos (more than double the compensation expenditures in 1989) (Alonso et al., 1994, Table 1).

In 1994, however, the government talked again of ending all but short-term compensation, and of pegging unemployment compensation (and social security) to the number of years people worked and their transferability to other jobs *(Granma International,* September 7, 1994, p. 2). There was mention of laying off one-tenth of the labor force (EIU 1995). Cubans polled by Gallup in 1994 indicated an interest in starting their own business (*Miami Herald,* December 18, 1994, p. 39A), which dovetailed with the state's interest in streamlining the official payroll. But islanders typically did not have the resources to go into business, and they continued to want the security that had come with official employment.

In announcing new layoffs Castro hinted that women workers would be affected more than men. In a 1995 speech he warned that "the danger is there that the will to be just with women will flag" (*Miami Herald,* March 9, 1995, p. 20A). Women had suffered more unemployment than men in years past (Eckstein 1994, p. 221), but the 1995 speech marks the first time that Castro publicly admitted that the official commitment to gender equality might wane.

In accordance with its campaign to reduce expenditures the government also announced plans to reduce enterprise subsidies and military outlays. It hoped to reduce subsidies to unprofitable enterprises by some 34 percent in 1994. But the government found it could not easily cut subsidies, for economic and not merely political reasons. If the government imported goods it could not produce efficiently and profitably, its hard-currency debt would mount *(Granma International,* August 17, 1994, p. 10). The hard-currency debt was more constraining than the domestic deficit.

The military cutbacks coincided with the transformation of the institution's historical mission from a nonproductive agency of national defense to a significant economic contributor. The transformed military became a key player immediately in the new agricultural-produce markets; it had become responsible for the production of nearly half the foodstuff in the Havana area.

Cutbacks also extended to investment financing—capital outlays designed specifically to stimulate much-needed production. In 1995 the government expected to invest 25.4 million pesos less than in 1994 *(Granma International,* January 4, 1995, p. 4), even though investment already had been severely slashed between 1959 and 1993. The fiscally strapped state placed its immediate investment future mainly in the hands of foreign capital.

To improve its fiscal base the government announced a major tax reform, aspects of which, if effectively implemented, would break dramatically with island tradition. Since 1967 few Cubans have paid direct taxes. Aware of the administrative difficulty of implementing tax collection, and of political opposition to taxes (as articulated at worker assemblies), the government projected that 77 percent of its 1995 income would come from increased prices, not taxes, and it postponed the implementation of the income tax.[8]

The fiscal reforms included taxes other than on income. The government planned to tax the exploitation of natural resources and luxury items, to charge transportation tolls, and to increase employer contributions to employee social-security coverage. It laid the groundwork for initiating worker contributions to the social-security fund as well. Prior to the Special Period social security expenditures had already exceeded respective revenues (Eckstein 1994, p. 229). The very social successes of the revolution had contributed to the social-security deficit: Cuba had the highest life expectancy and the most comprehensive social security system in Latin America.

For political as well as economic reasons the government relegalized private agricultural and then industrial-goods markets (which included on-site service repair work) in the fall of 1994. Officials understood that the markets might simultaneously address the liquidity, production, and fiscal crises, as well as a mounting moral crisis—and quickly. Politically, time was of the essence. Following the first large-scale riot under Castro, involving some 1,000 to 2,000 Havana residents, and then the attempted emigration of some 30,000 boat people, in the summer of 1994, the government recognized the need to address consumer grievances *(Cuba Business,* December 1994, p. 1). According to Raúl Castro, Cuba's main political, military, and ideological problem was food *(Cuba Business,* September 1994, p. 4). In June 1994 there were almost no vegetables in Havana's official markets.[9] For this reason the government released for immediate sale goods stored at warehouses for emergencies.

According to 1994 regulations, islanders could sell at the new markets any surplus they produced beyond their commitment to the state. Because vendors paid the government for market stands and tables, and their sales were taxed, the government hoped to stimulate production in a manner that brought money to its coffers. The first weekend of the new farmers' markets, functionaries took in about 700,000 pesos in sales tax alone, while charging 200 pesos for each stand and table *(Granma International,* October 12, 1994, p. 5 and December 14, 1994, p. 7). Because merchants could not sell produce the government intended for export and tourism, the state's hard-currency needs were not to be sacrificed for more profitable private domestic sales.

Reflecting official concern with the common citizen, the national leadership expressed displeasure with the high prices vendors charged. They recognized that the markets could not immediately be for everyone, but they claimed that the prices were lower than on the black market, and that prices would drop once production picked up. Ultimately they hoped the new markets would undermine the black market. The profitability of illegal sales had led farmers, middlemen, and distributors to siphon goods off from the official distribution system. Government efforts to regulate food distribution through law enforcement rather than reform were to no avail. The legally available food supply did not improve when the government placed armed guards on trucks and in the fields.

Theft had become so rampant that it undermined the government's moral authority. Indeed, to restore moral order the government announced a major campaign in 1994 to confiscate illegally obtained property. The campaign was announced at the same time as the politically unpopular tax and price reforms. Undoubtedly officials aimed thereby to convey a sense of justice while implementing hardships for ordinary folk.

Finally, the 1994 reforms included measures to regulate the dollarized economy, with the ultimate aim of instituting a fully convertible currency, in dramatic contrast to the heavy dependence on a nonconvertible currency for three decades. In this connection the government began to pay workers part of their income in a new peso, equivalent in purchasing power to the dollar.

Conclusion

Castro had relied on a mix of economic strategies prior to the collapse of Soviet aid and trade (Eckstein 1994, chaps. 2 and 3). What changed in the 1990s was the nature of the mix. Why the shift, and why did it occur while Castro remained publicly committed to socialism?

Castro came to deemphasize statist and collectivist strategies largely because in the context of the 1990s they no longer worked. The strategies depended on fiscal resources the government no longer commanded, and they created difficulties while leaving fundamental fiscal, production, and distribution problems unresolved. More than two-thirds of all state enterprises operated at a loss. They depended on inefficient, internationally uncompetitive Soviet technology, and they typically had bloated payrolls. Meanwhile, the state farms, combined with the urban labor mobilizations, drained fiscal resources while failing to avert a near-subsistence crisis. Average caloric intake dropped by some 30 percent between 1989 and 1993, while nutritional deficiencies arose, causing such new illnesses as optic neuritis.[10]

At the same time that the state sector was in crisis, foreign and domestic forces pushed for market reforms. With regard to the external sector, the government had little choice but to open up to market forces. All foreign trade came to be on a hard-currency basis; even former Soviet bloc countries and remaining communist countries insisted it be so. To develop an internationally competitive hard-currency sector the government had to turn to Western sources of capital and technology. To attract foreign capital the government absorbed investment costs, conceded ownership and managerial control, abandoned production for local consumption, and allowed foreign investors to appropriate revenue it desperately needed.

But the market reforms were driven by domestic pressures as well. Islanders did not rally for capitalism, but they covertly defied state rules and regulations in a manner that, more unintentionally than intentionally, served to usher in market features. The government extended new material incentives, including in hard currency (or hard-currency equivalent certificates), because established moral and material incentives no longer worked. The labor force lost interest in working for the earnings they had received until then. The new material incentives were designed to improve productivity under these circumstances.

At the same time islanders sabotaged state efforts to regulate distribution, in a manner that expanded market activity, albeit illegally. Scarcities drove up the black-market value of goods, inducing people to divert products from the official distribution system and to pilfer supplies from state enterprises and agencies for private dealings. Theft, corruption, and black marketing reached record levels, undermining official production and distribution. Crop theft became rampant, and an estimated 40 percent of the farm production sold to the state never reached official urban outlets (EIU 1991, p. 18; EIU 1994–1995, p. 20). Almost everyone participated in the black market, as buyer if not seller, and as the dollar became the de facto currency of choice, white-collar crime spread in the official hard-currency sector. The desire for dollars also led to the widespread return of prostitution.

In addition to undermining state production and distribution, the emergent informal and illegal market economy exacerbated the government's deficit and contributed to a "culture of illegality." To counter these tendencies the government initiated several market reforms. Law enforcement efforts had proved to be of no avail, despite periodic draconian crackdowns and a distribution of weapons to "peasant vigilance detachments." Repression had not worked because the underlying conditions that had generated the rule breaking remained intact. Under the circumstances the government opted to make legal what was transpiring illegally, in a manner that in principle would bring money to its coffers and reduce its expenses. Thus, when the government legalized the dollar as a domestic currency, islanders were to spend their hard currency in newly established state-run dollar stores; and when the government legalized self-employment and agricultural and artisan markets, vendors and other self-employed workers were to pay license fees and taxes. At the same time, the transformation of state farms into cooperatives and the release of state employees for independent work reduced fiscal expenditures.

The populace was not consistently, much less consciously, promarket and antistate. The effect of their involvement must be distinguished from their intent. When islanders turned to informal and illegal activity they typically were trying to make the best of a bad situation, and as moral and legal restraints broke down, the range of options they considered expanded. They were not calling for a capitalist transformation. Indicative of their selective support of market measures, they opposed government efforts to terminate guaranteed employment (and hefty unemployment compensation), and government efforts to impose an income tax.

Meanwhile, although the government publicly rationalized the precapitalist strategies it promoted in terms of internationally au courant environmental discourse, it did so to make virtue of necessity. The precapitalist strategies were promoted with survival needs in mind; unlike the market reforms, they were initiated neither in response to pressure from abroad or from civil society domestically.

Beneath the veneer of a strong, orthodox communist regime is a state much weaker and more flexible than conventionally conveyed. Global and domestic forces induced the government to reduce the role of socialist features and increase the role of market features. And beneath a veneer of formal political continuity, informal political power shifted. The importance of "reformers" grew, strengthened by ministerial shake-ups; each shake-up made the likelihood of additional market reforms the more probable. Nonetheless, the shift in strategy mix was not without its problems, given that policies often generated unintended consequences. As of mid-1995 it was too early to assess the full effect of the diverse Special Period strategies. Minimally, the sum effect of government strategies of the early 1990s was to transform socialism "as we know it."

The economy came to be based on a mix of statist/collectivist, capitalist, and precapitalist features. In the course of the 1990s the strategies most characteristic of a socialist economy waned in importance while market features, in particular, grew in importance, at the same time that the government remained publicly committed to socialism. But even as market features became of greater consequence, they were shaped by and adapted to preexisting institutions, including remaining features characteristic of a socialist economy. Paths from socialism hinge partly on the peculiarities of the political economy in which they are embedded. For historical reasons Cuba was not merely a mini-version of the Soviet Union.

The policy initiatives had some positive results. By the end of 1994 the money in circulation declined by about 16 percent *(Granma International,* December 21, 1994, p. 7), the budget deficit was reduced by some 72 percent, the black market peso/dollar exchange rate declined from about 120:1 in July to 25:1, food sales through legal channels improved, and the economy grew for the first time since the collapse of Soviet aid and trade (by .7 percent, with light industry increasing by some 13 percent).

However, the deficit was still equivalent to 10 percent of the national product, and life for the average Cuban had improved little. Moreover, the market reforms created as well as helped resolve problems. To attract foreign capital the government had to concede control over production and management, sacrifice revenue, and accept sectoral priorities not of its own choosing. On the domestic front the market reforms eroded the free cradle-to-grave welfare state and generated new inequality in the distribution of wealth. Policies that may appear economically rational for a government faced with global and domestic constraints are not necessarily politically tolerable.

Notes

1. EIU 1992–1993, p. 7; *Granma International,* May 5, 1993, 4. In the 1990s the armed forces became active in other economic sectors as well, for example in tourism (through Gaviota). For a discussion of the economic activities of the military prior to the Special Period, see Domínguez 1990.

2. The Cuban Communist Party published membership figures showing that there were over 706,000 card-carrying communists on the island in September 1994, up from about 597,000 in 1989. EIU 1995, p. 7.

3. In 1994 the sector still imported 70 percent of its needs.

4. As of 1993 about one-fourth of all enterprises were to be self-financing.

5. A tax on tobacco actually brought in 1.6 billion pesos in 1994. EIU 1995, p. 9.

6. For fiscal reasons supplies even of pencils, paper, and textbooks dwindled. Students had to share books or use them exclusively in libraries (*Granma Internacional,* October 5, 1994, p. 4).

7. *Cuba Business,* September 1994, p. 6. In Cienfuegos in 1993, for example, 9 percent of all teachers abandoned their jobs.

8. Through worker assemblies the government sought both to rally labor support for new legislation and to gauge opposition. Although workers had no way to guarantee that their grievances would be acted upon, through the assemblies they were able to make their sentiments known and on occasion convince the government to change its policy.

9. Crop output typically is low in the summer months, but the food available at official outlets in the summer of 1994 was exceptionally low.

10. In 1993 some 40,000 islanders lost their eyesight in conjunction with an epidemic of optic neuritis. The government quickly and effectively treated the illness and its cause, a vitamin B deficiency, through a mass distribution of vitamin pills free of charge.

◆ 9 ◆

The Cuban Economy in the Mid-1990s: Structural/Monetary Pathology and Public Policy

Archibald R. M. Ritter

◆

During the 1990s Cuba's economy became increasingly split between the traditional socialist economy based on the old peso, on the one hand, and the rapidly expanding, internationalized, dollar-oriented, and partially marketized economy, on the other. These two parts of the economy interacted so as to generate a number of pathological economic and social phenomena. It is necessary to reintegrate the economy if the harmful impacts of the split are to be reduced and ultimately eliminated. A reunification of the two components of the economy into a single mixed system is vital if economic recovery, adjustment, and transition are to occur.

Reintegration will require a battery of policy changes that will be economically, politically, and socially difficult in the short term. A number of the policies introduced in 1993 and 1994 appeared to be promising first steps in a process of reform, which offered hope of both healing the bifurcation and its negative consequences and launching Cuba on a path toward economic recovery and adjustment to the changed international realities. "Quick-fix" approaches to reintegration such as the forced replacement of the U.S. dollar by the "convertible peso"—as was being considered in the latter part of 1995—would likely generate more problems than would be solved, however.

This chapter explores the characteristics and consequences of Cuba's bifurcated economy and the impact on it of the policy reforms introduced by mid-1995. It goes on to identify and suggest policy initiatives that address this structural and monetary pathology so as to heal the split and reintegrate the economy more effectively.

The Structural and Monetary Pathology of the Cuban Economy

In the early 1990s the predominant characteristic of Cuba's economic structure was its bifurcation between the traditional socialist, peso-based

Table 9.1 Cuba's Bifurcated Economic Structure Circa 1995

	Traditional Socialist, Peso-Based Economy	Transitional Market Economy	Internationalized Dollar Economy
Institutions and Sectors	State-owned, centrally planned state agriculture; all industry; some services	Marketized parts of agriculture, industry, services, self-employment; underground economy, UBPCs	Sociedades anónimas; joint ventures; tourism; auxiliary services; remittances
Resource Allocation	Central planning remnants; sociolismo; improvisation	Market determined; price mechanism	Market oriented plus complex relations with socialist economy (e.g., dollar stores, restaurants)
Functioning			
Market structure	State monopolistic	Competitive markets	Some monopolistic, some competitive
Pricing	Complete price controls	Competitive market pricing	Major state controls
Ease of entry	State regulated	Low barriers to entry	High barriers to entry
Input procurement	Planned plus improvisation	Market determined	Market oriented
Labor remuneration	Wage and salary scale (convertible peso complication)	Market determined	Market oriented and state controls
Public Policy			
Exchange rate	1 old peso = U.S.$1.35 (or $1)	40 or 50 old pesos = U.S.$1 (market determined)	1 old peso = U.S.$1.35 (or $1)
Monetary system	Old peso: rapid emission, convertible peso complication	Old pesos and U.S. dollars at market determined rate	U.S. dollar predominates (plus convertible peso)
Taxation/subsidization	Major but declining subsidies	Improvised tax measures; no subsidies	Major hard-currency tax source; hidden subsidies (exchange rate)
Protectionism	Bureaucratic discretionary NTBs: from infinite to zero	Infinite NTBs (no rights to import)	Bureaucratic discretionary NTBs; Sociedades anónimas, easy NTBs at official exchange rate

economy and the internationalized, dollar-based economy (see Table 9.1). The former was in a state of depression and organizational decay or perhaps collapse. The internationalized, dollar-based part of the economy was expanding rapidly despite the recession. This expansion consisted of two elements: an increase in dollar-oriented activities (tourism, foreign businesses in joint ventures, various auxiliary goods and services, and dollar remittances from abroad), and the development of intermediate or transitional forms of market-oriented and quasi-market-oriented economic activity (including self-employment, both official and in the underground economy, and the economic activities operating through markets).

Characteristics

The traditional socialist, peso-based economy encompassed, in mid-1995, almost all industry, with the exception of self-employed artisanal and industrial workers and some export-oriented joint ventures. Services were largely in this sector, including all of finance, most business services, some personal services (except those provided through self-employment), most wholesaling and retailing (except for the agricultural, industrial, and artisanal markets), most transportation, and all communications. The role of the traditional socialist economy in agriculture was modified considerably in 1993, with the conversion of state farms into cooperatives *(*Unidades Básicas de Producción Cooperativa*,* or UBPCs). As a result, the state sector's share of total agricultural land fell from 75 percent to 34 percent and its share of cultivated land fell from 80 percent to 25 percent. The role of the state as the provider of inputs and auxiliary services and purchaser of output quotas at controlled prices is still significant, however; but it is not yet completely clear how authentically cooperative and autonomous the UBPCs will turn out to be.

Within the traditional socialist sector, resource allocation was undertaken prior to 1990 through the central planning system. The volume, mix, and destination of enterprise outputs, the mix and origin of enterprise inputs, the pattern of investment within and among sectors and industries, and the nature of the external interlinkages of the enterprises were all ostensibly determined by central planning. The impossibility of planning all this resulted in much improvisation and a heavy reliance on *sociolismo,* that is, the resolution of economic problems by the exchange of favors through circuits of friends. The official system deteriorated with the problems of the 1990s, to be replaced by improvisation and intensified sociolismo.

The allocation of consumer goods in this part of the economy occurs through the rationing system for some basic foodstuffs and household necessities (with decreasing quantities from 1990 to 1994). The prices of virtually all consumer goods provided through the rationing system were fixed at, or close to, their levels of 1960–1962. Labor has been allocated to sectors, industries, and specific activities not through decentralized market processes but through central determination, with some individual choice of careers and economic areas, and with the state guaranteeing first-time job seekers employment in the areas of their educational formation. In this sector, labor-force remuneration is confined to a relatively narrow wage and salary scale (from about 80 to 480 pesos per month), supplemented by the politically allocated items, at very low prices, and more recently with some hard-currency (and after December 1994, convertible peso) payments to workers in specific important sectors (electrical generation, oil production, some fishing, the ports).

The internationalized, dollar-based part of the Cuban economy consists of tourism and auxiliary services, foreign business operating with Cuban partners in joint ventures, and some of the large mixed enterprises (state-owned but financially and managerially autonomous conglomerate enterprises operating in the internationalized dollar-oriented economy and behaving much like private enterprises). The remittance economy, wherein workers receive dollars and spend them in the domestic market economy or the "dollar stores," would be included here. The domestic market economy—registered and unregistered self-employment, and the agricultural, artisanal, and industrial markets—are also part of this economy. The areas of the internationalized and domestic market economies would include the private sector of agriculture, which accounted for 14 percent of total agricultural land and a larger share of agricultural value added. The large role of the UBPCs in agriculture has already been noted, but the evolution of the UBPCs is still unclear, and they might be considered to be in an early transitional state. Some personal services are provided through the market mechanism and at prices determined by market forces. There appear to be no estimates yet available for the new and rapidly changing structure of employment or value added according to public or private sector, or marketized or nonmarketized activities. In this part of the economy, resource allocation occurs at least or partly through the market mechanism.

For the self-employed, and for exchanges in the agricultural and industrial markets, prices are determined by the forces of supply and demand within what often must be highly competitive markets with considerable ease of entry. The agricultural and industrial market transactions are by law supposed to be only in pesos, but money changers convert dollars to pesos conveniently and at the prevailing unofficial exchange rate. Transactions with those who are self-employed can occur in dollars or pesos, again at the unofficial exchange rate. The whole tourist sector as well as the foreign-business sector uses the U.S. dollar. The dollar stores include a number of chains of stores importing foodstuffs, clothing, footwear, appliances, consumer electronics and other durables and even candy, soft drinks, and alcoholic beverages, as well as restaurants for foreigners and Cubans alike. They are designed to "mop up" some of the dollars (and convertible pesos) in circulation, with a substantial tax-equivalent profit received by the state.

Remuneration and earnings in this part of the economy are determined largely by market forces. For those who are self-employed legally or illegally, incomes are determined by the relative demand for goods or services offered vis-à-vis the nature of competition and production costs on the supply side. For those in the tourist sector or providing auxiliary services, tips constitute the major remuneration and are paid in foreign currency. In the foreign-business sector, foreign factors of production must be paid in foreign currency; otherwise there would be no incentive to operate in Cuba. Cuban employees of foreign business are supposed to be paid in pesos; dollar supplements are illegal but hard to prevent totally when enterprises find that maintaining labor-force commitment requires such supplementation. Dollar remittances are, of course, not remuneration for services but gifts of relatives abroad.

Causal Factors

The bifurcation of the Cuban economy into the socialist, peso-based and internationalized, dollar-based components is the result of economic policies and the institutional structure of the economy, together with the economic *apertura*. With controlled low prices in the state sector for rationed goods and services, payments to people have exceeded the value of goods and services available for purchase. It was possible for the volume of peso payments to exceed the value of goods and services available in the socialist economy, because controls prevented any increase in prices and the government was willing to cover the operating deficits of state enterprises with grants that were financed by the printing of money or the creation of unredeemed and unredeemable credits. The creation of money, namely old pesos, for this purpose then generated the inflationary dynamics described earlier. The excess in remunerative payments over the value of rationed goods and services available increased from 1989 to 1994 as the volume of output shrank. This excess volume of money earnings then fed into the black market, putting upward pressure on the prices of goods and services in that part of the economy. As inflation continued and accelerated, reflecting the growing excess of money earnings over the value of goods and services available in the socialist economy, it increasingly devalued the peso with respect to the dollar. With worsening inflation, Cubans were losing faith in the peso as a currency and turning to the dollar for the performance of monetary functions.

The value of the U.S. dollar reached a high of 120 pesos in the unofficial market by summer 1994. This peso devaluation was the result of (1) the high demand for dollars by the *balseros* (rafters), who were trying to convert their assets to dollars for transfer out of the country, or for the purchase of rafts, (2) extreme shortages of items that could be legally purchased for pesos at the time, and (3) a growing air of pessimism, a loss of confidence, and desperation on the part of many Cubans with respect to the prospects for the economy. The unofficial exchange rate then declined, especially after the opening of the agricultural markets on October 1, 1994, which increased the demand for pesos and led to declines in the prices of foods vis-à-vis their earlier black-market levels. The rate fell as low as 30–35 pesos to the dollar by April 1995. After a variously explained decline in the value of the dollar—ultimately to about 7 old pesos briefly in July and August 1995—the rate appeared to be settling at around 25–30 pesos to the dollar in September 1995.

Exchange-rate policy and protectionism also play an important role in the generation of this bifurcation. The socialist, peso-based economy faces an exchange rate of 0.74 pesos to $1, a rate that makes imports of all sorts exceedingly cheap and would result in an impossibly huge demand for imports. Such an excess demand for imports is then limited by bureaucratic controls or nontariff barriers (NTBs), which can provide infinite protection. (These also permit other imports—medicines and foodstuffs, for example—at the official exchange rate so that their cost to Cuban consumers is maintained at a low peso purchase price.) Some imported products permitted to enter the country at a zero tariff have constituted a major subsidy for the enterprises receiving the rights to import at the official rate. With respect to exports from the traditional socialist economy, because the foreign-exchange earnings from exports are converted to pesos at the official rate, such enterprises have little incentive to expand and diversify exports.

Finally, the expansion of tourism and the growing presence of foreign business in the 1990s have contributed to the expansion of the internationalized, dollar-oriented economy. From 1990 to 1994, the number of tourists increased from about 340,000 to 619,000 (ONE 1995). Gross income from tourism increased from 1989 to upwards of $800 million, although the value added within Cuba was only about 30 percent of gross income by 1994. Likewise there were growing numbers of foreign businesses establishing branches or entering joint ventures with Cuban state enterprises.

Consequences of the Pathology

Income Distribution and the General Structure of Incentives

In the traditional socialist economy and at the unofficial exchange rate, the official wage and salary structure ranges from about $2.30 to $14 per month. Those who are able to earn or receive dollars can enjoy substantially higher real incomes. For example, tips for a bartender or elevator operator in the tourist sector might average $30 per month, and an engineer who drives a car as an unregistered taxi might earn $50 to $150 per month (or much more).

Those who are self-employed or who sell their goods or services through markets also usually receive higher incomes, because the prices at which their sales occur are market determined in the context of the excess money incomes most Cubans have after spending their peso incomes on the rationed commodities. However, these prices and hence the incomes of the self-employed are constrained by the relative freedom of entry into the registered (or unregistered) activities, with the large numbers of the self-employed forcing prices and incomes downward. Low barriers to entry, plus the increase in the number of potential entrants to this microenterprise sector (due to the present and prospective downsizing of state enterprises, public services, and some of the professions), should push prices and incomes to relatively lower levels in the future.

The dollar-oriented economy generates income levels that are usually high in comparison with the incomes generated in the traditional socialist economy. People's incomes in old pesos permit the purchase of rationed foodstuffs, but the rations available per month usually lasted only seven to fourteen days by 1994, leaving serious family food shortages. Incomes in old pesos typically also permit the purchase of other rationed goods, such as household and personal-hygiene products and some items of clothing per year. But for the purchase of foodstuffs from the agricultural markets (or prior to October 1, 1994, from the black market) and from the industrial and artisanal markets, large amounts of pesos are required because these prices are market determined. Dollars or convertible pesos are required for purchases of foodstuffs, personal-hygiene products, clothing, footwear, and consumer durables from the dollar stores.

The implications of this pattern of income distribution on the general structure of incentives that shape people's activities in their material lives are obvious: Cubans chase dollars. In practical terms, this means that professionals who speak English or another tourism-oriented language leave their jobs in the socialist sector to work in tourism. In general, people with jobs in the traditional socialist economy are under great pressure to earn or acquire dollars through self-employment or part-time provision of services or foreign travel (earning hard-currency per diems). From the standpoint of society, the incentive to perform those functions that are often of great value (in education, health care, agriculture, and industry, for example) are poorly rewarded, while other activities, some of which may be less important for society (such as selling cigars on the street), are highly rewarded. The irony of the situation is that those who have been among the strongest supporters and beneficiaries of the revolution in the traditional socialist economy (soldiers, workers, teachers, and health-care professionals) have been suffering material deprivation. On the other hand, Cubans who have maintained good relationships with family members abroad, small-scale entrepreneurs, and hustlers of various sorts receive or earn substantially higher incomes in dollars or through better rewarded self-employment.

Implications for Resource Allocation

The high incomes and resulting incentives for people to shift their energies to the dollar-oriented economy and out of the traditional socialist economy is ultimately a market-driven phenomenon. In some ways it is a natural response to the increased importance of foreign exchange and imports following the loss of some 70–75 percent of Cuba's capacity to import. Shifting resources toward the foreign-exchange-earning sector—tourism in this case—is a necessary part of the process of Cuba's structural adjustment.

In the internationalized sector the large, dollar-oriented conglomerates, or *sociedades anónimas* (SAs), also operate under the official exchange rates, and they are empowered to import commodities at zero tariff. These commodities are then sold to tourists, Cubans with dollars, and foreign businesspeople with a substantial price markup. So far the import bias of these conglomerates has been countered by various rules and directives designed to redirect their purchasing toward domestic sources. In contrast, the microenterprises have no right to import inputs at one of the official exchange rates, because they have not been in priority areas of the economy, nor have they yet organized themselves into lobby groups that could petition the government for access to some imports at the official rates. Indeed, the microenterprise sector does not even have the right to obtain imports directly from abroad at the black-market exchange rate—although inputs previously imported do make it through to this sector indirectly. Thus, Cuba is in the paradoxical situation of having a highly variable and discriminatory system of effective protection and subsidization of imports through bureaucratic NTBs and extreme exchange-rate overvaluation. The traditional socialist economy faces extreme variation in NTBs, plus the overvaluation; the transitional market economy faces virtually infinite NTBs; and the SAs often enjoy free importation of many goods at the very favorable official exchange rate.

Unfortunately, some of the key foreign-exchange-earning sectors, such as sugar, citrus fruit, and coffee, are in the traditional socialist economy, so that their revenues are in pesos at the official commercial rate. These sectors do not receive the hard currencies they earn for the country, nor the large resource infusions that characterize tourism, for example. Instead, their low remuneration in real terms results in shortages of inputs of all kinds (especially imported inputs) and accelerates the deterioration of the capital stock as well as the loss of human resources. This discrimination against most foreign-exchange-earning sectors must be one of the more destructive irrationalities in the functioning of the Cuban economy during the mid-1990s.

Although there is an underlying economic logic to the reallocation of resources to the internationalized and domestic market economy, there are also pervasive microirrationalities that add up to a giant economic dysfunctionality. Because of the controlled and very low prices in the socialist economy, a variety of goods and services can be purchased at the controlled prices and resold at higher, market-determined prices. Commodities in the socialist economy also leak out by theft or graft of various sorts and are resold at the high market-determined prices. Virtually any foodstuff acquired at the official price can be resold at a major profit. Any item imported at the official commercial exchange rate can be also resold at a higher black-market rate. The result of the myriad profit-making opportunities arising from price controls and imports at the official exchange rate is a massive volume of "rent seeking." It is highly remunerative for people to devote their creative economic energies to buying and selling between the two economies.

The second type of irrationality concerns the high cost in real terms that Cuba as a society pays to reallocate human resources to the internationalized economy. Although this reallocation needs to occur in current circumstances and cannot be without cost, those costs seem excessive under the dual-currency economy of the mid-1990s. For example, is it really appropriate to remunerate doctors, nurses, and factory workers in old pesos and within the old wage and salary structure while unskilled workers in tourism receive much higher real incomes through their tips? One hesitates to make value judgments of this sort, but it does appear that Cuban society devotes a large volume of real resources to motivate and remunerate such individuals in the dollar-oriented economy, while those in the fixed-price, peso-oriented economy are rewarded meagerly.

Social Consequences

As discussed in depth in Chapter 10, the structural pathology together with the contraction of the Cuban economy has produced a number of negative social consequences, including impacts on income distribution, work habits, and rent seeking. It has also led to the reemergence of social ills that had been virtually eliminated in the early 1960s such as begging, hustling, and prostitution or quasi-prostitution. The bifurcation of the economy and the economic contraction are also making it difficult to maintain a good-quality one-tier educational and health-care system. The public health system has deteriorated due to lack of imported inputs, and high absenteeism on the part of hospital staff. Medicines are also scarce in the peso economy. As a result, people with access to dollars find it necessary to purchase medicines in the dollar stores or when traveling abroad, and supplement the meals, supplies, and medical items available in the hospitals. In education there seems to have been a deterioration in quality as teachers have reduced their time and attention devoted to teaching in order to acquire dollars or income supplements in old pesos. In consequence, some parents increasingly pay for extracurricular instruction for their children as well as teaching them themselves. Finally, judging by anecdotal evidence, crime appears to have increased significantly.

Reintegrating the Economy

The intensifying economic pathology seems to have become clearer to the government only after the decriminalization of the use of the dollar in the summer of 1993. It is interesting that some of the main analyses of the Cuban economy before 1994 did not refer to or analyze this phenomenon (Carranza Valdes 1993; Lage 1993, for example). Although the economy contracted seriously from 1989 to mid-1993 (perhaps by 45 percent in per capita terms; see Table 9.2), there appears to have been almost a paralysis in public policymaking; no significant reformist policies were introduced. The Food Program of December 1990 was essentially an old-style campaign involving heavier planning for resource reallocation to agriculture. Its results were minimal, partly because the national economic contraction prevented the large infusion of imports and resources the program required. The government then placed its hopes for an economic turnaround on (1) an expansion of tourism (which occurred to some extent, but with an approximate 70 percent leakage of foreign-exchange earnings to the exterior); (2) the expansion of foreign-exchange earnings from biotechnological exports (which fell far short of expectations); (3) an expansion of exports into new markets (which was insufficient to counter the loss of old markets); and (4) an expansion of foreign investment (which also fell short of expectations). These did not arrest the downward spiral of the economy.

As the contraction continued, citizens were improvising their own survival strategies outside the formal planning system and the traditional socialist economy. The reform measures introduced from mid-1993 to mid-1995 usually legitimized the economic activities that Cubans themselves had undertaken. The reforms were essentially official responses to the grassroots behavior and pressures of Cuban citizens in a situation in which there appeared to be no other public-policy options that were reasonable, credible, or viable. The reform measures have strengthened the internationalized part of the economy and have permitted the emergence of what might be considered the third component of the economic structure, namely the domestically oriented and rapidly growing peso/dollar market economy.

Table 9.2 Main Economic Indicators in Cuba, 1985–1995

	1985	1986	1987	1988	1989	1990	1991	1992	1993	1994	1995
Estimated GDP ($ billion)	32.3	32.6	31.4	32.2	32.5	31.5	23.6	20.3	18.3	18.4[e]	
Estimated GDP per capita ($)	3,181	3,182	3,032	3,076	3,076	2,971	2,226	1,897	1,679	1,64[e]	
Change in GDP per capita (%)	+3.5	0	–4.7	+1.5	0	–3.4	–25.1	–14.8	–11.5	–2.3[e]	
GDP per capita, index (UN ECLAC)	100.0	99.7	95.4	96.5	96.4	92.5	68.7	58.6	52.4	51.8[e]	
Total exports ($ billion)	5.99	5.32	5.40	5.52	5.4	4.9	3.6	2.2	1.7	1.8[e]	
Total imports ($ billion)	8.04	7.60	6.58	6.58	8.1	6.7	3.7	2.5	2.2	2.3[e]	
External debt											
Hard currency ($ billion)	3.9	6.0	5.7	6.5	6.2	7.0	8.4	10.0	10.8		
Budget deficit (pesos, billion)	.3	.2	.6	1.1	1.4	2	3.7	4.2	5.1	1.4[e]	
Percent of estimated GDP	0.9	0.6	1.9	3.4	4.3	6.3	15.7	20.7	27.9	7.6	
Sugar harvest (millions MTs)	7.9	7.5	7.2	8.1	7.6	8.4	7.2	7.0	4.3	4.0	3.5[e]
Petroleum imports (millions MTs)	13.5	13.2	13.5	13.4	13.3	11.6	9.2	6.2	5.7		
Petroleum production (millions MTs)	.9	.9	.9	.7	.7	.7	.5	.9	1.1	1.3	1.4[e]
Total petroleum (millions MTs)	14.4	14.1	14.4	14.1	14.0	12.3	9.7	7.1	6.8		
Exchange rates											
Official tourist rate (pesos/$1)			1	1	1	1	1	1	1	1	1
Official commercial rate (pesos/$1)			.74	.74	.74	.74	.74	.74	.74	.74	1.0 (7)
Unofficial rate (pesos/$1)					5	7 (9)	20 (12)	35 (7)	55 (6)	100 (11)	35 (10)

Sources: CONAS 1994; Cómite Estatal de Estadisticas 1988; Terrero 1994; Centro de Estudios sobre la Economia Cubana. 1995; UN CEPAL 1995.
Note: "E" indicates estimates; numbers in parentheses indicate months.

The August 1993 decriminalization of the holding and use of the U.S. dollar again gave official recognition and legitimacy to what many Cubans were already doing. It also increased the use of the dollar in normal day-to-day transactions by removing the fear of prosecution. The consequent increase in the demand for dollars probably contributed to its initial rapid appreciation from mid-1993 to mid-1994, when it was as high as 120 pesos per dollar. Meanwhile, the subsequent liberalization of microenterprise self-employment meant that by late 1994 some 170,000 persons had registered as self-employed, with over 48,000 in Havana alone (*Granma*, February 14, 1995, p. 3). The expansion of this sector provided a growing outlet for the excess money incomes.

Of particular significance for the expansion of the market mechanism was the reestablishment of agricultural markets in October 1994. A related law of October 7, 1994, liberalized transportation by making it possible for any owner of transport facilities such as trucks to contract directly with farms to move foodstuffs to market (Ministerio de Transporte 1994). The markets increased food availability in urban areas, and reduced food prices to well below the black-market levels. The laws also provide incentives for farms to expand their production in coming crop years so that supplies should increase and prices fall further. The subsequent legalization of industrial and artisanal markets on December 1, 1994, had a less dramatic impact than the agricultural markets but has nevertheless included a considerable variety of fabricated products such as kerosene stoves, aluminum kitchen gadgetry, shoes, and clothing aimed at the domestic market. Craftspeople and artists produced a rapidly expanding variety of items for the tourist market and increasingly for the domestic market as well.

The legalization of self-employment, and the establishment of agricultural, transport, industrial, and artisanal markets has increased the role of the price mechanism and the scope of the market economy. This marketized component of the Cuban economy constitutes, to some degree, a fusion of the internationalized, dollar-oriented and the traditional socialist parts of the economy, and is undoubtedly a central part of Cuba's prospective economic system.

Public Policy: Complacency or Deliberativeness?

Despite the series of promising reforms introduced from mid-1993 to December 1994, the reform momentum appears to have slowed in 1995. Notwithstanding the high expectations and a considerable amount of optimism on the part of many citizens and observers, the measures introduced before October 1995 were rather modest in view of the dimension of the reform tasks facing Cuba. For example, the legalization and step-by-step liberalization of self-employment and the establishment of markets are still blocked by a number of restrictive provisions in the legislation. The limitation on the size of enterprises—officially self-employment, in practice sometimes family enterprises—is particularly restrictive. Many types of economic activity need to be larger if they are to operate effectively and efficiently. Second, the legalized range of self-employment is limited to activities that are mainly "low-tech" in character and excludes a broad variety of high-technology enterprises. Business-service enterprises in particular—technical consultants, management consultants, computer firms, accountants, law offices, marketing firms, surveying firms, office services, architects, geological exploration, etc.—all can provide important inputs to public- and private-sector firms in a cost-effective manner. These need to be legalized if Cuba is to develop a sophisticated modern economy. The legislation for microenterprises also prohibits private retailing, which dooms the sector to continued low-level operation because each producer must also be the retailer. Stores that would bring together a range of products and product varieties are effectively blocked. It would also be beneficial if property legislation were to be modified to permit retailers and producers to reestablish stores and specialized shopping areas. A liberalization of locational and rental arrangements for such enterprises would be useful for improving the quality of many services to the public.

The removal of a number of restrictions on the development of this sector would generate employment, improve the material quality of life for Cuban citizens, and stimulate productivity gains in large-scale public or private enterprises through the provision of business services. Lifting the limitations on the development of this sector would also permit an acceleration of entrepreneurial learning in the area of small-enterprise management. That learning process has been blocked since the 1960s and will be of vital importance when Cuba normalizes its relationship with the United States (and experiences a major inflow of Cuban American financial, technological, managerial, and entrepreneurial expertise). Finally, easing the restrictions on microenterprise development is also vital as a means of increasing the demand for pesos and the supply of goods and services available for the public. This would put downward pressure on market-determined price levels and on the black-market exchange rate for the dollar. In late 1995 there was talk of a further liberalization of microenterprise such that up to five employees could be hired. This would be an important change that would remove the current limitation of microenterprise size to one person (plus family labor).

Another significant recent policy change was the introduction of the convertible peso in December 1994 as part of a general strategy to replace the old peso. (The well-printed convertible peso does not state what it is convertible into nor at what exchange rate.) There is no hope that the new peso can absorb the old peso system and also maintain parity with the dollar—unless it incorporates a substantial devaluation of the old peso. Up to late 1995, the Central Bank has been able to maintain convertibility of the new peso with the dollar because of the low volume of emission. It will be difficult to restrain the volume emitted to a level that can maintain convertibility with the dollar. The resources acquired at no cost by the government through seigniorage are too attractive to turn off. The volume of new convertible pesos emitted will shortly—probably before the end of 1996—prove to be too high to permit their full and immediate redemption for real goods and services in the dollar stores, and a tier of convertible-peso stores will become necessary. When this happens, the psychological acceptance of the convertible peso as being as good as the dollar will cease, people will be unwilling to hold that currency for store-of-value purposes, and the convertible peso will devalue vis-à-vis the dollar.

A related monetary initiative that seemed to be "in the wind" in late 1995 was the demonetization of the U.S. dollar by requiring that all payments in import stores, tourist establishments, and the domestic economy be conducted exclusively in domestic currencies (old pesos and new, convertible pesos). The convertible peso would fully replace the dollar for legal transactions in the domestic economy. Cubans would likely be permitted to exchange their pesos (up to a possible maximum) but tourists, foreign businesspeople, and Cubans earning foreign exchange would likely have to exchange their hard currencies to domestic currency on entering the country. The primary objective of such legislation would probably be to complete the capture by the state of seigniorage (the first use of the resources that can be acquired by the authority empowered to create currency or new credit), and to reestablish control of the domestic money supply.

The risk of the forced movement out of the dollar and into the new peso would be quite high if complete and unquestioned convertibility of the new peso with the dollar could not be maintained. Maintaining such convertibility would indeed be impossible if the devaluation were insufficient to choke off the demand for imports, or if the government were unable to restrict rigorously the emission of the new pesos. If the new peso were to lose credibility and complete convertibility, then its value vis-à-vis the dollar on unofficial markets would decline. When this occurred there would be substantial profits to be made by exchanging dollars for new pesos at the better black-market rate and then using the new pesos in the import stores or tourist establishments. As this type of behavior expanded, the government would have to either liberalize the system again completely (by remonetizing the dollar) or install a complex system of controls on all exchanges of dollars by tourists, businesspeople, etc., similar to that of 1960s. This type of system would quickly kill off a significant proportion of tourism and reduce the interest of foreign businesses in the country. It would also further complicate the functioning of the economy with complex regulations and controls—which Cuba should be trying to ease rather than to intensify. A quick but artificial fix for Cuba's currency muddle could in fact lead to consequences more damaging to the economy than the original problem itself.

The new foreign-investment law approved September 5, 1995, legalizes 100 percent foreign ownership (though only on a case-by-case basis) in all sectors of the economy except defense, national security (undefined), health care, and education. After much debate, the National Assembly of Popular Power approved a provision that permits former Cuban citizens living abroad to invest in Cuba (Asamblea Nacional del Poder Popular 1995). Cubans within Cuba, however, are not permitted to invest in their country except within their "own-account" microenterprises and through the actions of state enterprises. It remains to be seen whether the new law will be able to outweigh the political and property-rights uncertainties that still limit much foreign investment and lead to a major surge of capital inflows. One might conclude, tentatively, that in the longer term this law may be of great significance, but in the near future it is unlikely to induce large increases in direct foreign investment.

Why the reform process has slipped into low gear is not completely clear. The official view is that the process is proceeding with deliberation in order to maintain equity, avoid the instabilities displayed by the countries of Eastern Europe in their reform processes, and maintain control of a process that could easily get out of control. Another interpretation is that those who champion reform in the government must face those who are not enthusiastic reformists, and must fight difficult political battles in order to move the process along. Moreover, it is likely that the first imperative of the revolution, as often reaffirmed by President Castro (*Granma,* July 13, 1995), remains the "construction of socialism" rather than further transition toward some sort of mixed economy. One may therefore question the depth of the commitment of the government to incorporate a significantly larger role for the market mechanism in the structure of the economy. In this interpretation, the market-oriented reforms that have been implemented so far are those considered necessary to make possible the continuation of as much of the status quo as possible.

An important factor that appears to have reduced the urgency of the reform process is the perception in Cuba that the economic contraction has ceased and that a recovery has begun. The measures enacted in 1994 by the Ministry of Finance to reduce the deficit have been effective. By cutting the deficit from about 5.1 billion pesos in 1993 (or perhaps 28 percent of estimated GDP) to an estimated 1.4 billion pesos in 1994 (or about 7–8 percent of GDP), the volume of new money pouring into the economy to finance the deficit was reduced significantly (Casals 1995).

The ostensible increase in GDP of 0.7 percent in 1994 and of 2.5 percent in 1995 seems to have created a sentiment that all is going well and that the process of reform can proceed deliberately and carefully. In his speech of July 26, 1995 (*Prensa Latina,* July 26, 1995), for example, Castro reported on this growth performance but made little mention of major economic change that might be necessary. Indeed, Castro referred to the economic changes introduced so far as operating to perfect the reforms in order to perfect socialism. It seems that in late 1995 a feeling of satisfaction with the recent evolution of the economy has promoted the conclusion that an ambitious and accelerating process of reform is not urgent or necessary at this time.

A cautious approach to policy in late 1995 and onward hardly seems appropriate, however. The economic contraction may not be over, and the alleged recovery may be a statistical mirage. If the estimates of economic growth in recent years took into consideration the rapid deterioration of the capital stock—if the measure employed were net domestic product instead of gross domestic product—the recorded growth would very likely be negative. The capital stock has depreciated rapidly as a result of the lack of imported inputs, replacement parts, and new equipment, which in turn has led to accelerated rundowns and cannibalization of the machinery, equipment, and physical plant. Moreover, low levels of capacity utilization—from 20 percent to 25 percent—also contribute to accelerated deterioration of machinery and equipment (Guzman Pascual 1995). The urgency of policy reform has not abated.

The Dimensions of Prospective Reform

A variety of public-policy initiatives and institutional changes will ultimately be required for the unification of the two parts of the economy and the healing of Cuba's central economic pathology. So far, some useful reform measures have been introduced, but a number of other measures will also be necessary. These measures are also relevant for the process of structural adjustment, transformation, and recovery. A few such changes will play an important part in the reunification of the socialist, peso-based and the internationalized, dollar-based parts of the economy. The more important changes of this sort, besides enterprise liberalization, will perhaps be privatization and cooperativization, and the redesign of the sociedades anónimas. Other institutional changes, such as reform of the financial and banking system, the establishment of a regulatory framework for the functioning of an expanding private sector, and the rewriting of property legislation, are important for an economic transition, but perhaps less central to the issue of the unification of the economy.

A particularly important policy change would be a further liberalization of small-scale enterprise. A removal of the prohibition of professionals working in high-tech activities requiring their expertise, an increase in the maximum size of such enterprises to five, ten or fifteen employees, an expansion of the permissible range of activities, allowing the establishment of retail enterprises rather than requiring fabricators to sell their own products, and a legalization of specialized retailing in permanent stores would all be useful initiatives.

An institutional reform that has considerable potential but that would have to be managed carefully would be a process of privatization or cooperativization of state-owned assets. This has already been undertaken with a large proportion of state farms and their conversion to cooperatives. There are many state-sector service facilities that operate on a small scale and already face effective competition from an expanding self-employment sector. Included here would be state retail shops of various kinds, repair shops, personal services such as beauty shops and barber shops, small bars, and coffee shops. Privatization of such facilities by sale to Cuban citizens would make sense in terms of the quality of the services that would be provided. Privatization would also permit the state to acquire significant amounts of old pesos, thereby reducing their supply and driving up their value vis-à-vis the dollar. The revenues acquired by the state would then engender reductions in fiscal deficits and monetary emission.

Privatization of medium- and large-scale enterprises is more contentious and more difficult. The Cuban government is already permitting partial privatizations to foreigners through the establishment of minority foreign ownership of joint ventures, often but not always for new investment projects. Privatization of existing assets to foreigners, even through joint ventures, has its drawbacks, namely the disposal at fire-sale prices of valuable assets, and the stream of profits that will be expatriated by the foreign owners into the future. Privatization to Cuban citizens may be advantageous, but Cuban citizens could not pay dollars for such assets. Other formulas such as cooperativization of some larger assets to Cuban citizens would be worth exploring. Privatization or partial privatization of natural monopolies (such as the sale of 49 percent of the telephone system to the Mexican firm, Domus) are even more difficult and require the creation of new public regulatory institutions to constrain their possible abuse of monopoly power.

The macroeconomic policies introduced to deal with the current situation include the fiscal policy outlined earlier and the introduction of the convertible peso. On the basis of the information available so far, it appears that fiscal policy has been quite successful. What might constitute a battery of macroeconomic policies designed to unify the structure of the economy and improve stability on a sustainable basis? Table 9.3 illustrates the types of relevant policies deserving consideration.

Such policies are necessary for the unification of the bifurcated economic structure as well as structural adjustment and ultimate economic recovery. Exchange-rate and commercial policy are particularly important from the standpoint of expanding and diversifying exports, and developing domestic substitutes for goods previously imported. A devaluation of the currently grossly overvalued exchange rate and the reduction (and eventual

Table 9.3 Macroeconomic Policy Options to Reduce Bifurcation

Fiscal policy
- Fiscal policy, aimed at deficit reduction, is basically on the right track and sustained efforts to lower the deficit are appropriate
- Alternatives to deficit financing, that is, bond sales to the public, could be developed
- Tariffication of nontariff barriers could be a revenue source in a transitional period
- Cost-recovery pricing by state enterprises is a necessary part of deficit reduction

Monetary policy
- Continuing limitation of the rate of emission of old pesos is necessary for continued anti-inflation purposes
- Emission of the new convertible peso should be small enough to maintain confidence in its par value with the U.S. dollar, and aimed only at capturing some seigniorage
- Other measures to increase the demand for the old peso and to put less downward pressure on market prices and the black-market exchange rate could include
  - establishing genuine markets for housing, cars, and other assets
  - liberalizing enterprise regulation
  - expanding the role of markets generally

Exchange-rate policy
- Maintain the convertibility at par of the new peso by strictly limiting its emission
- Promote actions to increase the use and value of the old peso vis-à-vis the dollar in black markets; for example, increase the demand for the old peso
- Begin a process of devaluation of the old-peso exchange rate
- Aim for the elimination in three or four years of the spread between the official and the market-determined exchange rate
- Unify the convertible peso and the old peso when the official and market-determined rates merge

Protectionism
- Phase out most or all discrimination in the implementation of (bureaucratic discretionary) protectionism by:
  - ending the zero-tariff/no-NTB privileges of the sociedades anónimas
  - standardizing tariff rates for all sectors (perhaps with special treatment initially for pharmaceuticals and some foodstuffs)
  - replacing NTBs with tariffs
- Begin the adjustment process with high tariff levels (for balance-of-payments and revenue-raising purposes), to be steadily lowered as the external sector improves and the economy recovers

Price policy and social security
- Continue to phase out price controls wherever they do not affect the cost of the basic set of rationed foodstuffs available (which had proceeded significantly by 1995)
- Continue raising the prices of nonfood rationed goods with the ultimate objective of price decontrol
- Move toward a system of income support for needy individuals or families rather than comprehensive untargeted general subsidization through rationing
- Coordinate the establishment of a targeted and income-support-oriented social-security system with price increase and price decontrol for goods currently rationed; for example, divert subsidies currently going to loss-making enterprises producing fixed-price rationed goods to income support payments for the most vulnerable groups

elimination) of the extreme discrimination inherent in the current system of protection is vital and urgent if Cuba is to break the tight foreign-exchange constraint on its economic recovery. A combination of a (continuing) tight fiscal policy and an innovative but anti-inflationary monetary policy could assist in increasing the use and demand for the old peso while constraining the increase in its supply. The result of this would be to reduce the black-market exchange rate in relative terms, probably to reduce market-determined prices from current levels, and thereby to modify the incentives for resource shifts between the traditional socialist and internationalized sectors to more appropriate levels. Also of great importance is the modification of the social-security system to protect those who are hurt by various policy changes, particularly price policy, with income-support payments rather than providing generalized subsidies to everyone via fixed-price rationed goods. The need for reform of the social-security system has been expressed by the minister of finance, J. L. Rodríguez (1995b).

Conclusion

This chapter has analyzed the central feature of Cuba's economy in the first half of the 1990s, namely the split between the traditional socialist, peso-based component and the internationalized, dollar-oriented and marketized component. The origins of this pathology lie in (1) the rapid expansion of tourism, foreign business (within joint ventures), and the SA conglomerates; (2) pre-1994 macroeconomic policies that produced large fiscal deficits, accelerating expansion of the money supply, rapid inflation in market-determined prices, and an extreme devaluation of the old peso vis-à-vis the U.S. dollar in unofficial currency markets while the official rate remained fixed; (3) exchange-rate and commercial policy that produced extreme discrimination in access to imports favoring certain parts of the internationalized sector (notably the SA); (4) the general weakness, loss of confidence, and contraction of the traditional socialist economy; and (5) the legalization of the use of the dollar, which expanded its use.

This structural and monetary pathology has important consequences for the functioning of the economy and society. First, there has been a major impact on income distribution; those Cubans who have access to dollars receive higher real incomes due to the high value of the dollar in unofficial exchange markets relative to those in the traditional socialist economy with incomes in old pesos. This income differential creates an overpowering and universal incentive for resources—most obviously human resources—to be attracted to the internationalized part of the economy. Whereas some reallocation of resources to the foreign-exchange-earning part of the economy is reasonable, the internationalized component is not identical to those activities that earn foreign exchange (e.g., sugar and tobacco) or produce potential substitutes for imports. The real rewards that society provides to those able to earn or acquire dollars appear to be out of line with the real value of their contributions to the economy or society. This schism contributes to pervasive rent seeking because individuals can earn more by arbitraging goods and services across the two economies, playing the differences between fixed and market-determined prices and the official and unofficial exchange rate. There are also negative social consequences of this bifurcation.

Quick-fix policies, such as a forced and possibly confiscatory conversion from the U.S. dollar to the convertible peso, may generate a variety of serious long-term problems that would likely overwhelm any short-term gains.

A number of public policies introduced since mid-1993 have tended to reduce the bifurcation, but a broader array of policies and institutional reforms is required. Of particular significance would be further liberalization of small- and medium-scale enterprise, continued cooperativization where appropriate, and privatization of small- and medium-scale enterprises of various sorts (especially in retailing and other services). These measures would expand the market economy, and would have beneficial macroeconomic effects that could be of major significance in lowering the black-market exchange rate and helping move the economy toward a more appropriate general structure of incentives. Of greatest importance, however, is macroeconomic policy (continued reduction of the fiscal deficit and reduced money creation) plus exchange-rate and commercial policy, all designed to unify the black-market and official exchange rates (at perhaps three pesos per dollar) and to standardize the system of protection and eliminate the strong discrimination inherent in its functioning at present. Price decontrol would also be part of such a package of policies, but this would have to be accompanied by the conversion of the current social-security system from one of generalized subsidization (through price controls on rationed commodities) to one of carefully targeted income-support measures for those who really are in need of such assistance.

This broader array of institutional and macroeconomic measures would also provide much of the needed policy changes for successful structural adjustment. The devaluation of the official exchange rate (plus the merger of the unofficial and official rates), together with further liberalization of small- and medium-scale enterprise and a standardization and ending of discrimination in commercial policy, should permit major expansion and diversification of production for both domestic and foreign markets. Such expansion of production for export and for substitution of imports is vital if Cuba's economic recovery is to be sustained and sustainable into the future.

◆ 10 ◆

Cuba's Second Economy and the Market Transition

Jorge F. Pérez-López

◆

The demise of communism in the former Soviet Union and Eastern Europe dealt a mortal blow to Cuba's socialist economy. Cut off from its normal sources of foreign trade and financing, the socialist, centrally planned economy went into a tailspin from which it has not yet recovered. The island's national output reportedly shrunk by about one-half from 1989 to 1993 (Terrero 1994) and probably fell again in 1994, notwithstanding Cuban official Carlos Lage's statement to a foreign audience that the economy grew by about 1 percent (*FBIS-LAT,* January 31, 1995, p. 4).

Meanwhile, the segment of the Cuban economy outside the central plan has grown by leaps and bounds. Not only have illegal activities (such as black-market operations) increased as consumers resort to extra-official means to make ends meet within an environment of generalized shortages, but government policies implemented during the Special Period in Time of Peace have broadened the scope of allowed economic activities for private gain, stimulating economic behavior outside the central plan—a second economy.

Because the second economy is the segment of the Cuban economy that responds most directly to market signals and operates most efficiently, it has the potential to play an important role in the island's inevitable transition to the market. The experiences of transition in Eastern Europe and the former Soviet Union suggest that the second economy can be a positive factor, serving as a source of entrepreneurial talent and a hothouse for small firms. But it can also be a negative factor kindling the misappropriation of state property, increasing corruption and crime, and creating a marginalized informal economy.

This chapter explores the potential role of the second economy in Cuba's transition to a market economy, relying heavily on the experiences of countries that have already started on the road toward transition. It summarizes, elaborates upon, and updates some of the arguments set out in previous work on this subject by the author (Pérez-López 1995). The first part of the chapter defines the contours of Cuba's first and second economies and discusses the order of magnitude of each and how Cuban government policies during the Special Period have contributed to the growth of the latter. The second part draws on the literature on transitions from socialism to sketch the role of the second economy in the move toward a market economy. The concluding part makes some general observations on the opportunities and challenges that the second economy raises for Cuba's transition to the market.

The First and Second Economies

The term "second economy" originates from the literature on centrally planned economies (CPEs). It has been used by scholars to comprise economic activities outside the first, official, socialist, or planned economy. Certain characteristics of CPEs—overwhelming government ownership of the means of production, tautness and rigidity of central plans, suppressed inflation—accounted for both the quantitative importance of the first economy and the pervasiveness of activities outside it.

Grossman (1977, p. 25) defined the second economy of the Soviet Union as including all production and exchange activity that was pursued directly for private gain, and/or was in some significant respect in contravention of existing laws. Grossman's definition has been criticized (e.g., by Holzman 1981) as being too expansive because it lumps together legal and illegal private economic activities. Grossman (1982, p. 111) has justified the inclusion of legal activities for private gain as part of the second economy on the grounds that it is intended to capture all forms of deviations from the model of a socialist command economy. Analogous definitions have been advanced by other scholars (e.g., Feldbrugge 1984, p. 529; Los 1987, p. 29; Holmes 1993, p. 74) who have studied economic activities outside the central plan in (formerly) socialist countries.

The national economy of a CPE is represented by the combination of the first and second economies. The first, socialist economy is the segment of a CPE that is under strict state control. Resources are owned by the state, and resource-allocation, production, and distribution decisions are made according to a central plan at predetermined prices and conditions. In the second economy, legal activities include agricultural production by private farmers and some forms of self-employment, such as repair work. Illegal activities are manifold: Although black markets tend to be the focus of attention, other forms of illegal activities include corruption, theft of state property, and economic crime.

Cuba's First Economy

Cuba's first economy consists of economic activities under the control of Cuba's socialist state and subject to the central plan. It has been estimated that in 1988 the Cuban state controlled 92 percent of the agricultural and 100 percent of the industrial, construction, retail-trade, wholesale and foreign-trade, banking, education, and transportation activities on the island (Rodríguez 1990b, p. 61).

The Cuban economy has been subject to Soviet-style central planning since at least 1961, with a central plan first elaborated for the year 1962 (Mesa-Lago and Zephirin 1971, p. 151). In the 1970s Cuba adopted a new economic-management and planning system (Sistema de Dirección y Planificación de la Economía, or SDPE), patterned after the Soviet model that incorporated some market-economy mechanisms (such as credit, interest, and taxes) and promoted limited decentralization of economic decisionmaking (Mesa-Lago 1981, pp. 29–30). The SDPE was the basis for the management of state economic activities in Cuba until the mid-1980s; it was set aside when the Rectification process dismantled market-oriented mechanisms and centralized economic decisionmaking (Mesa-Lago 1989; Pérez-López 1990).

Cuba's centrally planned economy was characterized by extensive misallocation of resources: investment projects that were never completed, vast underemployment in state enterprises, and shortages of labor in certain agricultural occupations. Prices of most commodities were fixed, a commodity-rationing system was in place, and shortages of consumer products were commonplace.

The 1979 Penal Code defined a wide range of crimes against the national economy and set penalties for each. Such crimes included speculation, hoarding, use of state financial and material resources for private gain, and misuse of power by employees of state enterprises. A new penal code enacted in 1987 also defined a new criminal offense, illicit enrichment, to attack corruption by government officials (Vega Vega 1988, p. 130).

Cuba's Second Economy

Socialist Cuba has permitted a limited range of economic activities for private gain to exist alongside the planned economy. The most significant area of private activity has been agriculture, where a portion of land is controlled by private farmers. The sale of certain personal services has also been permitted. Although they were very successful in bringing produce and other goods to consumers (Figueroa Arbelo and García de la Torre 1984; Rosenberg 1992), the farmers' markets and artisan markets of the early 1980s were closed down by the government in the mid-1980s as part of Rectification.

Cuba eased somewhat the restrictions on self-employment in the 1970s, allowing individuals to perform certain personal services on their own account, provided they did so alone or with the help of unpaid family members; registered with the state and paid a fee and taxes; had the qualifications to perform the services; and showed proper conduct, diligence, and work discipline, as evidenced by a certificate to this effect issued by the person's workplace. During the Rectification campaign of the mid-1980s President Castro condemned the high incomes earned by some self-employed persons, dooming this form of engagement for private gain.

The most significant illegal economic activities probably have been black-market operations, unauthorized use of government resources, and corruption. Black markets for consumer goods have existed in Cuba since the early 1960s, when commodity rationing was instituted. Misappropriation of government resources (theft, diversion of goods, short-changing of customers) has been one of the most common sources of goods and services exchanged in black markets. The extremely high concentration of resources in the state sector and the centralized nature of management, placed a great deal of power in the hands of government officials, creating ample opportunities for corruption.

There are no readily available measures or estimates of the magnitude of Cuba's second economy. An examination of official statistics on overall agricultural output, civilian employment, and the structure of population income suggests that private, legal economic activity in the 1980s probably accounted for about 6 percent of national product (i.e., the global social product), employed about 230,000 workers or about 6 percent of civilian employment, and accounted for about 5–6 percent of population income (Pérez-López 1995, p. 116). It is even more difficult to estimate the value of illegal economic activities. In Cuba, as in any other country, participants in illegal economic activities place a high premium on the anonymity of their actions and deal almost exclusively with cash transactions so as to avoid audit trails that could reveal their activities. Based on information on population income, it can be posited that illegal economic activities in Cuba may have been roughly the size of the cash holdings held by consumers, or approximately 17 percent of national income at the end of the 1980s (Pérez-López 1995, p. 117).

As the bottom fell out of the first economy, in the 1990s the second economy grew to fill the gap. Domínguez attributed the ability of ordinary citizens to adjust to economic adversity to the rise of what he called the "illegal market economy." Officially still illegal and subject to repression, in the 1990s illegal markets in fact have been tolerated—and even encouraged—by the Cuban government because of the contribution they make to the regime's survival (Domínguez 1993, p. 102).

A number of indicators point to a very large and growing Cuban second economy in the 1990s.

- The Institute of Internal Demand estimates that the value of black-market transactions rose from 17 percent of retail sales in 1990 to over 60 percent in 1992.

- The money supply reportedly rose by 47 percent in 1989–1991, while the availability of goods and services fell by 30 percent, adding to the already large excess-currency holdings by the population (Carranza Valdés 1992, p. 153). Excess currency in circulation at the end of 1993 was estimated at 12.3 billion pesos.
- In early 1991 there were 200,000 self-employed workers authorized by the State Committee on Labor and Social Security; overall, the number of self-employed workers was probably closer to 800,000 (*FBIS-LAT,* April 19, 1991, p. 2), or about 20 percent of a labor force of roughly 4 million persons.

These estimates of the magnitude and growth of the second economy predate the enactment of economic policies after 1993 and therefore underestimate the significance of the second economy toward the mid-1990s. The reforms implemented by the Cuban government since the early 1990s—the creation of Basic Units of Cooperative Production (UBPCs) (1993), joint ventures with foreign capital (1992), self-employment (1993), farmers' and artisans' free markets (1994), and the decriminalization of the use of the U.S. dollar (1993)—have stimulated the second economy in important ways. That each of these reforms tends to stimulate second-economy activities is not coincidental. Rather, the reforms reflect a recognition that the first economy is no longer viable in an economic environment in which there are no trade subsidies or economic assistance from the former Soviet Union and the Eastern European socialist countries, and that the second economy is the only available vehicle to slow down the economic decline and create the conditions for a potential economic recovery. However, consistent with its deep-seated ambivalence toward markets, Cuba also passed in May 1994 a strong antiprofiteering law that limits citizens' ability to accumulate wealth that might result from the economic-liberalization measures. The law granted the Ministry of Finance sweeping powers to confiscate all cash, goods, and assets of individuals found guilty of profiteering and provided for the retroactive application of sanctions for this offense. Such ministry decisions are not subject to judicial review.

The Second Economy and the Market Transition: Comparative Perspective

Positive Contributions

Demonstration effects. In the former Soviet Union, Grossman (1989, pp. 83–84) argued, the very presence of the second economy provided a major argument for the necessity of the economic reforms pioneered by then

General Secretary Mikhail Gorbachev. The second economy prepared the way for economic reform in several ways. It provided a living example of an alternative to the official command system, underscoring the efficacy of decisions based on supply and demand and profit orientation, and affirming market worth based on supply and demand and trade-offs rather than administratively set prices.

The second economy also dispelled the common myth that decades of Soviet rule had extirpated nearly all private initiative and enterprise, and demonstrated that Soviet citizens had ingenuity and could react quickly in pursuit of private gain. It demonstrated, at a very basic level, that economic relationships outside the official sphere and based on trust and cooperation could operate efficiently, and illustrated the growth of acquisitive, consumerist, and materialist tendencies in the Soviet population. This was a positive development for marketization given that a more acquisitive public makes for a market economy that is more governable by macroeconomic as well as microeconomic instruments, and less in need of administrative means of control.

Stabilizing force. Hungarian sociologist Endre Sik has posited that the existence of a second economy contributed to the nonviolent transformation of the Hungarian economy. Although the creation or tolerance of the second economy was originally a pacifying policy, aimed at overcoming obstacles and supporting mass consumption, according to Sik (1992, p. 173) it also had the positive effect of bringing about the birth of a petite bourgeoisie or a semiproletariat, a workers' elite, and a large group of professionals who had invested in and developed a sizable and asset-specific capital comprising skills, network, knowledge, and prestige. Such rational actors do not let their investments be ruined by violent transitions. Younger and well-educated state technocrats, state-enterprise managers, and some party bureaucrats shared this situation. The individualistic, wheeling-and-dealing, personalized subculture created by the second economy does not encourage the kind of collective action necessary for revolution and the violent overthrow of a regime.

During transition, as the allocation of goods and services shifts from the central plan to the market, power is mediated more by transactive exchanges and less by administrative fiat (Nee 1989 and 1991b). The growth of markets expands the range of opportunities outside the boundaries of the redistributive economy, changing the structures of opportunities and incentives and ultimately resulting in a reduction of social inequality associated with redistributive processes. However, under certain circumstances, particularly partial reform, social inequality may actually rise during the transition as existing structures crumble while redistributors continue to wield power.

Reservoir of entrepreneurs. The second economy is a hothouse for entrepreneurs. Discriminated against explicitly by the state and operating in a hostile environment, individuals involved in activities for private gain in socialist countries exemplify many of the qualities of entrepreneurs: ingenuity, flexibility, thriftiness, and willingness to take risks.

As Portes and Borocz (1988, p. 26) have observed, the second economy has a considerable impact on political mechanisms under state socialism. The second economy creates an avenue for civil society to manifest itself as distinct from the state, providing a short-term, individualistic alternative to a politically controlled command economy. For Kornai (1990, p. 40), the phenomenon of the second economy is a special kind of "civil disobedience movement," which raises its voice against senseless legal regulations and administrative restrictions.

Although socialist economic reforms in Poland failed in their objective of generating vigorous real economic growth, they did succeed in allowing the emergence of a small private sector that nurtured the entrepreneurial spirit in a largely hostile environment. According to Jan Krzysztof Bielecki, Poland's second postcommunist prime minister, the early economic reforms and the resistance to communism prepared Poles psychologically for the transition to capitalism by creating an entrepreneurial class (Nagorski 1993, p. 177).

A survey of Polish private-sector firms conducted by Johnson and Loveman over the period 1991–1993 revealed that 73 percent of private-sector entrepreneurs had left the state sector and found employment in private businesses before the radical economic-reform plan was implemented in January 1990 by the first Polish noncommunist government. During the 1980s, the authors explain, as partial communist reforms allowed private business to supply some of the goods and services that were in short supply, a generation of relatively young workers progressively moved into the private sector. Nearly 33 percent of entrepreneurs formerly held a high-level management position in the state sector (Johnson and Loveman 1995, pp. 13–14).

Source of small firms. One of the critical elements of the social transformation to a market economy is the development of a new middle class, whose core would be formed of industrious, thrifty entrepreneurs who want to move up in society. From among the owners of such small- and medium-sized businesses emerge the pioneers of economic progress and the founders of large enterprises, subject to the natural selection process of the market. Later, these entrepreneurs may be surrounded by people who do not themselves take part in the creation of new organizations, and do not found new firms, but are willing to invest in the economy through the purchase of shares or in other ways (Kornai 1990, pp. 50–51).

The Polish experience suggests that it is relatively easy to create conditions that allow the reservoir of entrepreneurs to quickly develop private businesses from scratch such as new shops, services, and small companies. At the end of 1991, two years into the transition to a market economy, retail trade in Poland was almost totally in private hands, as was 55 percent of the construction industry, and 24 percent of transport services. By the end of 1992, 56 percent of the overall labor force worked in the private sector, generating almost half of the country's gross domestic product. While some of the new entrepreneurs were hunting for short-term profits, many were plowing back whatever they made into their businesses and thinking about their long-term prospects, indicating the development of a healthier capitalist mentality (Nagorski 1993, p. 175).

Johnson and Loveman (1995) attribute Poland's successful economic recovery after shedding socialism (real GDP grew by 1 percent in 1992, 4 percent in 1993, and 4–5 percent in 1994) largely to the vigor of new private firms. Private-sector firms—meaning firms created from scratch and not through privatization—have done well in all sectors of the economy, but especially well in services-producing areas (domestic trade, business services, construction, international trade). Even in the manufacturing sector, the growth of the private sector has been impressive: In 1994 the private sector accounted for over 35 percent of industrial production, compared to 5 percent in 1981. Almost 30 percent of the entrepreneurs in the Johnson-Loveman survey worked for at least one private firm before starting their own enterprise, suggesting that entrepreneurial activity was positively correlated with previous employment in the private sector.

Similarly, the transition to a market economy in Hungary brought about a spectacular growth in the number of economic units: nearly a sixfold increase, from 10,811 units at the beginning of 1989 to 58,951 units by the end of March 1992. Nearly all of the new enterprises that were created were small companies. The major source of the emerging class of new private entrepreneurs was the state sector (where it was customary for workers to hold secondary jobs), participants in the second economy, members of industrial or agricultural cooperatives, and operators of agricultural household plots (Kiss 1992, pp. 1027–1028). More recent data indicate that the number of legal economic entities had grown to 97,000 in September 1994, while the number of unincorporated businesses rose from 245,000 in 1989 to 766,000 in September 1994; enterprises employing over 300 employees accounted for 19 percent of total legal organizations in 1989, but for only 1 percent in 1993 (Krueger and Lutz 1995, p. 13).

The success of Hungary's "small-privatization" program is further evidence of the tremendous ability of the second economy to form legal small businesses. Nearly half of the 10,000 units that were offered for sale to the public in the autumn of 1990 were already in private hands or were subject to a leasing contract. Thus, the small-privatization program merely legalized the status of second-economy enterprises that had been operating more or less within the rules (Kiss 1992, pp. 1020–1021). The number of newly created private and privatized economic organizations were estimated to account for 50 percent of economic activity in 1993 (Krueger and Lutz 1995, p. 13).

Small-business creation in the former East Germany has also been impressive. The bulk of the private enterprises operating in the new East German federal states in mid-1994 were the result of "bottom-up" transformation (i.e., the creation of new enterprises) rather than privatization of existing firms. Surveys of new East German enterprises confirm that at least 80 percent of these businesses are brand-new establishments that are the product neither of a privatization nor of the break-up of former state-owned enterprises (Brezinski and Fritsch 1995, pp. 25–26). By creating alternatives for employment outside of the state sector, the second economy empowers workers. It makes it more likely that their wages and conditions of work will result from transactive bargaining between workers and managers than be imposed from the center. This puts pressure on the first economy for change (Stark 1989, pp. 654–655).

Negative Consequences

Misappropriation of state property. One of the dilemmas posed by reform is that the spread of markets increases the payoff for opportunism for party officials, nomenklatura members, and economic bureaucrats (Nee 1991a, p. 19). Not only does illegal enrichment by the former nomenklatura during transition sap resources from the state, but it also makes an already difficult political process more so by creating a great deal of resentment among the population.

Economic reforms and the transition to a market economy create opportunities for the nomenklatura to ransack what they can from amid the chaos of disintegration and lack of regulation. Hungarian political scientist Attila Agh (1993, pp. 15–16) sees privatization from below, or spontaneous privatization, as a phenomenon that begins at a time when state socialism has weakened and there are still legal gaps and uncertainties in property regulations; influential people—often alliances between the old political and new managerial elite—find ways to privatize property during the chaotic period of transition for their own benefit. In a period of uncertainty, "those possessing economic power carve out for themselves and their clients valuable pieces of the state-owned cake" (Sik 1992, p. 158).

During the transition to a market economy in Poland, the importance of so-called nomenklatura companies rose. They tended to be small, linked to foreign trade or service activities, profitable, and largely free from the bureaucratic controls that saddled state enterprises. Thus, they were able to continue to exist—and even prosper—while large state enterprises went under as state subsidies were reduced or eliminated. In some instances, nomenklatura members proved to have management experience and talents that made it possible for the corporations they were associated with to thrive during the transition and subsequently (Nagorski 1993, pp. 72–73).

The phenomenon of former members of the nomenklatura emerging as owners or managers of private companies during the transition is not limited to Poland. In Hungary, on the eve of transition, managers of state-owned firms—most likely members of the Communist Party—initiated privatization themselves, "buying" the firms' assets from the state at very low prices, thereby severing ties with the state and becoming private corporations. Following a public outcry in 1989 against these abuses, Hungary set up a system whereby all privatizations had to be approved by the State Property Agency (Fischer 1992, pp. 237–238; Kiss 1992, p. 1018). According to rough estimates, nomenklatura buyouts accounted for 5 to 8 percent of state assets in Hungary and 15 to 20 percent in Poland before they were stopped (Agh 1993, p. 15).

Spontaneous privatization has also been a common phenomenon in the former Soviet Union, with managers—often members of the nomenklatura—the main beneficiaries (Johnson and Kroll 1991; Sachs 1991). Spontaneous privatization in the former Soviet Union has not been limited to large enterprises: Managers and employees of a state-owned restaurant, for example, might simply begin providing meals at prices negotiated with their customers. The state distribution network provides most of the food, but the managers and employees, not the state, get most of the profits. Soviet economists call it "privatization of profits" (Alexeev et al. 1992, p. 15).

Corruption and crime. Government corruption, the sale by government officials of government property for personal gain (Shleifer and Vishny 1993, p. 599), has been present in all societies and in all ages. As Heidenheimer et al. (1989) have documented, no society—developed or developing, East or West—is free from some sort of corruption, although the manifestations and intensity of corruption are likely to differ significantly from one society to another. Economic analysis of corruption was formalized in the 1970s (e.g., Krueger 1974; Rose-Ackerman 1985); recently there has been a resurgence of interest in the topic, in part because of the impact of corruption activities on economic-reform processes (e.g., Shleifer and Vishny 1993; Tanzi 1994).

The extremely high concentration of resources in the state sector, and the centralized nature of the management system, place a great deal of power in the hands of government officials of centrally planned economies. They also create a great deal of opportunity for corruption (Leitzel et al. 1995, p. 27). One of the major perils in the transition from socialism to a market economy is a large increase in corruption and crime. The root causes for the increase in these forms of deviant behavior are manifold, among them the lack of definition of property relationships, the widely held notion that it is natural, and almost a noble activity, to cheat the state, and the sudden disappearance of the police state. Indeed, in countries that have been centrally planned, the process of reducing the role of the state in the economy (by freeing prices, privatizing state enterprises, etc.) may itself produce enormous opportunities for bureaucratic corruption during the transition, when the institutions necessary to limit it have not been developed and the habits developed in the previous period may not have changed (Tanzi 1994, p. 16).

Examples of corruption in economies in transition abound. In Romania corruption is rampant: Bribes are common for making reservations in hotels, renting real estate, and getting a grave at a cemetery (Maass 1993). Hungary is affected by smuggling, counterfeiting, and tax cheating (Maass 1992). Corruption in China has reached new heights; government officials, who have been given permission to go into business, are able to take advantage of China's awkward economic status—neither completely market nor completely centrally planned—to abuse their position and power (Mufson 1994). Valuable parcels of public land are being "sold" to well-connected businesses at bargain prices (WuDunn 1993). Describing priorities for 1995, Vietnamese Communist Party leader Muoi told a Cuban journalist that "we must also give special attention to new issues emerging from the process of changing to a market economy, including fund embezzlement, squandering, and, above all, corruption, illegal commerce, and other crimes and social vices" (*FBIS-LAT,* January 10, 1995, pp. 3–5).

The enormous size and influence of organized crime in Russia—the *mafiya*—is well documented (e.g., Handelman 1994; Hersh 1994; Sterling 1994; Goldman 1995; Hockstader 1995a and 1995b). The onset of privatization of state property in Russia has brought about a free-for-all struggle to acquire assets, a struggle in which the mafiya is very active using corrupt, criminal, and violent methods. Because it already had accumulated large amounts of material wealth, Russia's mafiya can bid for the privatized assets in a proper, businesslike manner, at the same time that it extorts money from citizens—and foreign investors—in the form of bribes, protection, and so on (Grossman 1993, pp. 16–17). Not only is organized crime firmly entrenched within Russia, but it has broadened its reach to at least twenty-nine other countries, including the United States, Canada, and Sweden (Banerjee 1994; Hockstader 1995a).

The crime epidemic that has affected Russia also extends to Eastern Europe. Police forces are so outclassed by the criminal element in these countries that the Czech Republic and Poland are considering reviving their secret services—dismantled shortly after the fall of communism—in order to enlist them in combatting crime (Pomfret 1993).

The rise of informality. The systemic transformation to a market economy means that certain elements of the second economy of socialist countries automatically vanish. For example, currency convertibility and legalization of private imports close niches that used to be exploited by second-economy participants. However, during the transition period, characterized by uncertainties and regulatory gaps, an incipient taxation system, the privatization of enterprises, and rising unemployment, there are ample opportunities and motivation for second-economy activities to continue (Welfens 1992, p. 138).

With the actual disappearance of the socialist state, remaining second-economy activities are likely to take the form of the informal sector in capitalist countries. The motivation of some informal-economy participants may be subsistence strategies pursued by marginalized workers who are unable to find employment in the modern, formal sector. For others the motivation may to avoid registration requirements and taxation. Dummy small businesses established to avoid taxation, conceal revenue, or stow away property are on the rise in Eastern Europe, especially in Hungary and Poland (Ehrlich 1994, p. 43).

Sik sees the rise of informality in economies in transition as a negative development that tends to bring about increased inequality in income distribution. There are several reasons for such increased income inequality. Workers used to have an assured first-economy job and relied on the second-economy job for extra income; in a market economy, some of these workers may find that their first-economy job has disappeared and their income is limited to that from the second-economy job. Internationalization of the economy increases income inequality, because foreign capitalists tend to recruit a small group of workers who are loyal and overpay them compared to local income levels. High levels of corruption and tax evasion tend to increase income disparities, and inflation associated with marketization tends to have a disproportionately adverse impact on low-income individuals (1992, pp. 167–168).

Second-economy activities—and their successor informal activities—can be counterproductive for the macroeconomy of an economy in transition. Second-economy and informal activities may increase individual income, but they do not produce tax revenues because participants avoid income taxes, social-security taxes, and value-added taxes, the main sources of state revenue for an economy in transition (Rose 1992, p. 5). At a time of financial disequilibrium, the ability of the state to raise revenues to address budget deficits can be significantly impaired by informality.

Cuba's Second Economy and the Transition

The tailspin of the first economy, and the worldwide loss of confidence in the socialist model, augur well for Cuba's transition to a market economy.

Such change is inevitable, although its timing and modalities still remain cloudy.

Policies implemented by the Cuban government in the 1990s that have partially opened the economy to market influences and decentralized economic decisionmaking are positive developments for the transition. However, the Cuban government has been timid and slow in implementing such policies and, in fact, there has been some backtracking. A wide range of professional services—especially health services—are explicitly excluded from self-employment, and small businesses are not allowed to hire helpers. Not only are the standards for practicing a private trade very restrictive, but they also delve into matters related to conduct, such as "honorable social behavior."

Among the clearest examples of backtracking was the announcement in December 1993 that government authorities had ordered a shutdown of the private restaurants known as *paladares* that had sprung up all over the island as a result of the liberalization of self-employment—an estimated 1,000 to 2,000 such outlets in the city of La Habana alone and 4,000 nationwide (Farah 1994; Whitefield 1994). Most paladares seem to have been modest operations, serving the basic Cuban fare of rice, beans, pork, and cassava; however, there were also more upscale operations serving lobster, shrimp, seafood, and wine, and even offering musical entertainment (Whitefield 1994). During one of his many interventions at the December 1993 session of the National Assembly of Popular Power (Asamblea Nacional del Poder Popular), President Castro lashed out at the "excesses" that had occurred as a result of the legalization and expansion of self-employment:

> This happened in a Havana neighborhood. A restaurant was opened with 25 tables and 100 chairs and a cabaret. Some guy found himself a spot and charged 15 pesos to let people in . . . He charged in dollars, pesos, and what not. He had all the clients he needed. People from abroad would come in and bring friends and even family. I have already calculated how much the happy owner was making. He was making no less than 1000 pesos a day. And this is a conservative estimate. At least 1000 pesos a day. And all this because things had opened up a bit (*FBIS-LAT,* December 30, 1993, pp. 2–10).

The second economy, that segment of the economy that is already somewhat exposed to market forces, can play a key role in Cuba's transition to a market economy. Until very recently, Cuba's second economy was substantially smaller than that of other CPEs. For example, Poland's agriculture remained almost entirely in private hands during its socialist period, and in Hungary private plots were permitted within the larger structure of agricultural collectives; in both countries there were also substantial numbers of legal family-sized enterprises in retail trade and crafts and no restrictions on the size of private enterprises. In contrast, Bulgaria's agricultural sector was dominated by the state and the private sector was very small (Kochanowicz et al. 1994, p. 10; Adam 1994, p. 613). In this regard, Cuba's economic structure in the 1990s is closer to Bulgaria's than to Poland's or Hungary's as each of these countries began its transition to a market economy.

When marketization does occur in Cuba, second-economy participants have the potential for becoming the nucleus of an entrepreneurial class. However, Cuban citizens have not had as much exposure to market-oriented forms of economic organization—such as self-employment, franchises, and work partnerships—as their counterparts in Eastern European countries, which had larger private sectors or experimented earlier with market-oriented economic reforms. Economic reforms in Hungary and Poland before 1989 contributed to the emergence in these countries of markets, gradually introducing market mechanisms within the command economy by shifting allocative decisions from central authority to state enterprises. Especially in Hungary, this shift allowed managers of those enterprises to learn Western-style management, financial, and marketing techniques (Kochanowicz et al. 1994, p. 9). In contrast, Bulgaria had virtually no experience with market-like incentives and constraints within the all-encompassing state sector (Kochanowicz et al. 1994, p. 10). Nevertheless, the adaptability and ingenuity of Cubans, and their ability to make ends meet in the face of very unfavorable economic conditions, suggests that there is no shortage of entrepreneurial talent on the island. As a participant in the second economy told a U.S. journalist, "You have to be always looking for ways to get by. Cubans are very inventive—we make great entrepreneurs" (Speck 1993, p. 10A). Joint ventures are reportedly "islands of efficiency" and a training ground for Cuban managers (Villar 1993).

Recent actions by the Cuban government send some warning signals regarding possible efforts to promote the second economy as a way to slow down or derail Cuba's market transition. For example, legalization of self-employment has a salutary effect on the government's finances because transfer payments to such workers are reduced or terminated once they join the ranks of the self-employed. Fees and taxes levied on the incomes of self-employed workers constitute a new source of government revenue. Some analysts have intimated that the breakup of state farms into UBPCs may be a preemptive move to block potential claims on farmland by their prenationalization owners (Whitefield 1993a, p. 10A).

In Eastern Europe, many Communist Party members who became "businesspeople" fronting trading companies established with party funds have become immensely rich with the fall of communism (Pomfret 1994). The creation of *sociedades anónimas,* owned by elite individuals loyal to the government—or their children—suggests that the property grab by the nomenklatura that preceded marketization in Eastern Europe has already begun in Cuba. Reportedly, sixty-three sociedades anónimas (designated as SA) were in operation by the end of 1992 (Gunn 1993, p. 13). Two of the most prominent, Cubanacán SA and Gaviota SA, have extensive joint ventures with foreign investors in the tourism industry; Gaviota is reported to be connected to the Cuban military (Gunn 1993, p. 9). The SAs are controlled by high-level government officials Abraham Maciques and Antonio Benítez, respectively (Delgado and Seah 1994, p. 13). Former interior Minister Ramiro Valdés heads Grupo Cubano Copestel SA, the entity responsible for the production and sale of computer hardware and software (*El Nuevo Herald,* February 10, 1995, p. 1B). In perhaps the first documented case of a private domestic investor, singer and songwriter Silvio Rodríguez, allegedly sympathetic to the government, has provided financial backing for the establishment of a sound studio to provide for-pay recording services to national and international clients (*El Nuevo Herald,* February 12, 1995, p. 1B).

A disturbing development is that crime and corruption in Cuba are on the rise, replicating the pattern that has been observed in Eastern Europe, Russia, and China during transition. Decentralization policies have boosted the incentive for economic crime and the opportunities to divert resources for private gain (Whitefield 1993b). Criminalization is bound to increase as economic decentralization—including some forms of privatization—proceeds in a system in which the basic institutions that undergird a market economy are not present, as has occurred in Russia and the more orthodox CPEs (Intrilligator 1994a and 1994b; Rosefielde 1995). Increased government repression to fight crime and corruption may also squelch political dissidence and slow down the emergence of a political alternative to the regime. Criminologist Louise Shelley (1994, p. 343) argues that the penetration of organized crime into post-Soviet government structures undermines citizens' perceptions of democracy.

Growing social tensions in Cuba are also matters of concern. Access to hard currency has created a two-tier society; citizens who receive hard-currency remittances from abroad, work in tourism and earn hard-currency tips, or are employed by joint ventures or in sectors such as tourism, oil extraction, or tobacco in which incentives are paid in hard currency are able to shop in special stores and enjoy greater levels of, and more variety in, consumption. "Ostentatious behavior" by some of these individuals, or their families, is resented by the have-nots (*FBIS-LAT,* December 8, 1994, pp. 10–12).

Another privileged group is the *macetas* (black marketeers), who are able to command large amounts of domestic (or foreign) currency and thereby maintain high consumption levels; recently, farmers participating in the farmers' free markets have joined the macetas as the new rich. At the bottom of the consumption scale are pensioners, individuals out of the workforce, and workers in the first economy (whether still working or dislocated and receiving compensation) who earn salaries in domestic currency and do not have access to foreign currencies. For these citizens, the demise of the first economy—and the emergence of a foreign-currency-driven second economy—are matters that affect their basic consumption levels and their survival.

◆ 11 ◆

Economic Changes in Cuba: Problems and Challenges

Julio Carranza Valdés

◆

This chapter is not an exhaustive examination of current changes in the Cuban economy, nor is it a proposal for overcoming this process of change. Studies of that magnitude require much more space, such as I have tried to give to them in a recent and broader essay (Carranza et al. forthcoming). My intention here is to reflect on some of the problems and alternatives that exist within the sectors in which changes fundamental to restructuring the Cuban economy have come about and can be expected to continue.

The case of Cuba is extraordinarily complex. It is a situation for which there are no proven formulaic solutions. The most developed socialist experiences of Eastern Europe ended by restoring capitalism in the midst of the chaos brought on by a seemingly irreversible degeneration of social conquests. However, the specific conditions of Cuba—derived from its geography, its level of development, its geopolitical position, and its recent history—are not easily compared to other historical experiences. The restructuring of the economy and of Cuban society at large must be a creative act. This does not mean that international historical and theoretical experience is to be ignored. Such experience must be kept in mind to the extent to which it contributes to an understanding of how to face the challenges that are before us.

What Cuba needs is not just any kind of economic restructuring but a type that will, together with the recuperation of the economy's efficiency and productive yield, permit the more important social conquests of the revolution to remain intact. Neither the formulas of "real socialism," which failed in Europe, nor the return to a dependent form of capitalism and neoliberalism that reigns today in Latin America, can respond adequately to

---

This chapter was translated by Christopher Britt Arredondo.

the current challenges that face Cuba in its attempt to regenerate the viability of the national project and ensure an independent future in keeping with the interests of the majorities within the Cuban nation. What is needed is the sort of economic restructuring that would produce fundamental economic changes without abandoning Cuba's socialist essence. This can only come about by means of a collective effort including a vigorous debate regarding Cuba's current situation. Moreover, the younger generations ought to play a central role in this debate given that they are, in the final analysis, the social and political subject of the future of the Cuban revolution. The following reflections attempt to place themselves within the context of that debate.

The aggravation of the crisis during the past several years, expressed by strong imbalances in domestic finance as well as by the decrease in sugar production in 1993, has led to the formation of a greater consensus concerning the need for new and more profound changes in the organization of Cuba's domestic economy. Beyond any doubt, the Cuban government has proven capable in its management of a profound economic crisis over the past five years that has been aggravated by the economic blockade imposed by the United States. On an economic level Cuba has had to confront the three intimately related problems of adapting to a decrease in the availability of goods, modifying the economic insertion into the international economic arena, and promoting fundamental changes in the organization of the domestic economy.

To date, the fundamental successes of the strategy with which the government has confronted the crisis have been its capacity to sustain political stability; the more or less egalitarian distribution of the costs of the crisis; its encouragement of the use of currencies, first on the international and then on the domestic level; and its promotion of the country's reinsertion into the international economy.

The result is a complex and contradictory process that has significantly changed the economic and social dynamics of the country. Economic property has been diversified fundamentally by virtue of the presence of foreign companies, the generalized implementation of cooperative organizations in agriculture, and the extension of self-employment. New spaces within a free market have been opened up for the farming and ranching industries, as well as some smaller productive concerns. The relationship between the state and the economy has been modified: The state has become more of a regulator than a manager of industry, although it continues to hold a dominant place in industry given its ownership of many means of production. The use of currencies has been legalized, which has caused a fracture in the domestic market, and the system is less egalitarian, although its level of social equity is unequaled anywhere in Latin America or the Caribbean.

The major limitation of the reform project has been the lack of a sufficiently integrated, articulate, and explicit program for economic restoration. This can be explained by the tremendous complexities implicit not only in the conception of the project but also in its application and effective management.

Financial Equilibrium

When the economic crisis began in 1990, the Cuban government confronted it with a number of measures, the principal political objective of which was to attain an egalitarian distribution of the cost of the crisis. The point was to avoid the classical effects of inflation and unemployment that, as a rule, have been created by the policies of transition that were widely practiced throughout Latin America during the 1980s. Such policies placed the burden of the crises on the most vulnerable sectors of the society and economy. The Cuban government avoided the inflationary impact that the abrupt reduction of available goods could have brought about by generalizing the policy of rationing. This process permitted the government to control prices and to distribute products on an egalitarian basis.

Unemployment—which could have grown considerably with the paralysis of a good portion of industry due to the lack of energy, prime materials, and replacement parts—was impeded by a wide-reaching policy of reorientation and subsidy to avoid closing down factories affected by the crisis. This policy generated a great imbalance in domestic finance, demonstrated by an excess of money in circulation and the growth of Cuba's fiscal deficit. Toward the end of 1993 these indexes reached levels that were clearly incompatible with any policy that pretended to effect a global recuperation of the economy. The most evident effects of the economic imbalance have been a lack of discipline among workers and a decline in the productivity of labor; the growth of the black market, or what may be thought of as an economy submerged in inflationary conditions; and the loss of the national currency's value, which of itself has provoked negative effects not only in economic terms, but in political and ideological terms as well.

To regain economic equilibrium became the most immediate objective for economic policy. With regard to this issue, consensus already existed from 1993–1994, not only among the directors of the government and in the National Assembly of Popular Power, but also among the majority of the country's economists. Nevertheless, the issue of how to meet that objective and relate it to other necessary changes remains highly controversial.

The first point under discussion is the role to be played by financial transition in the process of economic restructuring. The reestablishment of financial equilibrium must be accompanied by a program of deeper changes, with the aim of modifying the dynamics of the national economy. Only a process of this scope will be able to create the conditions necessary for sustained growth and economic and social development.

The second point has to do with the roads that lead to a financial transition. There are at least two ways of approaching this issue. The first supposes a rather slow and gradual process, which is, in fact, the policy that was adopted in the second semester of 1994. Its principal contents are a price increase for certain products and services, generally those that do not satisfy the basic needs of the population; the elimination of certain subsidies and free services without actually undermining the social conquests won by the revolution; a new tax law; modifications in policy on subsidies; an attempt to restore financial discipline in the state sector, as well as among the population in general; and the liberalization of prices for a number of determined products.

At the end of 1994 this policy began to have some positive results. Examples are the considerable reduction of circulating currency and, above all, of the fiscal deficit. However, adequate levels are still far off, and some problems can be seen looming in the distance. An important portion of the profits recaptured by the state—81.2 percent—is due to the price increase for products such as tobacco and alcoholic beverages (José Luis Rodriguez, quoted in *Granma,* December 21, 1994). It is impossible to continue to recoup losses by such means. Moreover, the already unequal distribution of resources has led to significant differences in the capacity of different social sectors to weather the crisis. It is the well-off minority that is increasingly entering the spaces recently created for free-market exchanges (ranching, farming, and crafted and industrial goods); this in itself favors the concentration of wealth.

In this scenario the possibility for a currency change[1] that would accelerate and rectify the process is made all the more difficult. Once important spaces have been opened in the market it would be counterproductive to minimize the profits earned in these areas, given the government's commitment to these markets. This does not mean that a decision of this type would be impossible to adopt, but that the government would be obliged to find rather complicated formulas in order to make these earnings and the exchange of currencies compatible with the measures already taken.

A faster way of restoring financial equilibrium (which was rejected) would have considered the establishment of new rules governing the exchange of currencies to be but a first step.[2] It would probably have been more traumatic in the short run, but the political situation of the country toward the end of the first semester of 1994 would probably have permitted the application of such a measure with considerable support.

The alternative policy would have included the principal measures of the other policy, but would have prioritized currency exchange. This alternative would have allowed the government to produce an initial contraction in demand and maintain it at a level compatible with actual supply. The principal advantages to this alternative are that it would have been faster, and that it would have fundamentally affected the sector that has accumulated wealth on the basis of highly speculative and at times clearly illegal practices—the exchange rate having only affected savings above a level enjoyed by a small minority.

By allowing new spaces in the market after the exchange of currency, the government could have created a much more equitable opportunity for the population at large to enter the emerging markets. As a result, prices on the supply side would most probably be lower than they are today.

Because the process of liberalizing prices must be partial and progressive, it is important to consider that an inevitable tension is created by the coexistence of a number of products and services with free-market prices and others with regulated prices. The levels of income are greater when productive activity is associated with a free market. This fact explains, in part, the tendency among producers to concentrate resources for production of goods to be sold on that market as opposed to making them available to other industries that are extremely important to the nation's economy. The abrupt reduction of circulating specie brought about by the currency exchange would have diminished the differences in prices between the two sectors and would have created better conditions for a general structuring of prices. This in itself would constitute another necessary measure in economic restructuring.

The search for economic stability by any means has to be part of a larger and deeper program for economic reform that would immediately begin to modify the structural causes of the crisis. Otherwise, these causes would simply reproduce themselves at a time when it would no longer make sense to bring about a change in the currency. This issue probably had a great deal to do with the decision eventually made. The fundamental restructuring of Cuba's national economy is a complex and novel process that is not quite at the point of fruition.

Monetary Circulation

Monetary circulation is another of the issues central to the restructuring of the country's economy. The search for new sources of capital since 1990 encouraged the general circulation of foreign currencies, due to the growth of foreign investment and its relation to the national workforce and the growth of international tourism. In August 1993 this situation was officially recognized and the use of foreign currencies was legalized. The state's objective was to recuperate the greatest quantity possible of these concentrated resources in order to put them to use to the general advantage of the economy and society.

A measure of this sort is taken only in response to severe necessity, and should only be adopted temporarily, given the distortions it is bound to cause in the economy. The Cuban economy of the 1990s is characterized by the use of two currencies; that is, the coexistence of two sectors with differing logics. If reintegrating the national economy is a crucial step toward the successful development of the country, then the reinstitution of a single national currency is an essential component of that success.

The circulation of two currencies has expanded and accentuated the fractures of domestic markets. The number of stores and services in which only the dollar is accepted has grown, while the great majority of working people continue to be paid in the Cuban peso. In addition to its social and ideological impact, this situation affects the economy by discouraging people's interest in work that is socially useful, and bolstering their participation in activities that are sometimes illegal but that generate income in the more lucrative currency. Maintaining and increasing the productivity of labor is therefore extremely difficult. Furthermore, the existence of two currencies in circulation strongly distorts the system by which prices are set in the marketplace, and this permanently distorts the assignment of resources. A general consensus seems to have been reached regarding the need to restore a single national currency. Nevertheless, the timing and the means by which to achieve this goal are also a point of current discussion.

Many economists—and the government's policy seems to be leaning in this direction as well—are in favor of gradually establishing the circulation of a second national currency in order to replace the foreign currencies currently in use in the domestic market. The creation of a "convertible peso" in January 1995 is one step in this direction, although so far it has not replaced foreign currencies that are in circulation but only the various certificates for foreign currencies that have been in use for several years now.

The creation of this second national currency would certainly be a step foward, but it would not resolve the essential problem of having two currencies in circulation. There is at least one other way to confront this problem and to achieve with greater speed the shift toward the circulation of a single national currency. Such a solution could not be adopted in isolated pockets of the economy but would need to be part of a global project for restructuring the economy. It presupposes the following measures for lowering the pressures of accumulated demand: the exchange of currencies in order to reduce the amount of the national currency in circulation; an adjustment of prices; the establishment of an economically grounded exchange rate; a new policy concerning prices in the parallel markets (to be constituted, from that point on, by the establishments already using foreign currencies); and the support and extension of agricultural markets and industrial products.

This alternative would not eliminate (in its first stage) the rationed market, which would continue to exist as a guarantee of the basic basket, but it would immediately link the population at large to a single domestic market in which it would be possible to find—by means of one's work and within the reach of one's income—a complementary supply of articles to elevate the overall level of consumption. Paying directly for such goods and services with foreign currencies would be eliminated. Any Cuban or foreign person in possession of foreign currencies would need to exchange these at the set rate through the banking system established for that purpose. The price of goods in the parallel markets would be equivalent to those on the international market, but expressed in the national currency according to the established exchange rate, with an added charge intended to finance the imports. All those goods and services directly linked to tourism—travel packages and airline tickets—would be excluded from this overpricing so as not to affect the international competitiveness of this important sector of the economy. In this manner, the circulation of foreign currencies within the national domain would be restricted, at first, to certain operations in the reciprocal dealings between national and foreign companies; but here, too, it would eventually be eliminated. The convertibility of the new national currency would be a long-term goal to be achieved gradually and in direct relation to the development of the economy and the different stages of economic restructuring.

Firm-Level Reform

Reform of firms should constitute a central component of the process of economic restructuring. The formulation of the System of Direction and Planning of the Economy (SDPE) corresponded to Cuba's participation in the Council for Mutual Economic Assistance (CMEA). One of the goals of this system was to make the organization of the domestic economy compatible with its principal role in the international economy. The SDPE defined, among other things, rules to govern business within the context of the country's centrally planned economy. Companies were expected to move within a framework of relative self-management that was much more clearly defined in its theoretical conception than in its practical application during the 1970s and 1980s.

The permanence of a financial regime that was too soft and the excessive intervention of the government's central organizations were obstacles to developing a more efficient managerial and business environment. During the second half of the 1980s, as part of the process of Rectification, it was determined that the management system should be modified so as to restrict firms in terms of their monetary-market relations. At that time, however, an integral redefinition of the system was not formulated. Only in the experiment known as "perfecting firms," developed during those years in companies belonging to the armed forces, were certain modifications in the system attempted with positive results.

The central components of these were decentralization, extension of monetary-mercantile relations, and an expanded role played by financial indicators (Pérez and González 1988). This experience could prove to be extremely valuable to the future of business reform in the country; its fundamental limitation is that it basically referred to the intrafirm level as opposed to the interbusiness level at which companies must operate.

The growing influx of foreign investment and the necessity for different sectors of the economy to relate with these new economic agents obliged the government to introduce partial modifications in the organization of existing companies and their relation to the economy in general. The business structure that was formed by the revolution in the 1960s—including the fundamental modifications put into effect after 1975—virtually eliminated certain forms of business organization, such as the corporate structure. In the 1970s there were only thirteen Cuban stock companies overseas; these were used to facilitate commercial dealings abroad. They were regulated by Article 66 of Law 1323 of 1976. In 1979 CIMEX was created; it was the first Cuban stock company to be established on Cuban soil during the revolutionary period.

Since the end of the 1980s, and especially after 1990, as a consequence of the upsurge in joint investments with foreign capital, the number of stock companies in the Cuban economy began to increase. By 1994 approximately 200 of these companies existed, the majority on Cuban soil. Some are the product of joint ventures between Cuban and foreign capital, and some were formed by the capital of the Cuban government alone; these have been organized in terms of shares to facilitate these companies' overseas economic operation (*Opciones,* October 30, 1994, pp. 8–9). Stock companies coexist with the majority of firms, which are still managed according to the rules established by the SDPE. Each sector has used different forms of working, mechanisms of stimulation, levels of material security, subordination, and legal rules. These differences are another fundamental expression of the dual economy presently in effect in Cuba.

The most radical structural change within the Cuban economy is the creation of the Basic Units of Cooperative Production (UBPCs), which represent the fundamental form of property and organization in the rural sector. The new cooperative does not receive ownership of the land, which continues to be in the hands of the state, but is in effect the owner of the rest of the means of production as well as of the product. Its principal source of labor is its members. This opportunity for greater economic autonomy has found its complement in the creation in October 1994 of farming and ranching markets, where the cooperatives can sell their products after having met their obligations to the state. As the most extensive ranching and farming companies of Cuba the UBPCs are an example of the conditions the Cuban economy will need to adopt in order to develop in the years ahead. The principal limitations of the UBPCs stem from their being such a new experience and particularly from the contradictions inherent in the current national economy.

Finally, there is the sector of self-employed workers, which has expanded since the middle of 1993 but remains below the level it is sure to reach in the future Cuban economy.

The need for a new business structure capable of integrating all these sectors of the economy and creating greater efficiency is widely recognized. Perhaps the biggest problem has to do with the definition of property. Any alternative that seeks to restructure the Cuban economy on the basis of socialism, and preserve the social successes of the revolutionary period, also needs to defend the preeminence of social ownership of the fundamental modes of production. The current conditions in which Cuba must continue to live require, however, that other forms of ownership of nonfundamental modes of production be incorporated into the system, particularly where doing so would encourage greater efficiency.

It is necessary to reclassify the country's firms according to their technology, the impact of their activity on the economy at large, and their capacity to generate profits. Under current circumstances the state has the advantage of being able to establish the optimal dimensions for every company according to these factors. Once companies have been formed and are functioning within the new economy, the state would retain the right to discreetly intervene and either merge or divide those companies it owns in accordance with the dictates of both the domestic and the international markets.

To each type of company there would correspond specific forms of organization and different levels of subordination. Large and medium-sized companies whose activity has a great impact on the economy, of which very few exist in Cuba today, should be state owned (or jointly held with foreign investors in cases where this proves imperative). They should be centralized and directly subordinate to the central government and its ministries, but should also be allowed a degree of autonomy superior to that they have enjoyed to date.

The majority of medium-sized companies, whose activity impacts the economy to a lesser extent, should also remain state owned or jointly owned but should have far more autonomy and not be completely centralized. They would report their economic activity to the entities of the Popular Power. They should be profitable and their overall orientation should be determined in response to market signals.

Finally, a significant number of medium-sized and small companies which would only be made inefficient or uncompetitive by centralization, would need to be identified. Certain industries, crafts, services, and the greater part of ranching and farming would fit under this category. These should all be decentralized and different types of ownership applied to them: state, cooperative, private, individual, or mixed. The basic goal would be to create profitable business concerns. They would be guided by the market, although the government would be able to take discretionary measures, impose ceilings on some prices, and make other contractual demands. The principal function of the government with respect to these companies would be to create the conditions whereby they would be able to function effectively within a market context.

In the case of private companies, their growth would be subject to extra-economic limits as well as to economic regulations that impede the concentration of capital, which would run contrary to the system's socialist essence. The companies would be expected to function under the pressures of a strong financial regime that would drive them to maintain their profitability and the income levels of their management and labor forces (Alfredo González 1993). This would involve a new role and structure for banking in the financing of companies, and a new relationship between the companies and their budgets. The existence of a strong financial regime at the microeconomic level is a necessary condition for sustaining macroeconomic balance. Furthermore, the preservation of macroeconomic balance is a necessary condition for the stability of managerial policies within companies, as well as the realization of global economic goals.

The income of every worker should be directly related to the economic results of his or her labor and the management of the company. The development of the decentralized sector could significantly reduce, though not eradicate, the problem of unemployment. In keeping with the principle of the government's universal protection of the citizens, the state should support all workers who are temporarily unemployed, but with certain changes in the policy overseeing subsidies. Such workers would not be viewed as employees of companies who require subsidies—which involves many costs and affects the companies' profitability—but as citizens without a place of work. The subsidy should be minimal, just enough to meet the person's basic needs; when added to the free universal health care and education it would prevent anyone from becoming socially marginalized, a common and growing condition throughout Latin America. As a general rule, income based on subsidies should be maintained at a level inferior to income based on labor in any of the sectors of the economy.

The extension and development of the nongovernmental sector of the economy would seem to be imperative because it creates the space for certain productive forces that are latent in the population and cannot be organized adequately by the state. This is one of the economic forms that ought to contribute significantly to resolving one of the most delicate problems the Cuban economy will need to face in coming years: the excess of the workforce employed by the state. The new cooperative, private, and individual sector should not be considered a separate and unrelated addition to the other sectors of the economy but should be integrated into the whole as a dynamic element in a single national economy organized around state-owned, state-run companies. The state should regulate the activity of all sectors to prevent deformations of the system's social objectives.

Another important problem has to do with the development of foreign investment in accordance with the country's new organization of business. Given the current status of the economy and projections for its immediate future, the importance of this problem should not be underestimated. A new law governing foreign investment should be adopted that, in addition to enforcing the legislation already in effect, would contribute to a far more transparent and precise heuristic context. All companies with foreign capital invested in them ought to meet, as a general rule, the same standards eventually set for the national companies.

The New Role of the State

Planning must be an essential instrument of any strategy for developing the country economically and socially in the long term. The state should maintain the principal macroeconomic and regional balances and guard the growth of the economy's strategic sectors as well as the social system. The market, regulated by the state, should provide incentives for greater economic efficiency on the basis of dynamic competition among the diverse economic agents that coexist and will need to continue coexisting in Cuba.

To achieve a complementary relation between planning and the market is another of the major challenges that must be faced by all who are interested in restructuring the Cuban economy. The challenge here is to allow a larger space for the growth of monetary-market relations while changing the classical forms of centralized planning. What distinguishes socialism is not necessarily the absence of the market, but the suppression of the hegemony of capital.

The new economy that is to result from restructuring will redefine the functions of the state. The role of the state would still be to guide the fundamental variables of development, guarantee the social successes of the revolution, defend national interests, and maintain Cuban sovereignty. However, the forms by which these objectives are to be met would invariably have to change in accordance with the greater diversity of the new economy and society. What has occurred to date, in terms of decentralization, has been limited to the management of state-owned companies, the creation of new forms of ownership in specific industries and services, and the distribution of resources according to market principles on a microeconomic level.

But under the new conditions, the hegemony of the state will need to be exercised in a more complex manner, with greater emphasis placed on making use of economic instruments. It will need to be decentralized; the central government and the local governments will perform complementary functions. The latter in particular will need to be given greater control over the resources generated in their territory. The following are suggestions for the future functions of the state.

- The state would combine administrative and indirect methods of planning. The rest of the state's functions would be guided by these methods. The central government, with the active participation of local governments, would elaborate short- and long-term plans. The large companies to remain under centralized management would be an instrument for carrying out these plans in a direct fashion. By means of economic mechanisms and state orders for certain merchandise, such planning would influence all other economic agents in such a way as to achieve the projected objectives. The state would also plan the principal proportions of the economy.
- In its capacity as promoter, the state would promote the development of certain branches of the economy or companies by means of investment and policies regarding credit, tariff protection, and deposits. In this way it would also promote the development of specific regions.
- As regulator the state would establish the rules governing the market: antitrust regulations, management of contracts, ceilings on prices, quality standards, consumer protection, regulation of foreign investment, property management, ecological protection, regulation of a minimum wage and of labor management, and the implementation of an arbitrating system. In particular, the state's regulation of labor and working conditions is essential to any economic program that seeks to minimize the effects of the market on workers.
- The state would invest in those companies directly linked to the central government. Nevertheless, in the remainder of the productive sectors of the economy, the state would be permitted to invest directly even in companies that have been decentralized. It would assume risk, along with decentralized companies, in the face of economic uncertainty. It would also invest in social and productive infrastructure. Bidding for jobs could become a mechanism for selecting the recipients of central investments.
- The state would act directly as a business executive in centralized and decentralized state-owned companies. It could also become a partner in other companies not owned by the state. Its role as a direct administrator would be essential to strategic activities.
- By means of a newly formed bank of commerce and development the state would manage credit policies intended to sustain specific activities.
- The state would function as a stabilizing agent in that, by means of the management of the central bank's monetary policy, it also would be in

a position to manage fiscal policy governing taxes and expenditures, policy controlling prices and salaries, and foreign economic policy by means of import licensing, bids, and foreign exchange. All of this would be done with the aims of achieving accelerated growth, production, and employment, avoiding high inflation, and maintaining the balance of payments.

• The government would handle the redistribution of income by means of progressive taxes and subsidies to specific sectors of the population. It would also offer health and educational services, and in this way directly determine the portion of the gross national product spent on social consumption.

Any government, central or local, capable of shouldering these functions, some of which are completely new in terms of their content, would need to be highly qualified.

Conclusion

The examination of these issues demonstrates the complexities and contradictions inherent to the policies necessary to overcome the present crisis. It is also evident that the problem will not be solved merely by building consensus on the character of the Cuban future economy. In order to advance in that direction there is more than one alternative; the country should not avoid confronting them, evaluating them, and choosing the most effective ones. It is in this area that the debate has a central role: Not only is it necessary to making better choices, but it also permits greater consensus.

There are three undertakings that ought to be part of the present process of economic change. There is a need to transcend all partial and sectoral changes and produce fundamental changes in the mechanisms with which the system operates. This is a question of shifting from a socialist model to a new, as yet ill defined one.

The process ought to be integrated to allow for systemic change that would breathe life into each of its parts. This goes beyond the definition of the total number of measures needed for each stage of restructuring; it also has to do with the organization, rhythm, simultaneity, and sequencing of the work to be done.

An evaluation of all the alternatives is fundamental to the restructuring and the changes such a process will impose.

Since 1990 the government and the Cuban people have made an extraordinary effort to resist the effects of the crisis. The search for new international relations and new structures to regenerate the country's economy has progressed creatively. That process currently finds itself in one of its most complex and decisive stages: Political audacity and intelligence, which have never been lacking in Cuba's history, must impose themselves again in order to construct the necessary alternative.

Notes

1. By this Carranza Valdés means the creation of a new peso to replace the current currency, similar to the process seen in Eastern Europe after 1989 (eds.).

2. A measure of this type presupposes organizational precision and speed so as to minimize the possibility of an artificial dispersion of concentrated wealth.

◆ 12 ◆

The Economics of the Present Moment

Pedro Monreal

◆

The central phenomenon dominating Cuban life today is the process of economic reform. This process has ramifications beyond the economic sphere, and it has become the center of the national political debate. This chapter discusses the development (or lack thereof) of Cuban economic theory and its relationship to the reform process. A main thesis is that Cuba must develop new means with which to analyze economic reality if it expects to manage a successful transition. The current economic paradigm assumes the continued existence of a dual economic system, when what is needed is a new vision of a reformed and integrated economy.

From about the middle of 1993 it seemed that Cuba had begun a process of gradual transformation of its economy toward more market-oriented structures. What had begun at the end of the 1980s as a selective opening of the Cuban economy was now becoming a general economic reform. Cuba was in the throes of a profound economic crisis that seemed unable to be overcome simply by means of a series of specific measures.

The reform process has included three fundamental and interrelated phenomena: the accelerated development of international tourism, the reorientation of Cuba's foreign commerce, and the opening up of the economy to foreign investment (Monreal and Rúa 1994). This partial transformation toward the market coexists with a planned economic system that is still in effect, at least formally, in the majority of the sectors of the economy. The coexistence of evidently contradictory economic proposals determines the current existence, in Cuba, of a dual economy.

During the period 1990–1993 the only significant attempt to reform the Cuban economy was undertaken in the export sector. The reason for this was that in an economy such as Cuba's the difficulties in generating

---

This chapter was translated by Christopher Britt Arredondo.

economic surplus tend to be associated almost exclusively with a lack of hard currency. The initial measures taken in opening up Cuba's economy assumed the possibility of treating the export sector in isolation. The efforts to create an industrial policy and link exports to other sectors of the economy date from a later period and until 1993 they were relatively limited.

By 1993 it was evident that economic policy needed to move toward a new phase in structural transformation. During that year certain institutional reforms were implemented that more clearly indicated a shift in the domestic economy toward the type of changes that had so far been limited to the export sector. This explains the market orientation of the new laws and other legal dispositions that in 1993 began to extend beyond the sphere of foreign commerce, tourism, and foreign investment and to cautiously set foot in a changing internal economy where new economic agents were becoming active.

The decree of Law 140 of August 1993 and the regulations attendant to it, put forth by the National Bank of Cuba, legalized the holding of foreign currencies and regulated the use of these by Cuban citizens. Other important measures have been Law 141 of September 1993 and Combined Resolution 1, decreed by the State Committee on Work and Social Security and the State Committee on Finance, which established a new legal framework and general regulations for self-employment. The number of activities in which self-employment is authorized has been increased, and the taxation of these activities has become more precise.

It may be said that 1993 was the year in which the general economic reform of the Cuban economy first took on a decisive character. A key moment in that process was the decree of Law 142, which led to a massive decentralization of agricultural activity in Cuba by virtue of the formation of the so-called Basic Units of Cooperative Production (UBPCs). In essence this measure included two kinds of institutional transformations—organizational and normative—in that it allowed for the establishment of markets by encouraging cooperative, and to a lesser extent private, forms of production.

During the first half of 1994, Cuban economic policy concentrated on the design and cautious implementation of a program intended to reduce the fiscal imbalance. The new tax law approved in mid-1994 reached beyond the limits of purely financial considerations and recognized a diversity of economic agents. Another important measure was the creation, from December 1994 onward, of markets for industrial and trade products. But the most important measure adopted that year was the establishment in October of farming and ranching markets. As a result, these sectors became the principal focus of Cuba's economic reform and a factor in the extension of reform to other sectors of the economy.

The specific manner according to which recent economic policy in Cuba has evolved would seem to indicate the central role played by the opening of the export sector in launching and developing a cautious process of institutional modification. In the course of their own development these overran the initial emphasis on the external sphere of the economy. At the beginning of 1995 this process was still partial and remained in its initial stages, but it was becoming more general and no longer limited to the original export sector.

The fact that the term "economic reform" was not included in the official discourse on economic policy until recently does not mean that measures compatible with the notion of reform did not figure prominently in Cuba's economic policy; rather, it reflects the complexity of the political and ideological context. The point is not only that economic reform has an impact on politics and ideology but that it requires certain political and ideological premises that take time to formulate.

As is generally the case with drastic changes originating in crisis, the conceptualization and understanding of the partial reform of the Cuban economy has dragged behind the actual process. The debate concerning economic issues in Cuba has been characterized in recent years by a noticeable theoretical void; that is, the perceptual tools required by the new reality have not yet appeared. This is reflected on two levels: the relative lack of concepts and theoretical references that can be observed in the ongoing discussions, and the utter absence of a theory, or of serious efforts to create such a theory, capable of adequately explaining the economic reality that has been emerging in the country.

This theoretical vacuum is the most significant expression of a more general ideological crisis that can be observed on a national as well as an international level. It is indicative of a certain type of conceptual impasse that is normally linked to abrupt economic disruptions, and in this regard it demonstrates the profound and systemic nature of the crisis in Cuba. Moreover, the absence of a theory, or the difficulties of its formulation, point to the problems surrounding a definitive solution to the crisis—not because the formulation of a theory is a condition sine qua non for the transformation and initial recuperation of the economy, but because the configuration of the new conceptual system is likely to come about in accordance with the rate at which the economic reality matures.

It is interesting that the current vicissitudes of economic theory in Cuba are being discussed in the midst of one of the most intense economic debates in recent Cuban history and in the context of significant transformations. The debate, largely conducted outside formal academic settings, has had marked effects on the way the political system functions, on economic policy, on social conscience, and especially on the economic and social reality of the country. However, the debate has not been linked to economic theories relevant to the issues being discussed, nor has it generated a body of concepts that deserve to be categorized as a theory capable of explaining the nature and function of the Cuban economy of today or of the emerging economy. Until the beginning of 1995, the debate did not lead to the design of integral proposals of economic policy.

In the following pages I present an analysis of the different stages experienced by the Cuban economy since 1985 and the corresponding dominant paradigms that have served to guide policy.

The Economic Debate

A retrospective of the economic debate that has taken place in Cuba since signs of an impending economic crisis were first observed at the beginning of the 1980s suggests the existence of three clearly defined stages: the debate on the internalization of the international crisis (1982–1986); the rectification of the Cuban socialist model (1986–1991); and the debate on survival and adaptation (1991–1995). These stages coincide approximately with distinct economic policies, but more importantly with the themes of debate. Those themes reflect as much an interpretation of the essential causes of the crisis as of the means of overcoming it. Table 12.1 summarizes the most notable aspects of the stages of the economic debate in Cuba.

The debate has been permeated by pessimism regarding the equilibrium of the economy; even the socialist economy is suspected of lacking its often vaunted balance. In times of crisis, imbalance is perceived to be normal, and this perception has largely conditioned the terms of the Cuban debate, even though the notion of imbalance has not been properly conceptualized. The political economy's repeated failure over the past two decades to successfully recompose its balance by taking action in specific areas of imbalance (commerce with market economies, excesses in imitating the economic models of orthodox socialism, or the foreign sector of the economy) reinforced the intellectual pessimism that has influenced the search for solutions to the crisis. But such analyses could have led to the rise of new paradigms for discussing the crisis.

It is precisely this transition that the current economic debate in Cuba could be at the point of realizing. The theoretical activity, and the discussions that began in Cuba toward the beginning of 1995, indicate a growing understanding of the need for wide-reaching and well-articulated programs of economic activity. The increasing dissemination of concepts such as "the redimensioning of the economy" (Carranza et al. 1995) could be, independent of its limitations, the beginning of a turn in the economic debate toward a new stage. The central theme of this new stage would be general economic reform in which the crisis would be perceived not only as an external process but also as something derived from internal aspects that would require modifications of a relatively radical character.

The latest stage of the economic debate contrasts, in more than one way, with what occurred in Cuba since the mid-1980s. The economic problems of

Table 12.1 Stages of the Economic Debate in Cuba

Stage	Nature of Crisis	Policy
Internalization of crisis	External to socialism Can be resolved by adjustments in international relations without modifying the domestic system Possible to become more involved in the international socialist system	Relative isolation from capitalist world and increased integration with socialist global economy
Rectification of the Cuban model	External to Cuban socialism Can be overcome by changes in the economic system emphasizing its socialist character Deterioration of conditions for inclusion in the international socialist system	Rectification
Survival and adaptation	External to Cuban socialism Can be overcome by concessions in the economic system International socialism is not relevant	Concessions in increasing areas of economy

that time—much less grave than those that Cuba is currently facing—generated a discussion that was associated from the beginning with a specific set of concepts meant to explain the crisis in an integral fashion, as well as to propose a conceptual paradigm for grounding the reorganization of the economic system. Those concepts, in themselves certainly polemical, went beyond the strictly economic and were presented as a "great theory" that was assumed to be crucial to the effective correction of certain errors committed when first constructing Cuban socialism.

These characteristics can be explained to a large extent by the concrete conditions—national and international—around which the debate was organized. With respect to the national conditions, the impulse to reorganize the economy did not stem from a self-evident condition of crisis, although today with the wisdom of hindsight one might say that there did exist, at the very least, a latent crisis. The economic problems of that time were not perceived as the consequence of an important economic crisis, but were viewed in light of certain imperfections in the design and application of the economic model. The issue was never formulated as the need to create a new economic paradigm, but as an act of rescuing an already existing theoretical corpus and implementing the changes dictated by the circumstances of the moment.

With regard to the international conditions of the 1980s, the challenges then facing the socialist system were not interpreted as systemic by either government officials or by the predominant theoretical currents then in vogue in socialist countries, such as the Soviet perestroika, the Vietnamese *doi moi,* and the Cuban Rectification. This was so notwithstanding the significant differences that always existed among these projects with respect to the depth, pace, and reach of the changes, and with respect to certain ideological premises and the political processes attendant to these.

Substantial differences between these processes were not evident, however, until the end of the 1980s. It was then that the Soviet Union and the countries of Eastern Europe entered a political and social dynamic that definitively fractured the thesis of "perfecting" the system and led those countries to search for alternatives beyond the socialist paradigms. Conversely, the socialist countries of Asia as well as Cuba did not abandon the thesis of perfecting the system, although in each case it took on a meaning significantly different from its original sense. Some of the measures adopted in these countries seem to be more in line with a substantial redefinition of the socialist model than they are with the mere perfection of the model in force until then.

All of these cases are characterized by the absence of any great theory concerning contemporary socialism, including the conceptual ambiguities surrounding its economic system. In this sense, what is happening in Cuba should be understood as part of a more general phenomenon that can be explained not only in terms of the impasse that is normally reached in a context of traumatic economic changes, but also in terms of how disconcerting the new economic reality can be for the economic sciences. The peculiar behavior of the economy is not limited to the irregularities directly related to the crisis; it also reflects newer components of Cuban reality, many of which have no direct link to the crisis except as possible solutions to it.

In the process of overcoming a crisis, many practices that previously had been considered theoretical aberrations or temporal characteristics come to acquire a surprising permanence and centrality. The two examples par excellence of this theoretical discord in Cuba are connected to the growing role of the market and to the role played by foreign capital.

Adaptation or Fundamental Reform?

The principal consequence of the various attempts at overcoming the crisis has been the establishment of an accentuated economic duality. This has in turn created a schizophrenic social consciousness with respect to the economic reality of the country. The possibilities of creating an integral theoretical perspective capable of adequately explaining the national economy have, as their principal obstacle, the absence of an integral national economy. What current theory is attempting to explain no longer exists. This is, nevertheless, the point around which current economic debate should be organized.

Different conceptions of the crisis correspond to different solutions. In Cuba there are two principal ways of viewing the crisis: as an "imported" problem, that is, a problem external to the country's economic system; and as the result of the fatigue of that economic system. To the first conception corresponds a series of partial and sector-based solutions, whereas the second proposes a fundamental restructuring of the economy. The association of either of these points of view with a vocation for reform is imprecise, given that the term "reform" can be defined by both positions insofar as it would have a different meaning for each.

Nevertheless, the consequences of these two theoretical perspectives on the duality of the economy, which I have identified as the principal obstacle standing in the way of articulating an integral theory, could be extremely different. The first position tends to accentuate the duality; the second tends to eliminate it. There are considerable differences within the second position concerning how to integrate the new economic system, and these would certainly have repercussions on the form the new theory would eventually take.

The predominant perspective to date has been the first, although the facts would seem to indicate that the initial emphasis placed on specific sectors of the economy and the limitations placed on the mechanisms of the market attendant to this focus have undergone certain modifications. Every day the number of sectors to be doctored increases while the market also extends, although in many areas it continues to be limited.

The undercurrents of opinion still prevalent in the debate identify the current situation as a crisis of adaptation (basically to external situations), and many of the new realities are considered to be necessary concessions. These positions, which from a political point of view might have some significance, are irrelevant and incongruous from a theoretical point of view. The economic reality in Cuba that needs to be interpreted theoretically is by no means the result of a process of adaptation of the model previously in force to external conditions; it is the result of the replacement of the old model by the simultaneous and gradual action of two models.

From a theoretical point of view it is relevant to analyze the lessons of the past as well as the contradictions and potentialities of the present. The premise for such a study is that Cuba needs a fundamental economic restructuring to rationalize the dual system that has replaced the old integrated model. This premise is sufficiently endorsed by recent changes, which have represented not an adaptation but a radical transformation, notwithstanding its partial and incoherent character. The economic crisis of Cuba is not a crisis of adaptation but a double crisis: the "terminal" crisis of the old economic model, and the crisis associated with the emergence of a model for economic duality that is incapable of solving the various economic problems of the country.

A serious analysis of these crises could provide useful elements for the construction of a theory on the present economic reality and, consequently, on the economic system of the future. There are indications that the economic debate may be shifting toward a new stage in which the conceptual limitations that currently exist could be overcome and contemporary economic theory could be oriented toward the process of change necessary to the Cuban economy and society. At the beginning of 1995 the intellectual pessimism of earlier years seemed to be generating an intellectual perspective that is more positive with respect to Cuba's current economic reality and its potential for change.

PART 3

Postscript

Transition to What?

Manuel Moreno Fraginals

At the end of the conference we asked Professor Manuel Moreno Fraginals to speak on his impressions of present-day Cuba. His speech, reproduced here with some minor editing, was no doubt the most exciting moment of the conference. Whether or not one agreed with what he was saying, it was clear that this moment represented an emotional turn for the noted Cuban historian. For over thirty years he has demonstrated his loyalty to revolutionary Cuba. For many of us his expression of disillusionment served as a cathartic exercise that allowed us to communicate our sadness over the political, economic, and social realities described over the past two days. Some in the audience welcomed his words with acclamation. Our two contributors from Cuba asked for and were given time to respond. They challenged key points of the speech and argued that although Cuba was encountering difficulties, it still serves as an example for Latin American countries suffering through their own neoliberal revolutions. We include this short essay not because it necessarily conveys Cuban reality, but because it dramatically addresses the nature and scope of the crisis that any transition will have to confront. Perhaps more important, these are the words of a senior Cuban scholar who spent the best part of the past four decades studying Cuba from the perspective of an active participant in Cuban society.

—The Editors

Change in Cuba is a fundamental fact. What is happening in Cuba? This conference, among many, has been organized around the question of Cuba's transition, and with all due respect to the organizers of this seminar,

---

This chapter was transcribed by Elba Barzelatto and translated by Christopher Britt Arredondo.

I have to confess that I have always been against the use of the term "transition." I prefer to call the change in Cuba a disintegration.

"How is Cuba going to realize its transition?" a journalist asked me recently. I responded by asking "What do we mean by transition?" A transition presupposes a period of time between two points. A transition is supposed to have occurred when one comes to a completely different place. The transition in Cuba after the revolution, logically, does not include the revolution. Hence, the question arises: A transition to what? If it is toward a different state than that of the revolution, then there has been practically no transition whatsoever in Cuba.

What is presently taking place in Cuba is not a transition but a disintegration of Cuban civil society. I further believe that this disintegration, which has always been studied in terms of statistics, and particularly economic statistics, needs to be analyzed from a cultural point of view, that is, from a human point of view. The economic factor is definitely of extreme importance, but there are also certain factors that are not quantifiable. For example, I consider the exodus of Cuba's youth a cultural event of extraordinary importance in defining the process of disintegration.

The theme of the *balseros* (rafters) fascinates me, as does, in general, the subject of the Cuban diaspora. The first time I saw a balsero was from the air. I was in one of the planes operated by Brothers to the Rescue on one of their missions, and I must confess that it made an extraordinary impression on me. I believe I will never forget it: a man stretched out, or almost stretched out, on a piece of wood surrounded by the immensity of the ocean. I took a picture, which I have kept to this day.

After this experience I began to study the balseros of Guantánamo Bay. In order to do so, I took advantage of two things: First, I had in Guantánamo a nephew, the son of my eldest brother, among the balseros. Second, two of my students are also among the balseros. During a few visits to Guantánamo I distributed a number of questionnaires among the balseros. I believe the results of this survey provided me with a rather good picture of who these balseros are, why they left Cuba, and what their attitude is now with respect to Cuba.

I do not intend to bore you with erudition on the balseros. There are, simply, some facts that caught my attention that I would like to share with you. First of all, there is the age factor. As one would imagine, nearly 90 percent of the balseros are somewhere between twenty and thirty-five years old. I took those between fifteen and twenty-four as representing the reality faced by Cuba's youth today. These young people decided to risk their lives in order to go to a place they have heard about only by word of mouth or, in a negative light, from the Cuban press. Another group that profoundly surprised me and that made up a large number of the balseros are men ranging in age from thirty to thirty-five years.[1] This age is crucial, anywhere in the world, as a time when people define themselves with regard to their profession and their future. Consequently, the balseros are made up of a large group of people who at a critical juncture of their life have decided to leap into the unknown with the hope of a new beginning. Another trend that stood out concerns the number of children abandoned by their balsero mothers and fathers. Almost all the balseros either had children or had been married once, twice, even three times. The rate of divorce among them was found to be tremendously high—but this does not come as a surprise because, despite the fact that in Cuba this type of statistic is not commonly published, it is known that Cuba has one of the highest divorce rates in the world, with marriages averaging some three to four years. Finally, there was a question that my assistants asked the balseros: "If you can't get into the United States, will you return to Cuba?" The response, almost unanimously, was: "I will not return to Cuba." This simple phrase tells us more about the island than about those who have left.

Suicide is another example of the disintegration. Generally, in Cuba, statistics on this question are not published.[2] Some think that those who create statistics in Cuba, or those who manage these people, do not want to publicize certain facts that could discredit the revolution. The result is that those who do not fight against the revolution are also left without the proper statistics. Among the statistics that have not been published are Cuba's suicide rate, in particular the suicide rate among Cuba's youth. I began my study of suicide with great concern, because in one of Cuba's privileged schools—I use this term to refer to schools of the highest level such as the Escuela Lenin where my children studied—I found at least seven suicides in at least five years. In the swimming school, Camilo Cienfuegos, where another two of my sons studied, I remember there having been three suicides. I believe that few things can be more worrisome than to find a young man of seventeen, eighteen, or twenty years of age, with his entire life ahead of him, willing to end his life. Thanks to another study I conducted using the official interment books of Cuban cemeteries, I was able to confirm that, first, the government was hiding the number of suicides and second, during the current period the mortality rate increased while the number of years lived decreased.

All of these things may seem disconnected: the suicides, the exodus of Cuba's youth, the ideas on transition, and the ideas on disintegration. But they are pieces of a giant jigsaw puzzle and they are all part of a larger problem. This problem is central to the troubles the revolution is facing today. It is the problem of human deterioration, the problem of the total disintegration of the civil society, the disintegration of the family. This is a problem that has led to, as a friend of mine has put it, a situation in which "they have scarred our hope."

In many cases I believe that this assault on hope has not been intentional, or at least, the intention has not been to steal hope away from Cuba's youth. But when a regime is created in the image of a few people, these few people believe it to be their duty to direct others' lives from the cradle to the grave. People are told what to read, what they have a right to know, what they can and should do, where they need to go, how many should attend massive gatherings, or to go to a certain school to see a specific play, etc. When the capacity to direct one's own life is reduced, people either reach a point of desperation or become utterly ambivalent about their own lives. I believe that this is the fundamental problem in Cuba today. The double morality to which Marifeli Pérez-Stable has referred I prefer to call ambivalence. Because many times what people are faced with is not only a moral question, but a question of survival that leads them to maintain two separate attitudes, one official and the other personal. This is what happens, for instance, when people go to massive gatherings in order to be seen, when their true desire is to not attend such gatherings at all.

This ambivalence produces social disintegration that runs parallel to the physical disintegration of La Habana—the buildings that cannot survive a tropical rainstorm, and crumble to the ground because in thirty-five years they have not had the proper care or rehabilitation. The disintegration is not a single event, but a process. First it is a window that must be repaired, then it is the door; paint begins to chip and to peel off the walls; the yard is invaded by weeds. This is physical deterioration. It can be stopped, controlled. But when this physical deterioration is followed by moral deterioration, by a double morality or ambivalence, then the impact is much greater. Simply put, nothing works: The economy does not work, the national currency loses its value, statistics lie, the media lies (nothing has been published in Cuba in the past thirty-five years that can qualify as the free expression of a free press), young generations receive a pauperized education, and only revolutionaries or those who decide to make themselves seem to be revolutionaries are allowed privileges. The list goes on and on. Resentment is accumulating and becoming a social illness.

There are two movies that illustrate Cuba's disintegration very well. In both "Strawberry and Chocolate" and "Madagascar," leading characters announce: "I am leaving." It is interesting that audiences understand what they are leaving—it is not necessary to add "Cuba." When questioned as to where she plans to go, one character can only answer "to Madagascar." All of us know that to say "I am going to Madagascar" is the polite form in Cuba of saying "I am going to hell." It means that like many in the diaspora, like my nephew in Guantánamo and my two students there also, like all the suicides, she can say, "I will not return to Cuba."

So the question remains: Transition to what? The revolution did make gains. Will they also go to hell? What can be saved? Is the revolution going to be drowned and forgotten in the way many aspects of life prior to 1959 were senselessly erased? We know that history changes. After 1959 dates such as February 24, December 7, and October 10 were no longer commemorated.[3] Now they are returning. What will happen to July 26th?

What is to be restored? What is to be saved? The answer stems beyond the market and questions having to do with tourism and zinc. This process of disintegration and restructuring of Cuban society is the great task that looms before us, and each of us must play a part—those who are outside as well as those who are inside Cuba. I was angered today by a phrase in one of the papers read here. The sentence claims that "those who are absent are never right." If this were true then Martí could not have been right, because he lived outside his country. The point is that those who are absent are right; those who are present are right as well. I furthermore believe that to confront the harsh realities presently facing Cuba, what is needed is a certain openness to dialogue. It is only on the basis of such openness that the disintegration of this process that all of you are calling one of transition can be brought to a halt. That is all.

Notes

1. The group of women was relatively small, but not minute: 20 percent of the balseros.

2. Julie Feinsilver noted during the question period that these data are officially available (eds.).

3. These celebrate events from the War of Independence and the life of Antonio Maceo.

Reflections: May 1, 1996

Miguel Angel Centeno & Mauricio Font

Writing a book on anything as ephemeral as the last days of a revolution (and, not counting Carranza Valdés and Monreal, the majority of us suspect that we may be entering the last phase of the Cuban revolution) is always dangerous. Between the time we began planning the conference and the actual meetings, Cuba had experienced yet another mass exodus, the economy neared total collapse, market policies were ascendant, authorities on the island and moderate Cuban Americans were starting a new dialogue, and the Cuban and U.S. governments had agreed to resolve some long-standing disputes. By April 1995 (the date of the conference), we wondered whether the Cuban regime would survive until the publication of the book.

Another year brought a new cycle. As dissidents organized within Cuba and pressure for change mounted from the outside, the Cuban government shot down two small civilian planes flown by opponents from Miami and intensified a crackdown on dissidents organizing around the umbrella of Concilio Cubano. In response, the Clinton administration signed the Helms-Burton bill into law, thereby greatly hardening the embargo. Increasingly, dissidents found themselves under pressure, hard-liners were ascendant, and advocates of perestroika often unemployed; advocates of contact and dialogue were on the defensive in Miami as well as Havana, and the United States and Cuba are more antagonistic now than at any time in recent memory. Meanwhile, the economy was actually growing (even if modestly).

This shift actually confirms rather than contradicts the analysis in these pages, even if our intention was not to make tactical predictions on the day-to-day future of Cuba. The book aims at assessing underlying structures, dynamics, and enduring problems and issues expected to shape any transition scenario and process. The analysis of the Cuban reality at that level led us to fear and in some cases anticipate shifts, erratic turns, and even reversals in policy.

The institutional, structural, and historic continuities are clear. Cuba is still a largely monocultural economy, dependent on external sources for investment capital. It has an extremely well-educated and healthy workforce that is vastly underutilized. Cuban society is also still divided—between Miami and Havana, between the dollar and the peso economies, between black and white, between intransigents and moderates, between old and young. Reflecting and demanding to bridge the fault lines of Cuban society, the Cuban polity is defined by a powerful and highly centralized state claiming an organic relationship to the Cuban nation, immune and unresponsive to open debate, intolerant of political competition, and prone to subordinate all manner of policy to the logic of its own survival. This state is dominated by a single party and leader whose combination of political flexibility and ideological rigidity largely determines the future of the island.

The established pattern is that the Cuban state will experiment with all manner of reforms so long as they do not challenge or threaten the power structure. "All within the Revolution, nothing outside the Revolution," is the traditional motto. But reforms often generate their own problems, sometimes of comparable magnitude to those they seek to resolve, and market reforms in particular are likely to destabilize the power structure because they also transfer resources and decisionmaking away from the state and into the hands of private individuals and nongovernmental organizations. Besides unusual vision and commitment, it thus takes a pragmatic ideology and confident institutional framework to implement and sustain a serious market-oriented reform program. The most recent reversal in policy is partly explained by the very imbalances and dilemmas induced by the previous cycle of reform, even if the responses to the crisis of the Cuban economy were timid and cautions.

What direction will Cuba take? It is probably impossible to say. However, there is an almost universal, if often guarded, pessimism among many of the contributors regarding Cuba's ability to experience a smooth transition to either a revived revolution or a post-Fidel society. (The Cuban authors often stood alone with their hopes that the current system would triumph.) The divisions the island has lived with for so many years still represent seemingly insurmountable obstacles. Monoculture and dependence (whether based on tourism or sugar) ties the island to the international economy and effectively robs it of any significant economic autonomy. In the context of structural crisis, this makes it difficult to provide meaningful work for the greatest accomplishment of the revolution: the human capital represented by the Cuban people. A Caesaristic regime severely limits substantial or alternative involvement by Cuban citizens in the most important decisions of their lives. The recent shooting down of the Brothers to the Rescue planes not only revealed the level of distrust that exists on both sides, but how easily leaders on both coasts of the Florida Straits are willing to use human tragedy to maintain a political gulf. The price for continued economic growth may be forms of economic inequality that endanger precisely those goals embraced by the revolution. None of these problems can be ignored, nor will they be resolved through bravado or political machismo.

The contributions to this book have focused on how different aspects of the Cuban polity and situation will determine the future of Cuba. Centeno, Font, and Pérez-Stable have emphasized the institutional dynamics inside the current regime and how these need to be reorganized for substantial political or economic progress to be made. León and de la Fuente and Glasco remind us that the government is not everything in Cuba. Increasingly, different parts of Cuban civil society will have to be taken into account in defining the island's future. Gunn Clissold and Castro both emphasize the counterproductiveness of current U.S.-Cuba relations, but they also indicate that significant groups may oppose any improvement because it would threaten their interests. Eckstein reminds us that even authoritarian regimes have to balance their budgets and that any Cuba, present or future, will have to live within sharply constrained fiscal limits. For Pérez-López the underground economy represents both a promise and a threat: It teaches entrepreneurship, but also promotes illegal behavior and unproductive activities. Whatever economic model Cuba chooses, Ritter warns, must be internally consistent and cannot rely on the continued ability to maintain separate economies. Carranza and Monreal both clearly wish to maintain the many accomplishments of the revolution, but believe that some market mechanisms are imperative to do so. They represent an optimistic view of how the revolution can remain true to its ideals and yet survive.

A new Cuba will therefore have to reform its political and economic institutions, support the development of a new civil society to include all its citizens, reestablish a relationship with both the United States and the one million Cubans of the diaspora, balance its budget, create a consistent economic policy, and police its new markets. It must do all this while dealing with the insecurity and fear that accompany any process of change. We hope some of these can be accomplished, but we realistically conclude that the process will be an uneven and spasmodic one, with no guaranteed direction or destiny. We fear that too much jerkiness and too many failures could lead to disaster. Turning peril into opportunity, despair into hope, and imbalance into a new order will never be easy. But Cubans of all stripes have no choice but to try. There is little in recent history to encourage optimism about the successful harmonization of wills. Thus it will also probably take considerable help from friends and understanding from the international community as a whole to guarantee success. But that is a theme for another book.

Bibliography

Abbassi, Jennifer Dugan. 1994. "Changing Policies and Learning Lessons: Peasants, the State, and Cuban Socialism, 1959–1993." Ph.D. dissertation. University of California, Riverside.

Adam, Jan. 1994. "The Transition to a Market Economy in Poland." *Cambridge Journal of Economics* 18, no. 6 (December): 607–618.

Agh, Attila. 1993. "Europeanization Through Privatization and Pluralization in Hungary." *Journal of Public Policy* 13, no. 1: 1–35.

Aguirre, Benigno. 1984. "The Conventionalization of Collective Behavior in Cuba." *American Journal of Sociology* 90, no. 3.

Alexeev, Michael. 1994. "The Russian Underground Economy and Transition." Paper presented at the Fraser Institute Conference, "Impact of the Underground Economy." Vancouver, April 21–22.

Alexeev, Michael, Clifford Gaddy, and Jim Leitzel. 1992. "Getting the Picture Right: Soviet Collapse, Transition Problems, and Western Aid." *The Brookings Review* (Winter): 151–7.

Alonso, José F. 1993. "Further Potential Economic Reforms in Cuba." *Free-Market Cuba: Business Journal* 2, no. 6.

———. 1992. "The Free Farmers Market: A Rejected Approach, But a Possible Solution." *Cuba in Transition,* Vol. 2, August 13. Miami: Latin American and Caribbean Center, Florida International University.

Alonso, José, Ricardo Donate-Armada, and Armando Lago. 1994. "A First Approximation Design of the Social Safety Net for a Democratic Cuba." Paper presented at the Fourth Annual Meeting of the Association for the Study of the Cuban Economy, Florida International University.

Alonzo Tejada, Aurelio. 1994. "Las reformas cubanas y la introducción de la lógica de mercado." *Cuba en el Mes* Dossier 4: 85–86.

Alvarado Ramos, Juan A. 1995. "Estereotipos y prejuicios raciales (estudio en tres barrios habaneros)." Paper presented at the LASA Conference. Washington, D.C., September.

Analco, Gloria. 1993. "Castro and His 'Concessions.'" *Latin America News Update* 9, no. 8 (September): 31.

Andrews, George Reid. 1992. "Racial Inequality in Brazil and the United States: A Statistical Comparison." *The Journal of Social History* 26, no. 2 (Winter): 229–263.

———. 1991. *Blacks and Whites in São Paulo, Brazil 1888–1988.* Madison: Wisconsin University Press.

Asamblea Nacional del Poder Popular. 1995. *Proyecto de Ley para la Inversion Extranjera.* Havana.

ASCE (Association for the Study of the Cuban Economy). 1993. *Cuba in Transition,* Vol 3. Washington, D.C.: ASCE.

Ash, T. Garton. 1990. *The Magic Lantern: The Revolution in Warsaw, Budapest, Berlin and Prague.* New York: Random House.

Aslund, Anders. 1994. "Lessons of the First Four Years of Systemic Change in Eastern Europe." *Journal of Comparative Economics* 19, no. 1 (August): 22–38.

Azicri, Max. 1992. "The Rectification Process Revisited: Cuba's Defense of Traditional Marxism-Leninism." In *Cuba in Transition: Crisis and Transformation,* ed. Sandor Halebsky et al., pp. 37–54. Boulder, Colo.: Westview Press.

Balari, Eugenio R. 1992. *Cuba La Revolucion Acosada?* México: Fondo de Cultura Economica.

Baloyra, Enrique A. 1994. "Where Does Cuba Stand?" In *Cuba and the Future,* ed. Donald E. Schulz, pp. 33–49. Westport, Conn.: Greenwood Press.

———. 1993. "Socialist Transitions and Prospects for Change in Cuba." In *Conflict and Change in Cuba,* ed. Enrique A. Baloyra and James A. Morris. Albuquerque: University of New Mexico Press.

Baloyra, Enrique A. and James A. Morris, eds. 1993. *Conflict and Change in Cuba.* Albuquerque: University of New Mexico Press.

Baloyra, Enrique A. and Roberto Lozano. 1993. "Soviet–Cuban Relations: The New Environment and Its Impact." In *Conflict and Change in Cuba,* ed. Enrique A. Baloyra and James A. Morris. Albuquerque: University of New Mexico Press.

Bardach, Ann Louise. 1994. "Conversations with Castro." *Vanity Fair* 57, no. 3 (March): 128–135; 166–170.

Barrett, Michele. 1991. *The Politics of Truth: From Marx to Foucault.* Stanford, Calif.: Stanford University Press.

Bengelsdorf, Carollee. 1994. The Problem of Democracy in Cuba. New York: Oxford University Press.

Berliner, Joseph. 1994. "Perestroika and the Chinese Model." In *The Postcommunist Economic Transformation,* ed. Robert W. Campbell. Boulder, Colo.: Westview Press.

Bermeo, Nancy. 1995. "Sacrifice, Sequence and Strength in Successful Dual Transitions: Lessons from Spain." Princeton University, photocopy.

Bernel, David. 1994. "The Curious Case of Cuba in American Foreign Policy." *Journal of Interamerican Studies and World Affairs* 36, no. 2 (Summer): 65–104.

Blasier, Cole. 1993. "The End of the Soviet–Cuban Partnership." In *Cuba After the Cold War,* ed. Carmelo Mesa-Lago. Pittsburgh: University of Pittsburgh Press.

Booth, David. 1976. "Cuba, Color and the Revolution." *Science and Society* 11, no. 2 (Summer): 129–172.

Bransdwayn, Susan. 1993. "Cuba's Economic and Management Policy: Response to the Changing Global Environment." *Public Administration and Development* 13, no. 4 (October).

Brezinski, Horst. 1986. "Economic Relations Between European and the Less-Developed CMEA Countries." *East European Economies: Slow Growth in the 1980s.* Joint Economic Committee, U.S. Congress. Washington, D.C.: Government Printing Office.

Brezinski, Horst and Michael Fritsch. 1995. "Transformation: The Shocking German Way." Paper presented at the annual meeting of the Association for Comparative Economic Studies, Washington, D.C. January.

Brundenius, Claes. 1984. *Revolutionary Cuba: The Challenge of Economic Growth with Equity*. Boulder, Colo.: Westview Press.

Brundenius, Claes and Andrew Zimbalist. 1988. "Cubanology and Cuban Economic Performance." In *Cuban Political Economy: Controversies in Cubanology,* ed. Andrew Zimbalist. Boulder, Colo.: Westview Press.

Brzezinski, Zbigniew. 1989. *The Grand Failure*. New York: Charles Scribner's Sons.

Bugajski, Janusz. 1994. *Ethnic Politics in Eastern Europe: A Guide to Nationality Policies, Organizations, and Parties*. Armonk, N.Y.: M. E. Sharpe.

Bunck, Julie Marie. 1994. *Fidel Castro and the Quest for a Revolutionary Culture*. University Park, Penn.: The Pennsylvania State University Press.

Cabarrouy, Evaldo A. 1995. "Dimensión Fiscal de la Crisis Económica de Cuba 1986–1994." Paper presented at the Fifth Annual Meeting of the Association for the Study of the Cuban Economy. University of Miami, Coral Gables, August 10–12.

Cardoso, Eliana and Ann Helwege. 1992. *Cuba After Communism*. Cambridge, Mass.: MIT Press.

Carneado, José Felipe. 1962. "La discriminación racial en Cuba no volverá jamás." *Cuba Socialista* 2, no. 5 (January): 54–67.

Carranza Valdés, Julio. 1993. "Cuba: Los retos de la Economía." *Cuadernos de Nuestra América* 19: 131–159.

———. 1992. "Reform and the Future of Cuban Socialism." In *The Cuban Revolution into the 1990s,* ed. Havana: Centro de Estudios de América.

Carranza Valdés, Julio, Pedro Monreal, and Luis Gutiérrez. 1995. *Cuba: La reestructuración de la economía (una propuesta para el debate)*. Havana: Editorial de Ciencias Sociales.

Carriazo, George. 1994. "Cambios estructurales en la agricultura cubana: La cooperativización." *Boletín Informativo de Economía Cubana,* no. 18.

Casal, Lourdes. 1979. *Revolution and Race: Blacks in Contemporary Cuba*. Washington, D.C.: Woodrow Wilson International Center for Scholars.

Castañeda, Rolando H. and George Plinio Montalván. 1995. "Economic Factors in Selecting an Approach to Confiscation Claims in Cuba." Paper presented at the annual meeting of the Association for the Study of the Cuban Economy. Miami, August.

———. 1994. "Political Intransigence Versus Economic Reform." Paper presented at the annual meeting of the Association for the Study of the Cuban Economy. Miami, August.

Castellanos, Jorge and Isabel Castellanos. 1990. *Cultura Afrocubana: El negro en Cuba, 1845–1959*. Miami: Ediciones Universal.

Centeno, Miguel Angel. 1994. "Between Rocky Democracies and Hard Markets: Dilemmas of the Double Transition." *Annual Review of Sociology* 20: 125–147.

CIA (Central Intelligence Agency). 1993. *Cuba: Handbook of Trade Statistics*. Washington, D.C.: CIA.

Clytus, John. 1970. *Black Man in Red Cuba*. Coral Gables, Fla.: University of Miami Press.

Comite Estatal de Estadisticas. 1988. *Anuario Estadistico de Cuba, 1988*. Havana.

CONAS (Consultores Asociados). 1994. *Cuba: Inversión y Negocios*. Havana.

Cuban Economic Research Project. 1965. *A Study on Cuba*. Coral Gables, Fla.: Miami University Press.

Cuban Research Institute. 1992. *Transition in Cuba: New Challenges for U.S. Policy*. Miami: Florida International University.

Davis, D. and E. F. Vogel, eds. 1990. *Chinese Society on the Eve of Tiananmen: The Impact of Reform.* Cambridge, Mass.: Harvard Contemporary Chinese Series, no. 7.

De Groote, Jacques and Frank Moss. 1993. "Winds of Economic Change in Havana." *IMF* 3 (November 23).

Deere, Carmen Diana and Mieke Meurs. 1992. "Markets, Markets Everywhere? Understanding the Cuban Anomaly." *World Development* 20: 825–839.

Deere, Carmen Diana, Mieke Meurs, and Niurka Pérez. 1992. "Toward a Periodization of the Cuban Collectivization Process: Changing Incentives and Peasant Response." *Cuban Studies* 22: 115–150.

de la Fuente, Alejandro. 1995. "Race and Inequality in Cuba, 1899–1981." *Journal of Contemporary History* 30: 131–168.

de la Garza, Rodolfo O., F. Louis deSipio, Chris Garcia, John Garcia, and Angelo Falcon. 1992. *Latino Voices: Mexican, Puerto Rican, and Cuban Perspectives on American Politics.* Boulder, Colo.: Westview Press.

del Aguila, Juan M. 1994a. *Cuba: Dilemmas of a Revolution,* 3rd ed. Boulder, Colo.: Westview Press.

———. 1994b. "The Party, the Fourth Congress, and the Process of Counterreform." In *Cuba at the Crossroads: Politics and Economics After the Fourth Party Congress,* ed. Jorge Pérez-López. Gainesville: University Press of Florida.

Delgado, Natalia and Susan L. Seah. 1994. "Foreign Investment Today." *Latin American Law and Business Report* 2, no. 12 (December 31): 12–15.

Díaz-Briquets, Sergio. 1994. "Emigrant Remittances in the Cuban Economy: Their Significance During and After the Castro Regime." In *Cuba in Transition,* Vol. 4, ed. ASCE. Washington, D.C.: Association for the Study of the Cuban Economy.

Dilla Alfonso, Haroldo. 1994. "Cuba Between Utopia and the World Market: Notes for a Socialist Debate." *Latin American Perspectives* 21, no. 4 (Fall).

Domínguez, Jorge I. 1994. "U.S. Policy Toward Cuba in the 1980s and 1990s." *The Annals of the American Academy of Political and Social Science* 533 (May).

———. 1993. "The Secrets of Castro's Staying Power." *Foreign Affairs* 72, no. 3 (Spring): 97–107.

———. 1990. "The Cuban Armed Forces, the Party and Society in Wartime and During Rectification (1986–1988)." In *Cuba After Thirty Years,* ed. Richard Gillespie, pp. 45–62. London: Frank Cass.

———. 1978. *Cuba: Order and Revolution.* Cambridge, Mass.: Harvard University Press.

Duharte Jiménez, Rafael and Elsa Santos García. 1995. *Cuba y el fantasma de la esclavitud: Testimonios sobre los prejuicios raciales.* Unpublished.

Eckstein, Susan E. 1994. *Back from the Future: Cuba Under Castro.* Princeton, N.J.: Princeton University Press.

EIU (Economist Intelligence Unit). 1995. *Cuba Country Profile 1994–1995.* London.

———. 1995. *Cuba, Dominican Republic, Haiti, Puerto Rico Country Report I, II, III.* London.

———. 1994. *Cuba, Dominican Republic, Haiti, Puerto Rico Country Report II.* London.

———. 1993. *Cuba Country Profile 1992–1993,* p. 7. London.

Edquist, Charles. 1985. *Capitalism, Socialism and Technology: A Comparative Study of Cuba and Jamaica.* London: Zed Books Ltd.

Ehrlich, Eva. 1994. "Private Sector and Privatization in Some Central and East European Countries: Peculiarities in Hungary." In *Privatization in NACC:*

Defense Industries Experiences and Policies and Related Experiences in Other Fields, pp. 41–55. Brussels: NATO Economics Directorate.

Espino, María Dolores. 1994. "Tourism in Cuba: A Development Strategy for the 1990s?" In *Cuba at the Crossroads: Politics and Economics After the Fourth Party Congress,* ed. Jorge Pérez-López. Gainesville: University Press of Florida.

Espinosa, Juan Carlos. 1995. "Markets Redux: The Politics of Farmers' Market in Cuba." Paper presented at the meeting of the Association for the Study of the Cuban Economy. Miami, August.

Evenson, Debra. 1994. *Revolution in the Balance: Law and Society in Contemporary Cuba*. Boulder, Colo.: Westview Press.

Fagen, Richard R., Richard A. Brody, and Thomas J. O'Leary. 1968. *Cubans in Exile: Disaffection and the Revolution.* Stanford, Calif.: Stanford University Press.

Falcoff, Mark. 1994. "Cuba and the United States: Thinking About the Future." In *Cuba and the Future*, ed. Donald Schulz, pp. 117–126. Westport, Conn.: Greenwood Press.

Fedarko, Kevin. 1995. "Open for Business." *Time* (February 20): 50–55.

Feinsilver, Julie M. 1993. *Healing the Masses: Cuban Health Politics at Home and Abroad*. Berkeley: University of California Press.

Feldbrugge, F. J. M. 1984. "Government and the Shadow Economy in the Soviet Union." *Soviet Studies* 36 (October): 528–543.

Fernández, Damián. 1993. "Civil Society in Transition." In *Transition in Cuba: New Challenges for U.S. Policy,* ed. Lisandro Pérez. Miami: Florida International University.

Fernández Robaina, Tomás. 1990. *El negro en Cuba 1902–1958: Apuntes para la historia de la lucha contra la discriminación racial.* Havana: Editorial de Ciencias Sociales.

Figueras, Miguel Alejandro. 1992a. "The Transformation of the Cuban Sugar Complex." In *The Cuban Revolution into the 1990s,* ed. Havana: Centro de Estudios de América.

———. 1992b. "Structural Changes in the Cuban Economy." In *The Cuban Revolution into the 1990s,* ed. Havana: Centro de Estudios de América.

Figueroa Arbelo, Víctor and Luis A. García de la Torre. 1984. "Apuntes sobre la-comercialización agrícola no estatal." *Economía y Desarrollo* 83 (November–December): 34–61.

Fischer, Stanley. 1992. "Privatization in East European Transformation." In *The Emergence of Market Economies in Eastern Europe,* Christopher Clauge and Gordon Rausser, eds., pp. 227–243. Cambridge, Mass.: Blackwell.

Fitzgerald, Frank T. 1994. *The Cuban Revolution in Crisis: From Managing Socialism to Managing Survival.* New York: Monthly Review Press.

———. 1990. "Cuba's New Professionals." In *Transformation and Struggle: Cuba Faces the 1990s,* ed. Sandor Halebsky and John M. Kirk. New York: Praeger.

Flisfisch, Angel. 1985. "Reflexiones algo oblícuas sobre el tema de la concertación." In *Concertación Social y Democracia,* ed. Mario Dos Santos, pp. 17–45. Santiago, Chile: Centro de Estudios del Desarrollo.

Frank, Marc. 1993. *Cuba Looks to the Year 2000.* New York: International Publishers.

García, María Cristina. 1990. *Cuban Exiles and Cuban-Americans: A History of an Immigrant Community in South Florida, 1959–1989*. Ph.D. thesis. University of Texas.

Gellner, Ernest. 1993. "Homeland of the Unrevolution." *Daedalus* 122, no. 3: 142.

González, Alfredo. 1993. "Modelos económicos socialistas: Escenarios para Cuba en los años 90." Havana: Instituto Nacional de Investigaciones Económicas.

Graziano, Luigi. 1994. "Pluralismo em Perspectiva Comparativa: Notas Sobre as Tradiçoes Européia e Americana." *Revista Brasileira de Ciências Sociais* 9, no. 26 (October): 7–17.

Greene Walker, Phyllis. 1994. "The Cuban Armed Forces and Transition." In *Cuba and the Future,* ed. Donald E. Schulz. Westport, Conn.: Greenwood Press.

Grenier, Guillermo J., Hugh Gladwin, and Douglas McLaughen. 1995. *The 1995 FIU Cuba Poll.* Miami: Florida International University.

Grossman, Gregory. 1993. "The Underground Economy in Russia." *International Economic Insights* 4, no. 6 (November–December): 14–17.

———. 1989. "The Second Economy: Boon or Bane for the Reform of the First Economy." In *Economic Reforms in the Socialist World,* ed. Stanislaw Gomulka et al., pp. 79–98. Armonk, N.Y.: M. E. Sharpe.

———. 1982. "Comment on 'The Second Economy in CMEA: A Terminological Note' by Franklyn Holzman." *The ACES Bulletin* 24 (Spring): 114–115.

———. 1977. "The 'Second Economy' of the USSR." *Problems of Communism* 26 (September–October): 25–40.

Gunn, Gillian. 1995. "Cuban NGOs: Government Puppets or Seeds of Civil Society?" *Georgetown University Briefing Paper Series.* February. Washington, D.C.

———. 1994a. "Balancing Economic Efficiency, Social Concerns and Political Control." *La Sociedad Económica* 42 (June).

———. 1994b. "In Search of a Modern Cuba Policy." In *Cuba and the Future,* ed. Donald E. Schulz. Westport, Conn.: Greenwood Press.

———. 1993. *Cuba in Transition: Options for U.S. Policy.* New York: Twentieth Century Fund.

———. 1992. "Cuba's Search for Alternatives." *Current History* (February).

Guzman Pascual, Arturo. 1995. "Notas Tomadas en la Conferencua Sobre el Reordenamiento y Ajuste de la Economia Cubana." Mimeo (March 15).

Halebsky, Sandor et al., eds. 1992. *Cuba in Transition: Crisis and Transformation.* Boulder, Colo.: Westview Press.

Halebsky, Sandor and John M. Kirk, eds. 1990. *Transformation and Struggle: Cuba Faces the 1990s.* New York: Praeger.

Handelman, Stephen. 1994. "The Russian 'Mafiya.'" *Foreign Affairs* 73, no. 2.

Havel, Václav. 1985. "The Power of the Powerless." In *The Power of the Powerless: Citizens Against the State in Central-Eastern Europe,* ed. John Keane, pp. 23–96. Armonk, N.Y.: M. E. Sharpe.

Hechter, Michael. 1994. "Theoretical Implications of the Demise of State Socialism." *Theory and Society* 23, no. 2 (April): 155–167.

Heidenheimer, Arnold J., Michael Johnston, and Victor L. LeVine, eds. 1989. *Political Corruption: A Handbook.* New Brunswick, N.J.: Transaction Publishers.

Hernández, Daniela. 1995. "Relaciones raciales en Santa Clara." Paper presented at the LASA Conference. Washington, D.C., September.

Hernández, Gladys. 1993. "Cuban Nickel: Market and Production Outlook." *La Sociedad Económica Bulletin* 26 (January): 1–4.

Hernández-Catá, Ernesto. 1995. "Julio Carranza and Pedro Monreal on Economic Change in Cuba: A Critique." Paper presented at the annual meeting of the Association for the Study of the Cuban Economy. Miami, August.

———. 1993. "Economic Policy in Cuba's Transition to a Market Economy: Lessons from the Russian Experience." In *Cuba in Transition,* Vol. 3, ed. ASCE. Washington, D.C.: Association for the Study of the Cuban Economy.

Hersh, Seymour M. 1994. "The Wild East." *The Atlantic Monthly* 273, no. 6 (June): 61–86.

Holmes, Leslie. 1993. *The End of Communist Power*. New York: Oxford University Press.

Holzman, Franklyn. 1981. "The Second Economy in CMEA: A Terminological Note." *The ACES Bulletin* 23 (Spring): 111–113.

House of Representatives. 1996. *Cuban Liberty and Democratic Solidarity Act of 1996.* 104th Congress, 2nd Session, March 1. Report 104-468.

Huntington, Samuel P. and Jorge Domínguez. 1975. "Political Development." In *Handbook of Political Science. Vol. 3: Macropolitical Theory,* ed. F. I. Greenstein and N. W. Polsby. Reading, Mass.: Addison-Wesley.

Intrilligator, Michael. 1994a. "Reform of the Russian Economy: The Role of Institutions." *Contention* 3, no. 2 (Winter): 153–170.

———. 1994b. "Privatisation in Russia Has Led to Criminalisation." *The Australian Economic Review* (2nd Quarter): 4–14.

Jenkins, Gareth. "Beyond Basic Needs: Cuba's Search for Stable Development in the 1990s." In *Cuba in Transition: Crisis and Transformation,* ed. Sandor Halebsky et al. Boulder, Colo.: Westview Press.

Johnson, Simon and Heidi Kroll. 1991. "Managerial Strategies for Spontaneous Privatization." *Soviet Economy* 7, no. 4 (October–December): 281–316.

Johnson, Simon and Gary Loveman. 1995. "Private Sector Development in Poland: Shock Therapy and Starting Over." Paper presented at the annual meetings of the Association for Comparative Economic Studies. Washington, D.C., January.

Jordan, David C. 1993. *Revolutionary Cuba and the End of the Cold War*. Lanham, Md.: University Press of America.

Karl, Terry Lynn and Phillipe C. Schmitter. 1991. "Modes of Transition in Latin America, Southern and Eastern Europe." *International Social Science Journal* 43, no. 2 (May).

Kiss, Yudit. 1992. "Privatisation in Hungary: Two Years Later." *Soviet Studies* 44, no. 6: 1015–1038.

Kochanowicz, Jacek, Kalman Mizsei, and Joan Nelson. 1994. "The Transition in Bulgaria, Hungary, and Poland: An Overview." In *A Precarious Balance: Democracy and Economic Reforms in Eastern Europe,* ed. Joan Nelson, pp. 1–23. San Francisco: Institute for Contemporary Studies Press.

Kornai, Janos. 1992. *The Socialist System: The Political Economy of Communism.* Princeton, N.J.: Princeton University Press.

———. 1990. *The Road to a Free Economy: Shifting from a Socialist System—The Example of Hungary*. New York: Norton & Norton.

———. 1986. *Contradictions and Dilemmas*. Cambridge, Mass.: MIT Press.

———. 1980. "'Hard' and 'Soft' Budget Constraint." *Acta Oeconomica* 25: 231–246.

———. 1979. "Resource-Constrained Versus Demand-Constrained Systems." *Econometrica* 47: 801–819.

Krueger, Anne O. 1974. "The Political Economy of the Rent-Seeking Society." *American Economic Review* 64, no. 3 (June): 291–303.

Krueger, Thomas and Mark S. Lutz. 1995. "Hungary: Developments and Challenges." Paper presented at the annual meetings of the Association for Comparative Economic Studies. Washington, D.C., January.

Lane, Charles. 1994. "The Long, Long Good-Bye." *The New Republic* (October 3): 15–18.

Larzelere, Alex. 1988. *The 1980 Cuban Boatlift*. Washington, D.C.: National Defense University Press.

Leitzel, Jim, Clifford Gaddy, and Michael Alexeev. 1995. "Mafiosi and Matrioshki: Organized Crime and Russian Reform." *The Brookings Review* (Winter): 26–29.

León, Francisco. 1995. "The International Reinsertion of Cuba: Emerging Scenarios." In *Cuba in the International System: Normalization and Integration,* ed. Archibald R. M. Ritter and John M. Kirk. London: Macmillan.

———. 1994. "Cuba: Una opción latinoamericana de inserción internacional." *Revista del Instituto de Estudios Internacionales de la Universidad de Chile* 27, no. 107/108 (July–September/October–December): 1–6.

León, Francisco and Archibald R. M. Ritter. 1994. "Presentación." *Revista del Instituto de Estudios Internacionales de la Universidad de Chile* 27: 1–6.

Levinson, Sandra. 1995. "Gallup Poll in Cuba." *CUBA Update* (February–March): 9.

Linden, Ronald H. 1993. "Analogies and the Loss of Community: Cuba and East Europe in the 1990s." In *Cuba After the Cold War,* ed. Carmelo Mesa-Lago. Pittsburgh: University of Pittsburgh Press.

Lipset, Seymour Martin, and Gyorgy Bence. 1994. "Anticipations of the Failure of Communism." *Theory and Society* 23, no. 2 (April): 169–210.

Liss, Sheldon B. 1994. *Fidel! Castro's Political and Social Thought.* Boulder, Colo.: Westview Press.

Los, Maria. 1987. "The Double Economic Structure of Communist Societies." *Contemporary Crises* 11: 25–58.

———. 1982. "Crime and Economy in the Communist Countries." In *White-Collar and Economic Crimes,* ed. Peter Wickman and Timothy Dailey, pp. 121–137. Lexington, Mass.: Lexington Books.

McCormick, Barrett L. 1990. *Political Reform in Post-Mao China: Democracy and Bureaucracy in a Leninist State.* Berkeley: University of California Press.

Mainwaring, Scott, Guillermo O'Donnell, and J. Samuel Valenzuela, eds. 1992. *Issues in Democratic Consolidation: The New South American Democracies in Comparative Perspective.* Notre Dame: University of Notre Dame Press.

Martínez Heredia, Fernando. 1989. *Rectificación y profundización del socialismo en Cuba.* Buenos Aires: Ediciones Dialéctica.

Martínez, T. Vivian. 1994. "Entrevista al dramaturgo Alberto Pedro: El tetro es una conspiración." *La Gaceta de Cuba* (June): 8–11.

McFadyen, Deidre. 1995. "The Social Repercussions of the Crisis." *NACLA Report on the Americas* XXIX, no. 2.

Mesa-Lago, Carmelo. 1994a. *Breve Historia Económica de la Cuba Socialista.* Madrid: Alianza.

———. 1994b. *Are Economic Reforms Propelling Cuba to the Market?* Miami: University of Miami North-South Center.

———. 1993a. "The Economic Effects on Cuba of the Downfall of Socialism in the U.S.S.R. and Eastern Europe." In *Cuba After the Cold War,* ed. Carmelo Mesa-Lago. Pittsburgh: University of Pittsburgh Press.

———. 1993b. "Cuba's Economic Policies and Strategies for Confronting the Crisis." In *Cuba After the Cold War,* ed. Carmelo Mesa-Lago. Pittsburgh: University of Pittsburgh Press.

———. 1991. "El proceso de rectificación en Cuba: Causas, políticas y efectos econmicos." *Revista de Estudios Políticos,* no. 74 (October–December): 497–530.

———. 1989. "Cuba's Economic Counter-Reform (*Rectificación*): Causes, Policies, and Effects." *The Journal of Communist Studies* 5 (December): 98–139.

———. 1981. *The Economy of Socialist Cuba.* Albuquerque: University of New Mexico Press.

Mesa-Lago, Carmelo, ed. 1993. *Cuba After the Cold War.* Pittsburgh: University of Pittsburgh Press.

Mesa-Lago, Carmelo and Horst Fabian. 1993. "Analogies Between East European Socialist Regimes and Cuba: Scenarios for the Future." In *Cuba After the Cold War,* ed. Carmelo Mesa-Lago. Pittsburgh: University of Pittsburgh Press.

Mesa-Lago, Carmelo and Luc Zephirin. 1971. "Central Planning." In *Revolutionary Change in Cuba*, ed. Carmelo Mesa-Lago. Pittsburgh: University of Pittsburgh Press.

Meurs, Mieke. 1992. "Popular Participation and Central Planning in Cuban Socialism: The Experience of Agriculture in the 1980s." *World Development* 20, no. 2: 229–240.

Michnik, Adam. 1985. *Letters from Prison and Other Essays.* Berkeley: University of California Press.

Monreal, Pedro. 1993. "Cuba: To Market, to Market." *Hemisfile* 4, no. 3 (May–June): 10–11.

Monreal, Pedro and Manuel Rúa. 1994. "Apertura y reforma de la economía cubana: Las transformaciones institucionales (1990–1993)." *Cuadernos de Nuestra América* XI, no. 21 (January–June).

Montaner, Carlos A. 1976. *Informe secreto sobre la revolución cubana.* Madrid: Ediciones Sedmay.

Moore, Carlos. 1988. *Castro, the Blacks, and Africa.* Los Angeles: UCLA Center for Afro-American Studies.

———. 1964. "Le peuple noir a-t-il sa place dans la Révolution Cubaine?" *Presence Africaine* 52: 177–230.

Morley, Morris and James Petras. 1992. "Cuban Socialism: Rectification and the New Model of Accumulation." In *In the Time of Cholera,* ed. Morris Morley and James Petras, pp. 93–127. New York: Routledge, Chapman and Hall.

Mosak, Esther. 1991. "Al tiempo hay que ayudarlo." *Cuba Internacional* 258 (June): 34–37.

Murrell, Peter and Mancur Olson. 1991. "The Devolution of Centrally-Planned Economies." *Journal of Comparative Economics* 15, no. 2.

Nagorski, Andrew. 1993. *The Birth of Freedom.* New York: Simon and Schuster.

Nee, Victor. 1996. "The Emergence of a Market Society: Changing Mechanisms of Stratification in China." *American Journal of Sociology*, 101, no. 4.

———. 1991a. *Sleeping with the Enemy: Why Communists Love the Market.* Working Papers on Transitions from State Socialism No. 92-1. Ithaca, NY: Mario Einaudi Center for International Studies, Cornell University.

———. 1991b. "Social Inequalities in Reforming State Socialism: Between Redistribution and Markets in China." *American Sociological Review* 56, no. 3 (October): 267–282.

———. 1989. "A Theory of Market Transition: From Redistribution to Markets in State Socialism." *American Sociological Review* 54, no. 5 (October): 663–681.

Nee, Victor and Peng Lian. 1994. "Sleeping with the Enemy: A Dynamic Model of Declining Political Commitment in State Socialism." *Theory and Society* 23, no. 2 (April): 253–296.

Nuñez Rodriguez, Lupo 1995. "Evolución de organización empresarial agropecuaria en la Cuba revolucionaria." Paper presented at the meeting of the Latin American Studies Association. Washington, D.C., September.

Oficina Nacional de Estadisticas. 1995. *La Economia Cubana, 1994.* Havana.

Oi, Jean C. 1989. *State and Peasant in Contemporary China: The Political Economy of Village Government.* Berkeley: University of California Press.

Oppenheimer, A. 1992. *Castro's Final Hour.* New York: Simon and Schuster.

Pastor Jr., Manuel and Andrew Zimbalist. 1995. "Cuba's Economic Conundrum." *NACLA Report on the Americas* 22, no. 2 (September–October): 7–12.

Pedraza, Silvia. 1995. "Cuba's Refugees: Manifold Migrations." In *Origins and Destinies: Immigration, Race, and Ethnicity in America,* ed. Silvia Pedraza and Rubén G. Rumbaut. Belmont, Calif.: Wadsworth.

Peña Castellanos, Lázaro and José Alvarez. 1995. "The Transformation of the State Extensive Growth Model in Cuba's Sugarcane Agriculture." Paper presented at the annual meeting of the Association for the Study of the Cuban Economy. Miami, August.

Pérez, Armando and Berto Gonazález. 1988. "El perfeccionamiento empresarial en el MINFAR." *Cuba socialista,* no. 36.

Pérez, Lisandro. 1992. "Cuban Miami." In *Miami Now: Immigration, Ethnicity, and Social Change,* ed. Guillermo Grenier and Alex Stepick. Gainesville, Fla.: University Press of Florida.

Pérez-Díaz, Victor. 1993. *The Return of Civil Society: The Emergence of Democratic Spain.* Cambridge, Mass.: Harvard University Press.

Pérez-López, Jorge. 1995. *Cuba's Second Economy: From Behind the Scenes to Center Stage.* New Brunswick, N.J.: Transaction Publishers.

———. 1992a. "The Cuban Second Economy: Methodological and Practical Issues Related to Quantification." In *Cuban Transition,* Vol. 2, ed. ASCE. Miami: Florida International University.

———. 1992b. "The Cuban Economy: Rectification in a Changing World." *Cambridge Journal of Economics* 16, no. 1 (March).

———. 1991. *The Economics of Cuban Sugar.* Pittsburgh: University of Pittsburgh Press.

———. 1990. "Rectification at Three: Impact on the Cuban Economy." *Studies in Comparative International Development* 25 (Fall): 3–36.

Pérez-López, Jorge F., ed. 1994. *Cuba at the Crossroads: Politics and Economics After the Fourth Party Congress.* Gainesville: University Press of Florida.

Pérez-López, Jorge F. and Carmelo Mesa-Lago. 1990. "Cuba: Domestic Counter Reform Leads to Crisis." *Transition* 1, no. 8 (November): 6–8.

Pérez Martín, Ezequiel. 1992. "Estados Unidos: El racismo corriente." *Prisma Latinoamericano* (June): 10–11.

Pérez-Stable, Marifeli. 1993a. *The Cuban Revolution: Origins, Course, and Legacy.* New York: Oxford University Press.

———. 1993b. "Legislative and Electoral Dynamics: Reforms and Options." In *Transition in Cuba: New Challenges for U.S. Policy.* Miami: Cuban Research Institute, Florida International University.

———. 1990. "Socialism and Democracy." In *Transformation and Struggle: Cuba Faces the 1990s,* ed. Sandor Halebsky and John Kirk. New York: Praeger.

———. 1985. "Politics and Conciencia in Revolutionary Cuba, 1959–1984." Doctoral dissertation. Stony Brook: State University of New York at Stony Brook.

Perry, Joseph M., Jeffrey W. Steagal, and Louis A. Woods. 1995. "Small Business Development in Post-Transition Cuba." Paper presented at the annual meeting of the Association for the Study of the Cuban Economy. Miami, August.

Petras, James F. and Morris H. Morley. 1992. "Cuban Socialism: Rectification and the New Model of Accumulation." In *Cuba in Transition: Crisis and Transformation,* ed. Sandor Halebsky et al. Boulder, Colo.: Westview Press.

Planas, J. Richard. 1994. "Why Does Castro Survive?" In *Cuba and the Future,* ed. Donald E. Schulz. Westport, Conn.: Greenwood Press.

Portes, Alejandro and Joszef Borocz. 1988. "The Informal Sector Under Capitalism and State Socialism: A Preliminary Comparison." *Social Justice* 15 (Fall/Winter): 17–28.

Preeg, Ernest H. with Jonathan D. Levine. 1993. *Cuba and the New Caribbean Economic Order*. Washington, D.C.: Center for Strategic and International Studies.

Pridham, Geoffrey and Tatu Vanhanen. 1994. *Democratization in Eastern Europe: Domestic and International Perspectives*. London: Routledge.

Przeworski, Adam. 1991. *Democracy and the Market: Political and Economic Reforms in Eastern Europe and Latin America*. New York: Cambridge University Press.

Przeworski, Adam and Fernando Limongi. 1994. "Democracia e dsenvolvimento na América do Sul, 1946–1988." *Revista Brasileira de Ciências Sociais* 9, no. 24: 31–48.

———. 1993. "Political Regimes and Economic Growth." *Journal of Economic Perspectives* 7: 51–71.

Puerta, Ricardo A. and José Alvarez. 1993. "Organization and Performance of Cuban Agriculture at Different Levels of State Intervention." In *Cuba in Transition,* Vol. 3, ed. ASCE. Washington, D.C.: Association for the Study of the Cuban Economy.

Quijano, Carlos. 1995 "Reforms in Cuba and Vietnam." Paper presented at the annual meeting of the Association for the Study of the Cuban Economy. Miami, August.

Rabkin, Rhoda. 1991. *Cuban Politics: The Revolutionary Experiment*. New York: Praeger.

Rathbone, J. P. 1993. "The Cuban Economy: A Twelve-Month Review." *La Sociedad Económica Bulletin* 33 (August 23): 2.

Reed, Gail. 1995. "Cuba's Economy 1995: Critique and a Crystal Ball." *Cuba Update* (February).

Reznick, Rosalind. 1993. "Bringing the Law Back Home: Cuban Exiles Prepare for the Day Castro Falls." *National Law Journal* (June 28): 15.

Ritter, Archibald R. M. 1993. "Exploring Cuba's Alternate Economic Futures." *Cuban Studies* 23.

———. 1992. "Cuba in the 1990s: Economic Reorientation and International Reintegration." In *Cuba in Transition: Crisis and Transformation,* ed. Sandor Halebsky et al. Boulder, Colo.: Westview Press.

———. 1991. "Perspectivas para el cambio económico y político en Cuba durante los noventa." *Sintesis* 15 (September–December): 375–393.

———. 1990. "The Cuban Economy in the 1990s: External Challenge and Policy Imperatives." *Journal of Interamerican Studies and World Affairs* 32 (Fall): 117–149.

———. 1974. *The Economic Development of Revolutionary Cuba: Strategy and Performance*. New York: Praeger.

Roca, Sergio G. 1993a. "The 'Comandante' in His Economic Labyrinth." In *Conflict and Change in Cuba,* ed. Enrique A. Baloyra and James A. Morris. Albuquerque: University of New Mexico Press.

———. 1993b. "The End Is Near? Why Cuban Socialism Failed!" In *Cuba in Transition,* Vol. 3, ed. ASCE. Washington, D.C.: Association for the Study of the Cuban Economy.

———. 1992. "Cuba's Socialist Economy at Thirty: Assessments and Prospects." In *Cuba in Transition: Crisis and Transformation,* ed. Sandor Halebsky et al. Boulder, Colo.: Westview Press.

———. 1988. *Socialist Cuba: Past Interpretations and Future Challenges*. Boulder, Colo.: Westview Press.

———. 1976. *Cuban Economic Policy and Ideology: The Ten Million Ton Harvest*. Beverly Hills: Sage Publications.

Rodríguez, José Luis. 1995a. "Panorámico de la situación del país." In *Conferincia "La Nación y la Emigracíon": abril 22, 23 y 24, La Habana, Reeba, 1994.* Havana: Editora Política.

———. 1994. "The United States and Cuba: From a Strategy of Conflict to Constructive Engagement." In *Cuba and the Future,* ed. Donald E. Schulz. Westport, Conn.: Greenwood Press.

———. 1992. "Cuban Ecoonmic Policy in the Process of Rectification." In *The Cuban Revolution into the 1990s,* ed. Havana: Centro de Estudios de América.

———. 1990a. "Aspectos Económicos del Proceso de Rectificación." *Cuba Socialista* 44 (April–June): 86–101.

———. 1990b. *La estrategia del desarrollo económico en Cuba.* Havana: Editorial de Ciencias Sociales.

———. 1988a. "The Antecedents and Theoretical Characteristics of Cubanology." In *Cuban Political Economy: Controversies in Cubanology,* ed. Andrew Zimbalist. Boulder, Colo.: Westview Press.

———. 1988b. *Crítica a Nuestros Críticos.* Havana: Editorial Ciencias Sociales.

Rodriguez Calderón, Mirta. 1995. "Life Under the Special Period." *NACLA Report on the Americas* XXIX, no. 2.

Rodríguez Chavez, Ernesto. 1992. "El patrón migratorio cubano: Cambio y continuidad." *Cuadernos de Nuestra América* 9, no. 18 (January–June): 77–95.

Rodríguez Mesa, Gonzalo. 1985. *El proceso de industrialización de la economía cubana.* Havana: Editorial de Ciencias Sociales.

Rose, Richard. 1992. *Divisions and Contradictions in Economies in Transition.* Studies in Public Policy No. 206. Glasgow: Center for the Study of Public Policy, University of Strathclyde.

Rose-Ackerman, Susan. 1985. "The Economics of Corruption." *Journal of Public Economics* 4: 187–203.

Rosefielde, Steven. 1995. "Russian Enterprise Optimization Under Kleptocratic Collectivism." Paper presented at the annual meeting of the American Economic Association. Washington, D.C.

Rosenberg, Jonathan. 1992. "Cuba's Free-Market Experiment: Los Mercados Libres Campesinos, 1980–1986." *Latin American Research Review* 27, no. 3: 51–89.

Rothschild, Joseph. 1993. *Return to Diversity: A Political History of East Central Europe Since World War II.* New York: Oxford University Press.

Rout, Jr., Leslie B. 1976. *The African Experience in Spanish America.* Cambridge: Cambridge University Press.

Rua, Manuel and Pedro Monreal. 1993. "La Apertura Económica Cubana." *Cuba Foreign Trade* 1: 1–11.

Rupesinghe, Kumar, Peter King, and Olga Vorkunova, eds. 1992. *Ethnicity and Conflict in a Post-Communist World: The Soviet Union, Eastern Europe, and China.* New York: St. Martin's Press.

Sachs, Jeffrey D. 1991. "Spontaneous Privatization: A Comment." *Soviet Economy* 7, no. 43 (October–December): 317–321.

Sanguinettiy, Jorge A. 1995. "Economic Education for a Market Economy: The Cuban Case." Paper presented at the annual meeting of the Association for the Study of the Cuban Economy. Miami, August.

Scalopino, Robert A. 1992. *The Last Leninists: The Uncertain Future of Asia's Communist States.* Washington, D.C.: The Center for Strategic Studies.

Scarpaci, Joseph L. 1995. "On the New Economic Geography of Havana's Food and *Paladar* Markets." Paper presented at the annual meeting of the Association for the Study of the Cuban Economy. Miami, August.

Schroeder, Susan. *Cuba: A Handbook of Historical Statistics.* Boston: G. K. Hall.

Schulz, Donald E. 1994. "Postcript: The Cuban Crisis in the Summer of 1993—An Opportunity for the United States?" In *Cuba and the Future,* ed. Donald E. Schulz. Westport, Connecticut: Greenwood Press.

———. 1993. "Can Castro Survive?" *Journal of Interamerican Studies and World Affairs* 35, no. 1.

Serrano Peralta, Lourdes. 1995. "Estructura y relaciones raciales en un barrio popular: Mujer, instrucción, ocupación y color de la piel." Paper presented at the LASA Conference. Washington, D.C., September.

Shelley, Louise I. 1994. "Post-Soviet Organized Crime." *Demokratizatsiya* 2, no. 3.

Shleifer, Andrei and Robert W. Vishny. 1993. "Corruption." *Quarterly Journal of Economics* 108, no. 3 (August).

Sik, Endre. 1992. "From the Second to the Informal Economy." *Journal of Public Policy* 12, no. 2: 153–175.

Smith, Wayne. 1992. "Castro: To Fall or Not to Fall." *SAIS Review* 12, no. 2.

Sola, Lourdes, ed. 1993. *Estado, Mercado e Democracia: Política e Economia Comparadas*. Rio de Janeiro: Paz e Terra.

Solchaga, Carlos. 1994. "Transition in Cuba." *Actualidad Económica* 17 (October).

Stark, David. 1992. "Path Dependence and Privatization Strategies in East Central Europe." *East European Politics and Societies* 6: 17–54.

———. 1989. "Bending the Bars of the Iron Cage: Bureaucratization and Informalization in Capitalism and Socialism." *Sociological Forum* 4, no. 4: 637–664.

Stark, David and Victor Nee. 1990. "Para una análise institucional do socialismo de estado." *Dados* 32, no. 2: 181–209.

Sterling, Claire. 1994. "Redfellas." *The New Republic* 210, no. 15 (April 11): 19–22.

Stokes, Gale. 1993. *The Walls Came Tumbling Down: The Collapse of Communism in Eastern Europe*. New York: Oxford University Press.

Strout, Jan. 1995. "Women, the Politics of Sexuality, and Cuba's Economic Crisis." Unpublished.

Suárez, Luis. 1994. "Crisis, reestructuración y democracia en Cuba: Apuntes para un debate." *Cuaderno de Nuestra America* 20 (July–December).

Suchlicki, Jaime. 1992. "Possible Scenarios of Change in Cuba." In *Cuba's Transition to Democracy: Lessons from the Former Soviet Bloc,* ed. CANF. Miami: Cuban American National Foundation.

Sugar, Peter F., ed. 1980. *Ethnic Diversity and Conflict in Eastern Europe*. Santa Barbara: ABC-Clio.

Sutherland, Elizabeth. 1969. *The Youngest Revolution. A Personal Report on Cuba.* New York: The Dial Press.

Svejnar, Jan and Jorge Pérez-López. 1993. "A Strategy for the Economic Transformation of Cuba Based on the East European Experience." In *Cuba After the Cold War,* ed. Carmelo Mesa-Lago. Pittsburgh: University of Pittsburgh Press.

Szelenyi, Ivan and Balazs Szelenyi. 1994. "Why Socialism Failed: Toward a Theory of System Breakdown—Causes of Disintegration of East European State Socialism." *Theory and Society* 23, no. 2 (April): 211–232.

Tanzi, Vito. 1994. *Corruption, Governmental Activities, and Markets*. IMF Working Paper WP/94/99 (August).

Terrero, Ariel. 1994. "Tendencias de un ajuste." *Bohemia* 85, no. 22 (October 28): B30–39.

Tomás, Angel. 1994. "El gobierno cubano pide a los ciudadanos 'honrados' que combata a todos los 'elementos antisociales.'" *Diario 16* (August 9).

Torres, María de los Angeles. 1986. *From Exiles to Minorities: The Politics of the Cuban Community in the United States*. Ph.D. thesis. University of Michigan.

Touraine, Alain. 1994. *Qu' est-ce que la democratie?* Paris: Fayard.

Travieso-Diaz, Matias and Alejandro Ferraté. 1995. "Recommended Features of a Foreign Investment Code for Cuba's Free-Market Transition." Paper presented to the Association for the Study of the Cuban Economy. Miami, August.

Treml, Vladimir G. and Michael V. Alexeev. 1994. "The Growth of the Second Economy in the Soviet Union and Its Impact on the System." In *The Post-communist Economic Transformation,* ed. Robert W. Campbell. Boulder, Colo.: Westview Press.

———. 1993. *The Second Economy and the Destabilizing Effect of Its Growth on the State Economy in the Soviet Union: 1965–1989.* Berkeley-Duke Occasional Papers on the Second Economy in the USSR no. 36 (December).

Tu Wei-ming, ed. 1994. *China in Transformation.* Cambridge, Mass.: Harvard University Press.

Turits, Richard. 1987. "Trade, Debt, and the Cuban Economy." *World Development* 15, no. 1 (January): 163–180.

Turley, William S. and Mark Selden, eds. 1993. *Reinventing Vietnamese Socialism: Doi Moi in Comparative Perspective.* Boulder, Colo.: Westview Press.

UN CEPAL. 1994. *Preliminary Overview of the Economy of Latin America and the Caribbean.* Santiago, Chile: CEPAL.

Valdés, Nelson P. 1992. "Cuban Political Culture: Between Betrayal and Death." In *Cuba in Transition: Crisis and Transformation,* ed. Sandor Halebsky et al. Boulder, Colo.: Westview Press.

———. 1988. "Revolution and Paradigms: A Critical Assessment of Cuban Studies." In *Cuban Political Eonomy: Controversies in Cubanology,* ed. Andrew Zimbalist. Boulder, Colo.: Westview Press.

Vega Vega, Juan. 1988. "El delito de enriquecimiento ilícito." *Cuba Socialista* 35.

Walder, Andrew G. 1994. "The Decline of Communist Power: Elements of a Theory of Institutional Change." *Theory and Society* (April): 297–323.

Walton, John. 1989. "Debt, Protest, and the State in Latin America." In *Power and Popular Protest: Latin American Social Movements,* ed. Susan Eckstein, pp. 299–328. Berkeley: University of California Press.

Welfens, Paul J. J. 1992. "The Socialist Shadow Economy: Causes, Characteristics, and Role for Systemic Reforms." *Economic Systems* 16, no. 1 (April): 113–147.

White, Gordon. 1993. *Market Reform and the Emergence of Civil Society in Post-Mao China. Working Paper* no. 6 (September). Brighton, UK: IDS.

Wong, Raimundo Francisco. 1974. *The Political Behavior of Cuban Migrants.* Ph.D. thesis. University of Michigan.

Wong, Y. C. Richard. 1994. "Reform and China's Underground Economy." Paper presented at the Fraser Institute Conference, "Impact of the Underground Economy." Vancouver, April 21–22.

Yeltsin, Boris. 1994. "The Economic Policy of Russia." Speech delivered to the Federal Assembly, Moscow, February 24. As reproduced in *Vital Speeches of the Day* 60, no. 12 (April 1): 354–360.

Yopo H., Boris. 1993. "Latin American Perspectives on the Cuban Transition." *Cuba Briefing Paper Series* 3 (July).

Zhang, Baohui. 1994. "Corporatism, Totalitarianism, and Transitions to Democracy." *Comparative Political Studies* 27, no. 1: 108–136.

Zimbalist, Andrew. 1994. "Treading Water: Cuba's Economic and Political Crisis." In *Cuba and the Future,* ed. Donald E. Shulz. Westport, Conn.: Greenwood Press.

———. 1993. "Dateline Cuba: Hanging on in Havana." *Foreign Policy* 92 (Fall).

———. 1992a. "Introduction to Part 2." In *Cuba in Transition: Crisis and Transformation,* ed. Sandor Halebsky et al. Boulder, Colo.: Westview Press.

———. 1992b. "Teetering on the Brink: Cuba's Current Economic and Political Crisis." *Journal of Latin American Studies* 24, no. 1 (May).

———. 1988a. "Cuba's External Economy: Reflections on Export Dependence, Soviet Aid, and Foreign Debt." *Comparative Economic Studies* 30, no. 2 (Summer): 21–46.

———. 1988b. "Cuban Political Economy and Cubanology: An Overview." In *Cuban Political Economy: Controversies in Cubanology.* Boulder, Colo.: Westview Press.

———. 1987. "Cuban Industrial Growth, 1985–84." *World Development* 15, no. 1 (January).

Zimbalist, Andrew, ed. 1988. "Interpreting Cuban Planning: Between a Rock and a Hard Place." *Cuban Political Economy: Controversies in Cubanology*. Boulder, Colo.: Westview Press.

Zimbalist, Andrew, ed. 1987. *Cuba's Socialist Economy Toward the 1990s*. Boulder, Colo.: Lynne Rienner Publishers.

Zimbalist, Andrew and Claes Brundenius. 1989. *The Cuban Economy: Measurement and Analysis of Socialist Performance*. Baltimore: Johns Hopkins University Press.

Zimbalist, Andrew and Susan Eckstein. 1987. "Patterns of Cuban Development: The First Twenty-Five Years." In *Cuba's Socialist Economy Toward the 1990s,* ed. Andrew Zimbalist. Boulder, Colo.: Lynne Rienner Publishers.

About the Contributors

Julio Carranza Valdés is senior economist and former deputy director at the Centro de Estudios de América in Havana. He has published extensively on Cuba.

Max J. Castro is a research associate at the North-South Center of the University of Miami. He has written numerous works on Cuba and the exile community.

Miguel Angel Centeno is assistant professor of sociology at Princeton University. He is the author of *Democracy Within Reason: Technocratic Politics in Mexico.*

Alejandro de la Fuente is a Ph.D. candidate in the History Department of the University of Pittsburgh and has published several articles on Cuba.

Susan Eckstein is professor of sociology at Boston University. She is the author of several books and articles including her recent *Back from the Future: Cuba Under Castro.*

Mauricio Font is associate professor of sociology, Graduate Center and Queens College, City University of New York. His work on Brazil includes *Coffee, Contention, and Change.*

Laurence Glasco is a Ph.D. candidate in the History Department at the University of Pittsburgh.

Gillian Gunn Clissold is director of the Georgetown University Caribbean Project in the Latin American Studies program at Georgetown University. She has published many articles on Cuba-U.S. relations.

Francisco León is a senior economist at CEPAL, the UN Economic Commission for Latin America and the Caribbean. He is the author of several works on Cuba and Latin American issues.

Pedro Monreal is a research associate at the Centro de Estudios de América in Havana. He is the author of various works on the Cuban economy.

Manuel Moreno Fraginals is arguably the leading Cuban historian, has received many international prizes, and is a widely respected authority on slavery and the sugar economy.

Jorge F. Pérez-López has published numerous articles and books on Cuba and is past-president of the Association for the Study of the Cuban Economy.

Marifeli Pérez-Stable is associate professor of sociology at SUNY-Old Westbury. She is the author of *The Cuban Revolution: Origins, Course and Legacy*.

Archibald R. M. Ritter is in the Economics Department at Carleton University in Ottawa, Canada. He is author of several articles and books on the Cuban economy.

Index

About the Book

How can the political and economic transitions of the 1990s in Cuba best be understood? And where are they leading? In this thorough overview of contemporary Cuba, the authors provide a systematic analysis of recent changes, the ways in which present circumstances will shape the future of the island, and the extent to which Cuba fits, or defies, current models of transition.

After summarizing conditions within their areas of specialization, each author discusses how the various political, social, and economic sectors might respond to a variety of transition scenarios. They also offer their own visions of Cuba's future. A final chapter, by one of the country's most respected intellectuals, discusses recent events in Cuba and their implications for the social legacy of the revolution.

Miguel Angel Centeno is assistant professor of sociology at Princeton University. He is author of *Democracy Within Reason: Technocratic Politics in Mexico*. **Mauricio Font** is associate professor of sociology in the Graduate Center and Queens College, CUNY. His work on Brazil includes *Coffee, Contention, and Change*.